IMAGES of America

RAYTHEON COMPANY
THE FIRST SIXTY YEARS

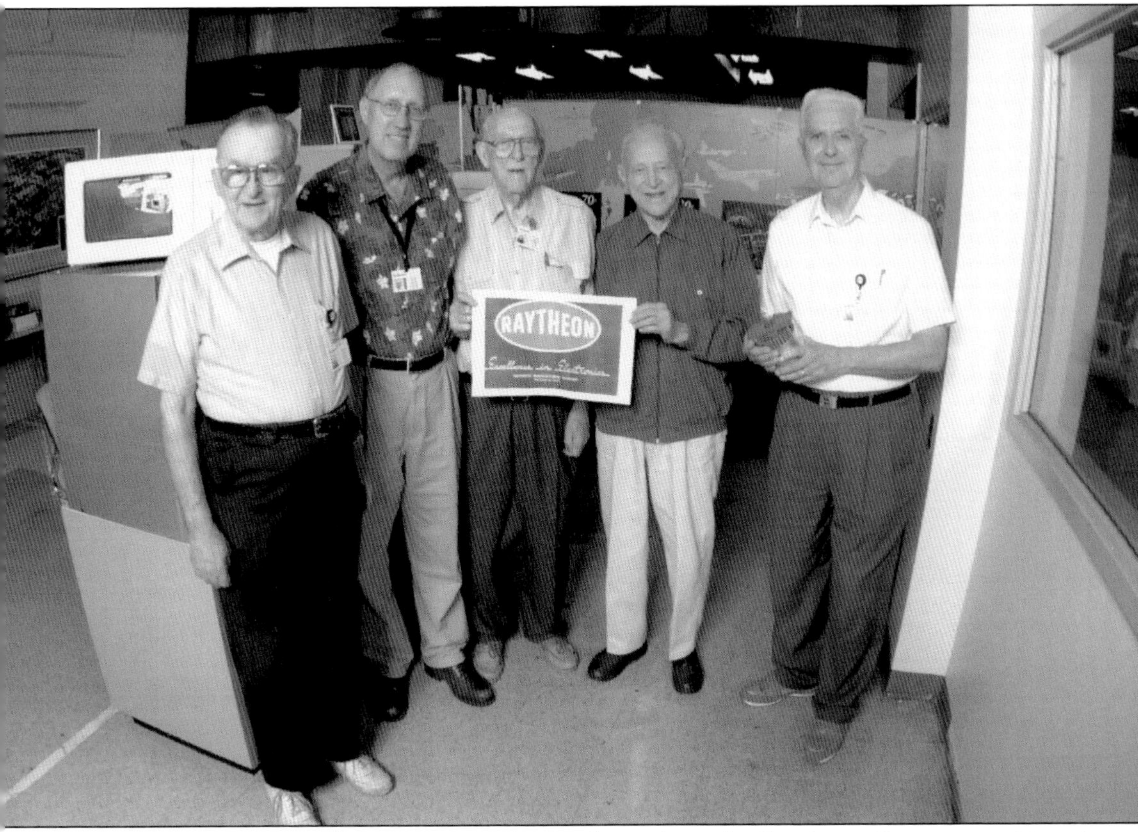

The photographs and documents in this book are from the Raytheon Company archives in Waltham, Massachusetts. Shown above are personnel who volunteer in the archives, helping to catalog material, establish product displays, and respond to inquiries. They are, from left to right, Alden Mayo, Harold Galberg, Lucien Theriault, Norman Krim (chief archivist and former vice president of Raytheon), and Robert E. Edwards (coauthor of this book).

IMAGES
of America

RAYTHEON COMPANY
THE FIRST SIXTY YEARS

Alan R. Earls and Robert E. Edwards

ARCADIA
PUBLISHING

ISBN 978-0-7385-3747-4

Published by Arcadia Publishing
Charleston, South Carolina

Printed in the United States of America

Library of Congress Catalog Card Number: 2004116470

For all general information contact Arcadia Publishing at:
Telephone 843-853-2070
Fax 843-853-0044
E-mail sales@arcadiapublishing.com
For customer service and orders:
Toll-Free 1-888-313-2665

Visit us on the Internet at www.arcadiapublishing.com

Contents

ACKNOWLEDGMENTS

This book is based on material from the Raytheon Company archives in Waltham, Massachusetts. The authors are deeply indebted to Raytheon for granting permission to use these archives. Moreover, we are forever grateful to chief archivist and former Raytheon vice president Norman Krim, who began his career at the company in 1935 and who has been a fountain of information on Raytheon's early days. He started the archives in his own garage and has built and maintained them for over 25 years. We also thank the following retirees and archive volunteers for their assistance: Lucien Theriault, who began working at Raytheon in 1933; Alden Mayo, who worked for the company for 44 years; and Harold Galberg, a Raytheon employee for 38 years.

Thomas Phillips, former CEO and president of Raytheon, provided helpful insight into the company's objectives during its major growth years. Raytheon's principal fellow Eli Brookner reviewed and augmented the technical background information on radar and missile systems that is presented here. Raytheon corporate photographer Don Bernstein took many of the photographs featured in these pages and contributed additional samples to the archives from his own departmental files. James Fetig of Raytheon Corporate Communications reviewed the original outline for the book and granted corporate approval for the project.

Besides the extensive photograph files of the archives, numerous Raytheon publications provided important sources of images and stories. These included *Raytheon News*, *Electronic Progress* magazine, *Missile Messenger* magazine, annual reports, and manuscripts of interviews with Tom Phillips, Norman Krim, and Fritz Gross from a Raytheon oral history project undertaken by Sharon Mercer in 1988. Also helpful was *The Creative Ordeal*, by Otto Scott, a detailed company-sponsored reference book on Raytheon history up to 1973. The book we have written differs from Scott's in that it is a pictorial history and in that it emphasizes the broad scope of newer company activities up into the 1980s. Another excellent reference was *Journey to the Moon*, by Elton C. Hall, which explores mankind's greatest expedition, the Apollo program, including Raytheon's manufacture of the guidance computer that helped deliver the astronauts safely there and back.

The excellent support of the people at Arcadia Publishing, particularly our editor, Kaia Motter, and the photographic and layout staff, is very much appreciated. Finally, we thank our wives, Karen and Francine, for their help and patience through the many hours required to assemble this book.

To those workers and retirees who do not find their particular endeavor or products represented here, we apologize. We may not have had a pertinent photograph in the archives or we simply may not have had room to include it—an inevitability, given the broad range of Raytheon's programs.

It should be noted that even with the large number of photographs included herein, no book can do full justice to the diversity and talent of a company like Raytheon. Furthermore, the photographic record is inconsistent. Thus, some programs are well represented, while others that are equally or perhaps more worthy are omitted. In all cases, we have endeavored to be as equally representative as possible.

INTRODUCTION

While there is perhaps no such thing as a typical company, Raytheon is in many ways a very atypical company. At a time when science was viewed by most people as something far removed from commerce, Raytheon was launched by scientists with a determination to wrest a living from scientific advances that pushed the limit of the state of the art. As the company grew, it frequently found itself competing with established giants and struggling for recognition. But through pluck, intelligence, and plain hard work, it often ended up in the lead.

There were times when a fortunate stroke of technical or managerial ingenuity saved the company and opened doors to dynamic new fields. One of the intentions of this book is to display Raytheon's unbelievably wide variety of programs and products, including radio and television, educational publishing, lifesaving medical equipment, public service weather radars, and military defense equipment.

Summarizing the rich history of such a company is no small task. The important eras could be summarized in terms of their dominant technologies. Indeed, the pictorial record, upon which this book is based, invites such an approach. For instance, in the 1920s and 1930s, the company's chief product was radio tubes. These products did not subsequently disappear; in some ways they grew more important. From the 1940s onward, Raytheon became synonymous with more and more complex radar and guidance systems. The history illustrated by the company's most important hardware is also reflective of the remarkable cast of business and technical leaders that made Raytheon unique over the decades.

The founding triumvirate of Laurence K. Marshall, Vannevar Bush, and Charles G. Smith, later joined by brothers Percy and Al Spencer, provided an impression of quintessential technical entrepreneurship that was carried on by the likes of Fritz Gross and Norm Krim. Business success was always their goal, but imagination coupled with a mastery of engineering made them alive to new possibilities and ever ready to seize new opportunities for leadership.

In the years following World War II, these larger-than-life personalities were supplemented by—and, in some cases, eclipsed by—a new generation. Charles Francis Adams, scion of the famous New England Adamses, became a helmsman of vision, first as president (1948–1960 and 1962–1964) and then as chairman of the board (1964–1975). In all, his involvement with the company lasted for more than half a century. Then, emerging from the engineering ranks in the early 1950s, Thomas Phillips infused the company's newest projects, its missile systems, with energy and purposefulness. He later assumed broader responsibilities under Adams's tutelage. While there were many talented men involved with the company's management in these years, it was this pair in particular that became synonymous with Raytheon's growth from a collection of loosely linked electronic product lines into a model for disciplined expansion and diversification. Indeed, one might fairly describe the period from 1948 to 1992 (when Phillips retired) as the Adams-Phillips era.

No one would have thought that a company that began in 1922 with three founders, $50,000 in raised capital, and nothing more than hope for the success of its single product (a new refrigerator that proved to be unworkable) would mushroom into the Fortune 500 corporation it is today.

Today, Raytheon Company, with sales of $18.1 billion in 2003, is an industry leader in defense and government electronics, space, information technology, technical services, and business and special-mission aircraft. With headquarters in Waltham, Massachusetts, Raytheon employs 78,000 people worldwide.

One

The Early Years

The American Appliance Company, as Raytheon was originally called, was founded in 1922, but it had been conceived through a series of intersecting relationships dating back more than a decade. In 1911, Vannevar Bush—the future dean of engineering, vice president of the Massachusetts Institute of Technology (MIT), and World War II science adviser to Pres. Franklin D. Roosevelt—had been roommates at Tufts College with Laurence K. Marshall. Bush went on to MIT to pursue his doctorate and to teach. Meanwhile, with partial support from Tufts, a group of men launched a company in 1913 called American Radio (or Amrad). The group included C. G. Smith, Al Spencer (a technician with the gifts of an inventor), and, eventually, Bush himself, who served for a time as research manager. One of the firm's major innovations was the development of the S tube (generally credited to Smith), which ultimately eliminated the need for batteries to supply direct current for radios. The company prospered during World War I, but in 1920 there was a brief but severe economic depression, and Amrad's fortunes turned for the worse. It closed its facilities in the Boston area, although remnants of the company survived for a few more years in New York.

Following the disappointment of Amrad, Al Spencer, who had invented a simple thermostatic control called the Klixon Disk, launched the Spencer Thermostat Company. He was helped by Marshall—who had gone into industry after Tufts and then served as an officer in the U.S. Army during World War I—and by Bush. The company prospered, selling the Klixon Disk in large quantities for use in appliances such as electric irons. This phase of the company's history was important, as it established this small group as successful entrepreneurs.

Only then did Raytheon's lineal antecedent, the American Appliance Company, finally come into being. Smith came up with a design for a highly advanced refrigerator with no moving parts, and Bush and Marshall came aboard to help launch a company around the invention, much as they had done with Spencer. Alas, after a period of research and development, the refrigerator proved to be one Smith innovation that did not work out. The new company was left without a product.

The founders had raised $50,000 in capital to start the company and had spent half of it on the refrigerator's development; they needed a new direction to pursue. So they secured the rights to manufacture an updated version of Smith's S tube and went into electronics manufacturing, bringing Al Spencer on board in the process. By 1925, the company, propelled by this combination of talents, was earning a profit. They were even able to recruit Al Spencer's younger brother Percy, who was a self-made engineering talent, to join the company. Percy had begun learning about electricity as a youth when he helped to wire a factory in his home state of Maine. Inspired by the role of radio in mitigating the *Titanic* disaster, Percy joined the U.S. Navy and became a radioman. He later worked for the Submarine Signal Company (SubSig), where he acquired further skills in electronics.

Along with its new product, the company also had a new name. It was renamed Raytheon Manufacturing Company in 1925 to avoid a conflict with another company called American Appliance, based in the Midwest.

Throughout the 1920s, the company prospered with its line of rectifier and radio tubes. The depression years of 1929–1933 were difficult. Raytheon survived with Percy Spencer's new line of transmitting tubes and Marshall's management skills, but the company was still overshadowed by the giants of the industry, such as General Electric and RCA. Indeed, from 1930 to 1940, the company barely managed to maintain profitability.

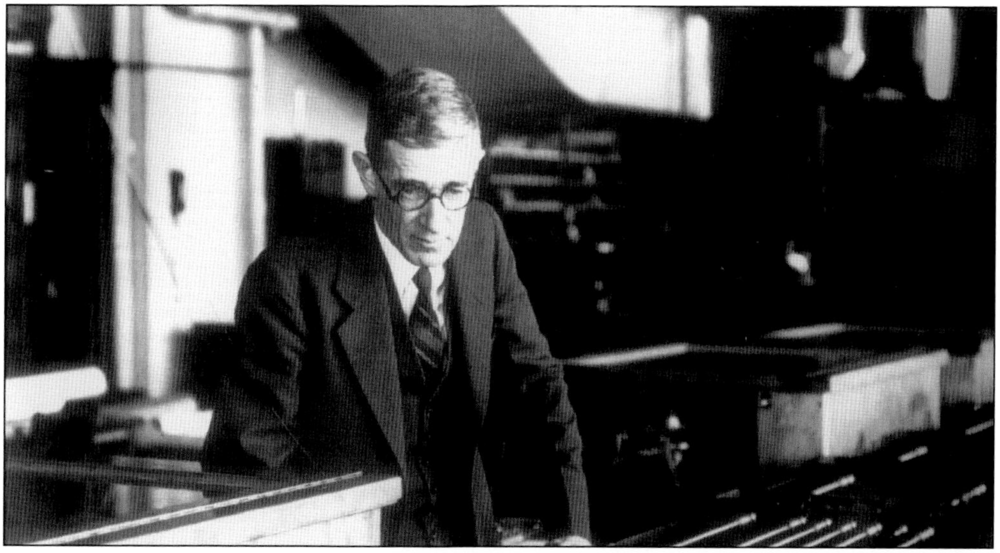

From its inception, Raytheon has been built by unusually talented people. Vannevar Bush was one of Raytheon's founders. He and another founder, Laurence K. Marshall, had been roommates at Tufts College in 1911. They stayed in touch over the years. Bush went on to obtain his doctorate and to teach at MIT; he served as Pres. Franklin D. Roosevelt's chief scientific adviser during World War II. In this photograph from the 1930s, he works at MIT on his early version of an analog computer called the Differential Analyzer, which attempted to solve differential equations mechanically.

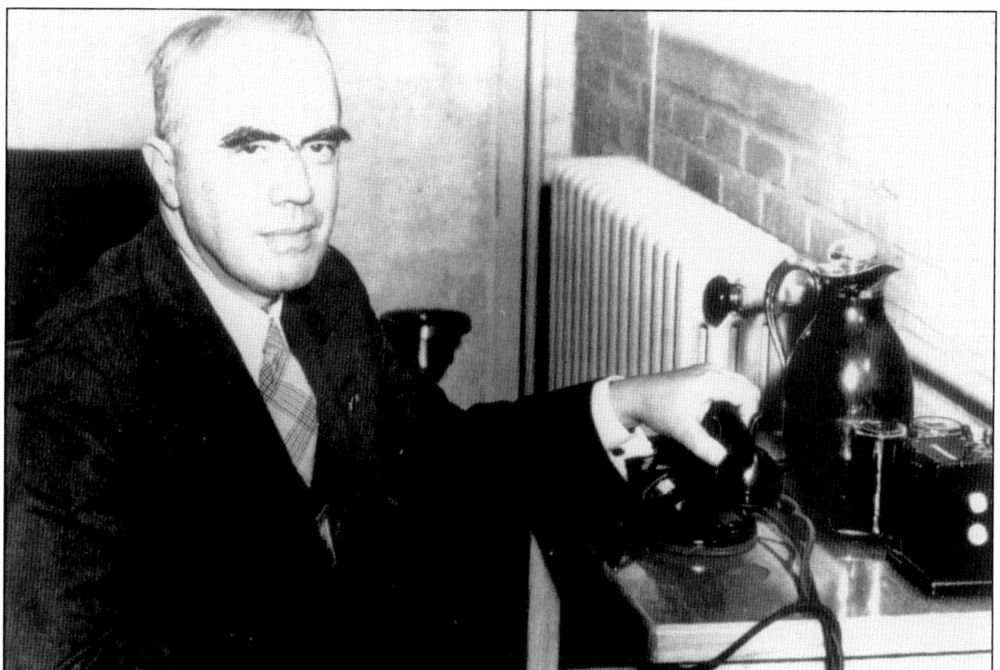

Laurence K. Marshall was the entrepreneur of the three founders. His energy, business insight, and financial acumen saw Raytheon through many difficult years. He was company president from 1928 until 1948.

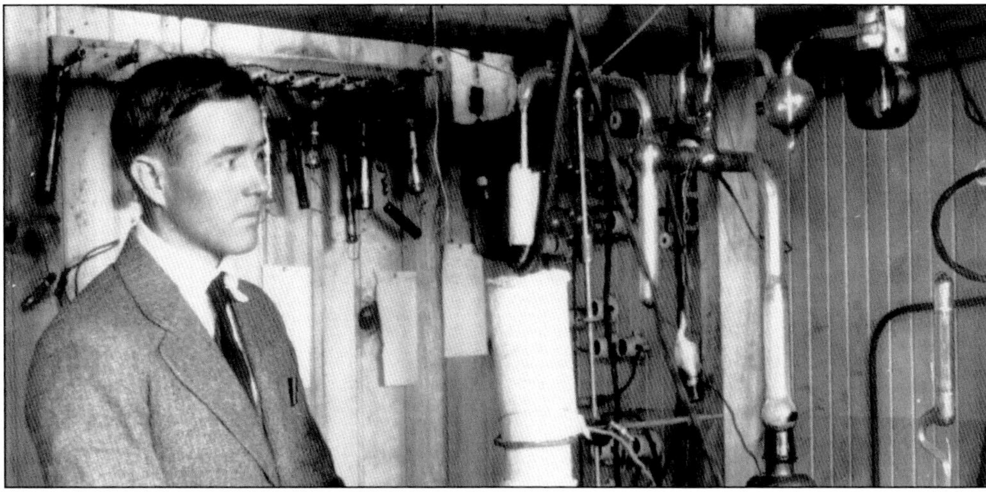

C. G. Smith, the third of the original Raytheon triad, had a concept for a refrigerator with no moving parts, which led to the 1922 formation of the American Appliance Company. The three founders had to find a new product when the refrigerator proved unsuccessful. Fortunately, Smith had invented the S gas rectifier tube while he was employed at Amrad. The founders obtained the rights to the patent, and with some improvements by Smith, it became a highly successful product. The tube eliminated the need for large and expensive batteries that had, until then, supplied the current for all home radios. This was the true beginning of Raytheon Manufacturing Company (as American Appliance was renamed in 1925).

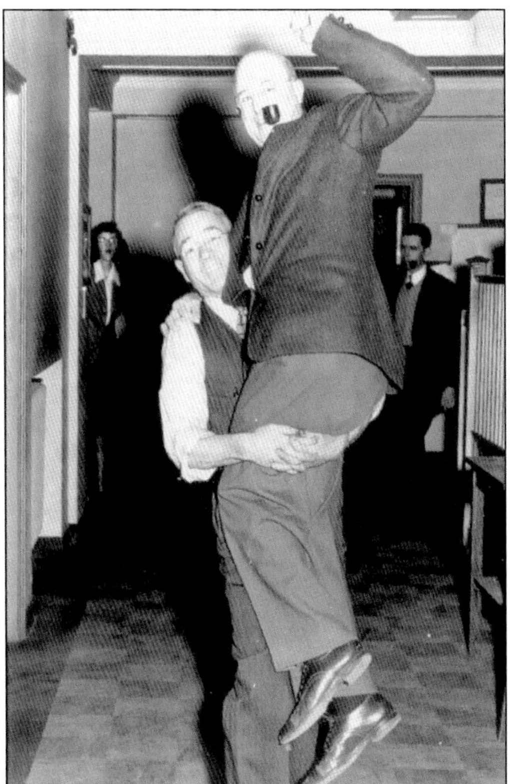

Scientist C. G. Smith not only pushed the boundaries of electronics but was also proud of developing his physical strength. He always insisted on having a high metal bar across his office doorway so that he could do chin-ups every day. Here he is effortlessly hoisting financial backer Billy Gammell, who served as Raytheon president from 1924 to 1928.

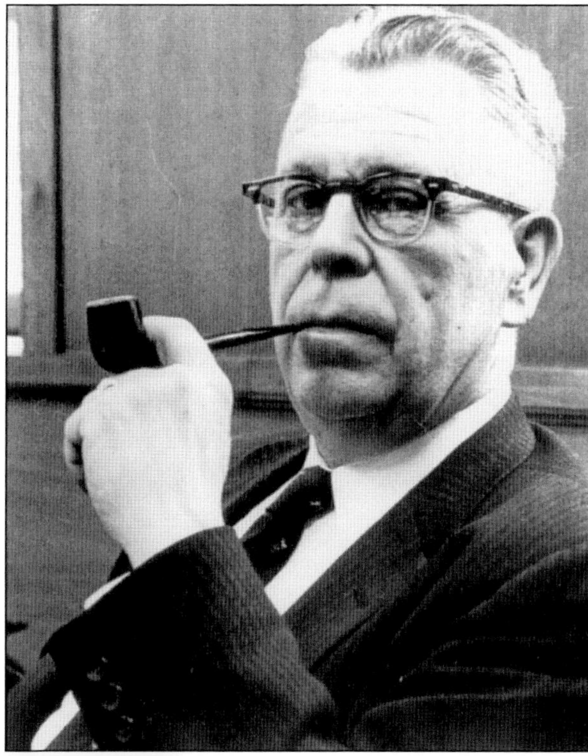

Percy L. Spencer was very important to Raytheon's development. He was hired by Raytheon at the suggestion of his older brother, John. Percy saved the company by converting the B tube rectifier to the BH design to run at the new, higher operating voltage of 180 volts. During the 1930s, he developed a full line of radio transmitting tubes for amateur radio use. In 1940, he introduced a method of producing magnetron tubes using sheet-metal laminating, which broke a production bottleneck in the application of microwave radar and helped to win World War II. He invented the microwave oven in 1945. He had more than 140 patents and was inducted into the National Inventors Hall of Fame posthumously in 1999.

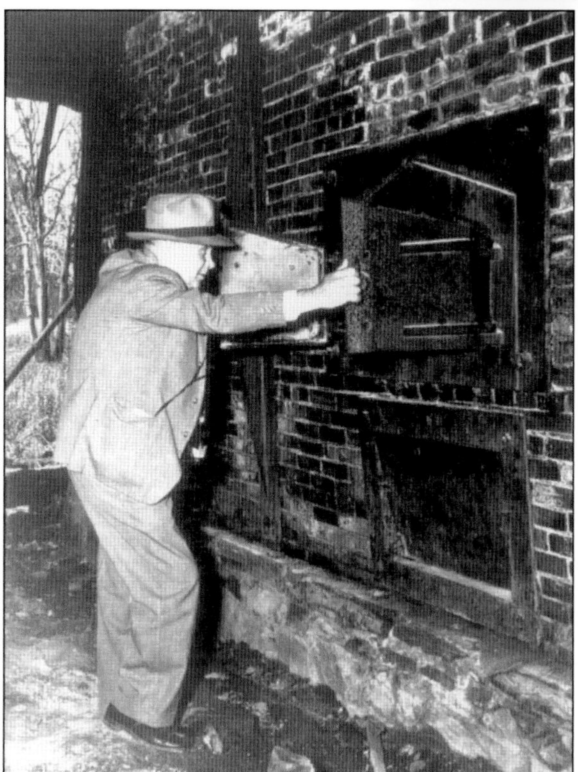

John (Al) Spencer conceived his snap-disk thermostat when he was only 15 and was tending a furnace in a mill in northern Maine. He noticed that when the furnace cooled, the door snapped from concave to convex. By 1921, when he was 29, he had made a working sample snap-disk about the size of a quarter that snapped in the same way at a specific temperature. This invention, promoted by Laurence K. Marshall and Vannevar Bush as the Klixon Disk, led to the founding of the Spencer Thermostat Company, whose success demonstrated the entrepreneurial skills of this small group. The original furnace incident is re-created here by John Spencer. He later became Raytheon's first manufacturing manager.

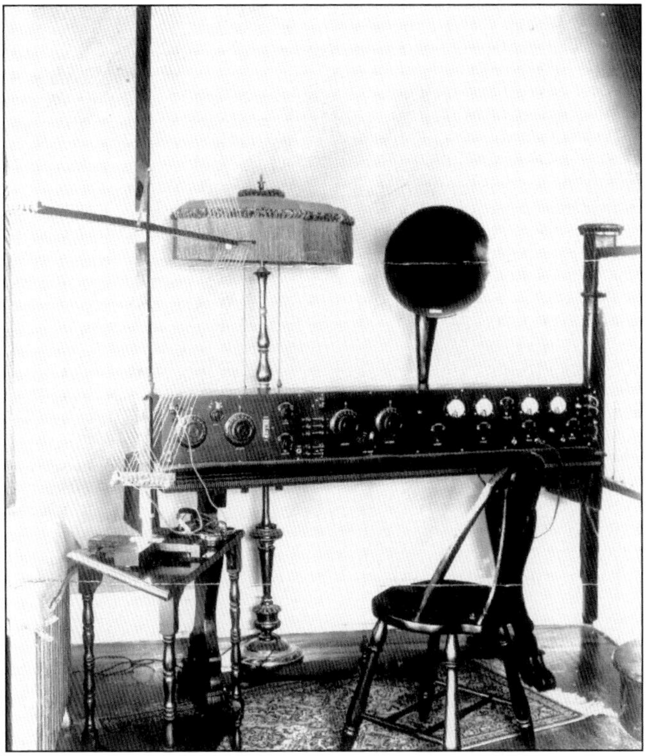

Here is a view of a 1920s radio setup, a far cry from today's shirt-pocket transistor radios. Note the gigantic antenna at the left and the high-style floor lamp in the background. Although radio was popular, at this date it was still an emerging industry.

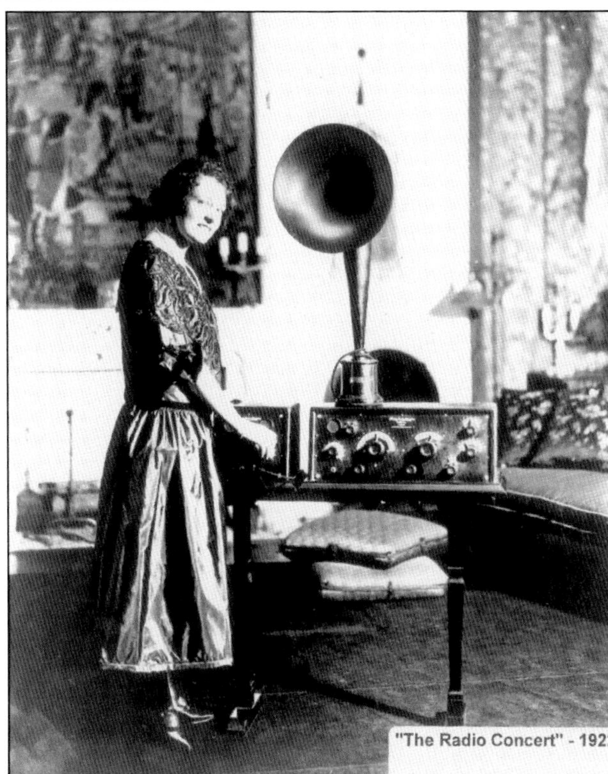

One of the factors limiting the expansion of the radio business was that all early radios were battery powered, as seen in this 1922 photograph. The constant expense and annoyance of replacing batteries—a frequent occurrence, given the tremendous power requirements of vacuum tubes—created a demand for a more practical power source. Raytheon's rectifier tubes, which converted household AC current to the DC used in radio tubes, provided the answer and helped boost sales of radio products.

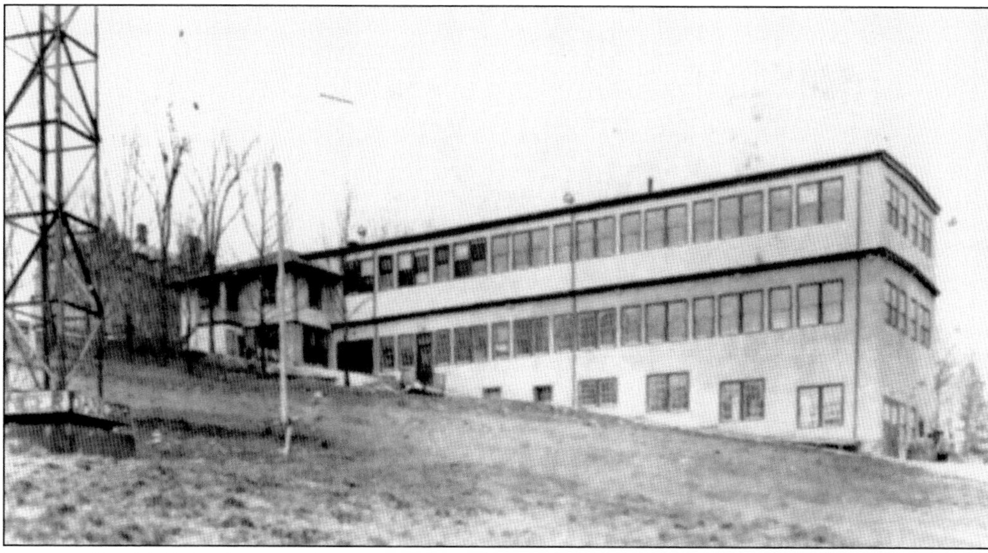

During World War I, Amrad was busy producing radio receivers and transmitters for the military. This 1920 view of the factory, located adjacent to Tufts College in Medford, was taken shortly before the company suffered serious setbacks due to economic problems. It was at Amrad that C. G. Smith developed the gaseous rectifier S tube. After Smith joined Raytheon and Amrad's patent rights were purchased, an improved version of this tube became the first successful product for the fledgling company in the mid-1920s. Amrad operated Boston's first commercial radio station.

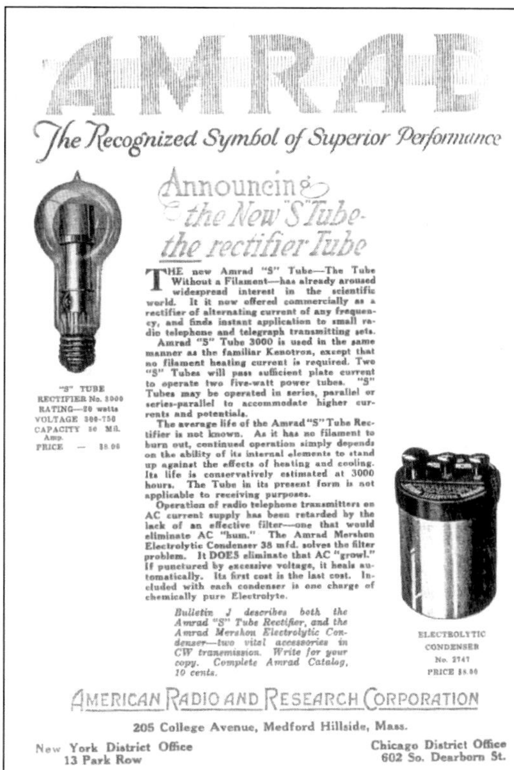

This advertisement presents the S tube rectifier, invented by C. G. Smith at Amrad. Unfortunately, the customer base for radio products was not sufficiently developed to sustain the company when the country was hit by the financial depression of 1920–1921, causing major cutbacks in Amrad's business. In particular, financier J. P. Morgan withdrew his funding. C. G. Smith left in 1922 and became one of the three founders of the American Appliance Company (later renamed Raytheon).

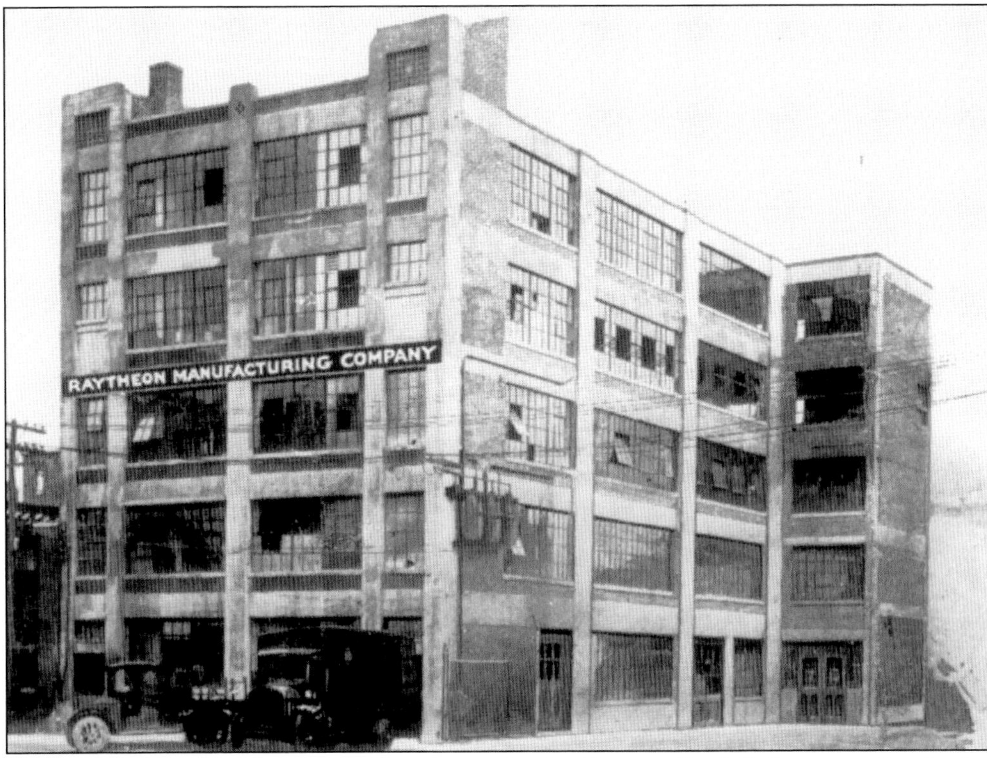

The first Raytheon production facility was in this building in Kendall Square in Cambridge, Massachusetts, shown in 1928. Note the vintage trucks.

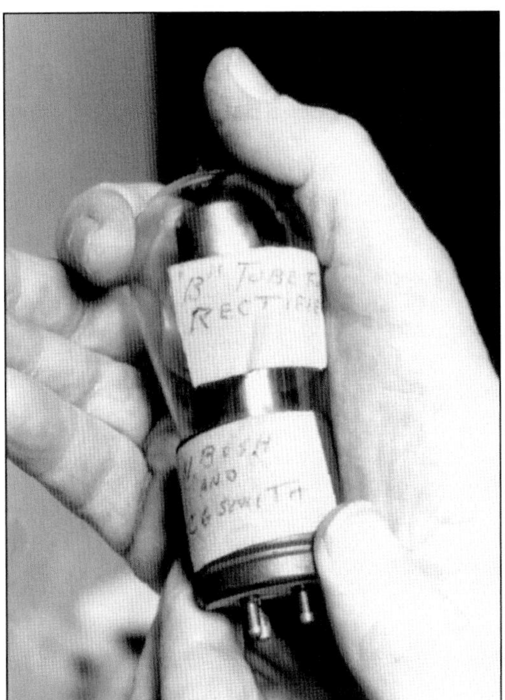

Raytheon (or the American Appliance Company, as it was first known) went on to develop its B tube gaseous rectifier based on an improved version of C. G. Smith's earlier S tube, which made household radios more practical.

In a move that some believe was aimed squarely at Raytheon, RCA, a dominant maker of radios, raised the standard rectifier operating voltage from 135 to 180 volts in 1925, providing more power for radios, but also threatening to make the Raytheon B tube obsolete. However, Raytheon's Percy Spencer quickly responded by redesigning the B tube to comply, resulting in this BH rectifier. This saved the company's primary business and resulted in a very profitable period in the late 1920s.

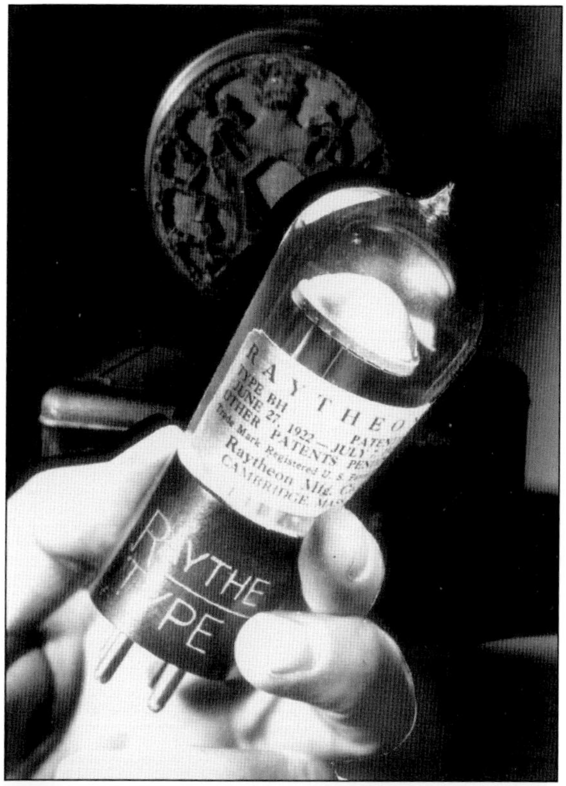

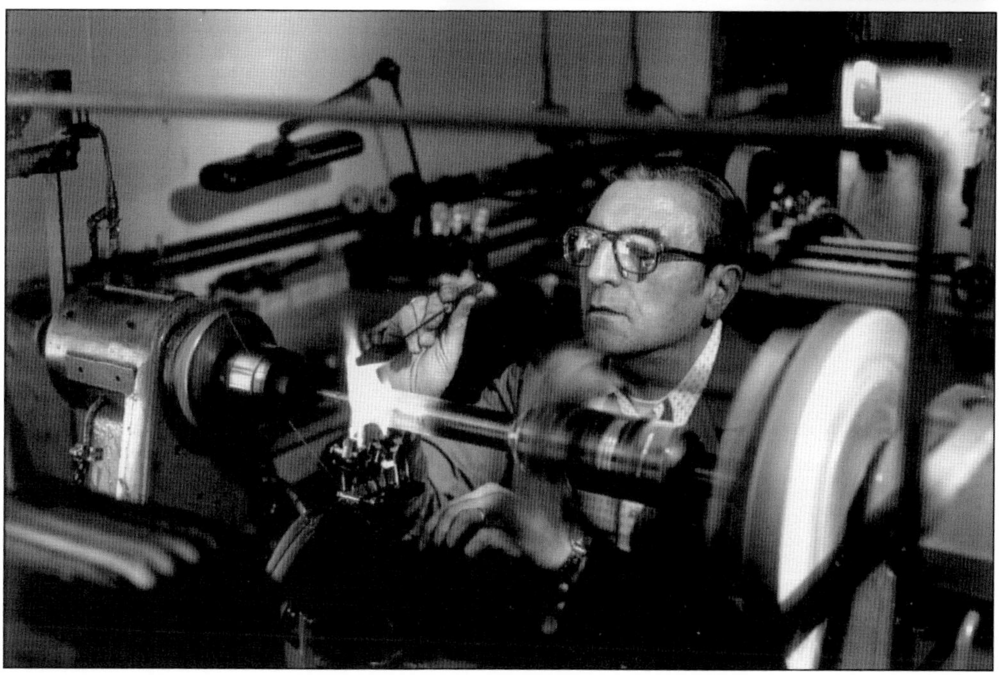

Hand glasswork was an integral part of tube manufacture throughout the company's history. While no photographs of early glass workmanship exist in the company archives, this later picture shows the typical artistry required of the highly skilled workers in this occupation.

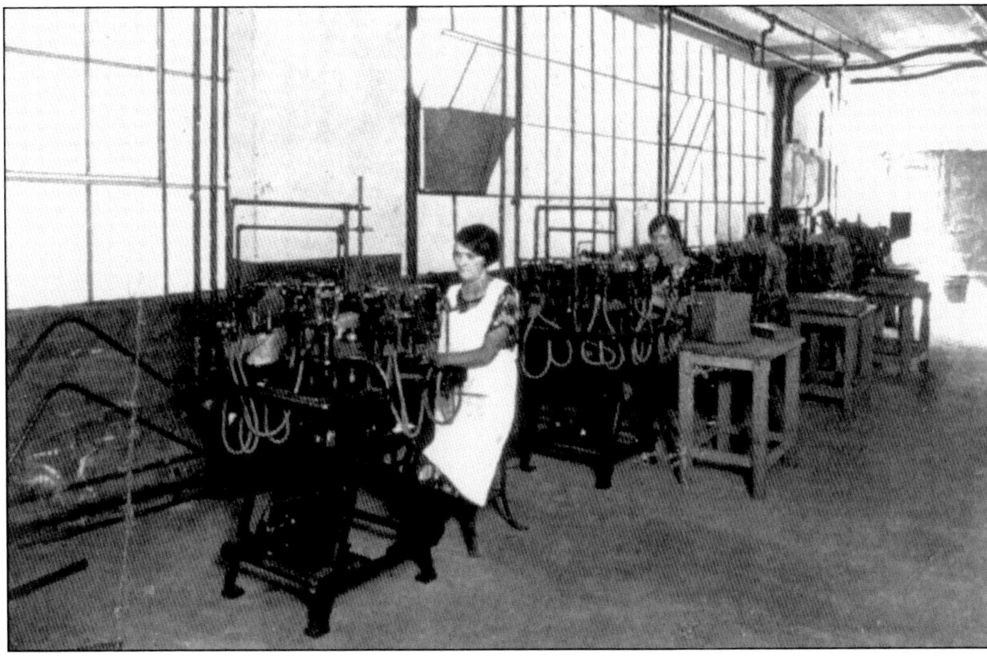

This bare-bones tube-production line was typical of Raytheon's early manufacturing facilities in the mid-1920s. Glass "stems" are being sealed to internal tube elements by these workers.

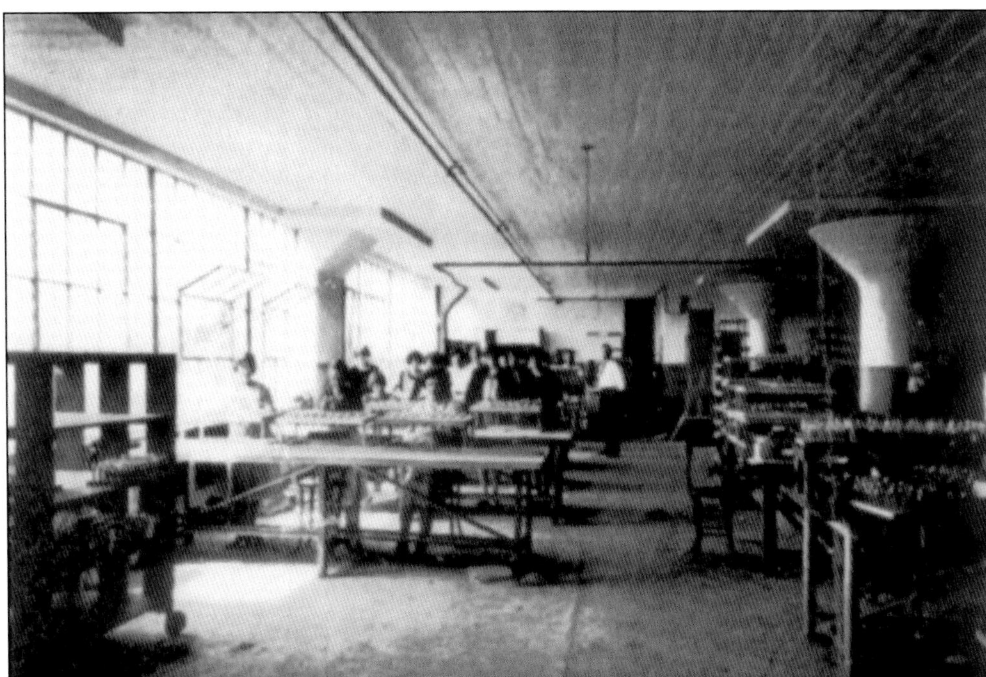

This is an interior view of the Cambridge factory of Raytheon Manufacturing Company in the mid-1920s. Workers are cleaning and performing final inspection of Raytheon rectifier tubes in preparation for shipment.

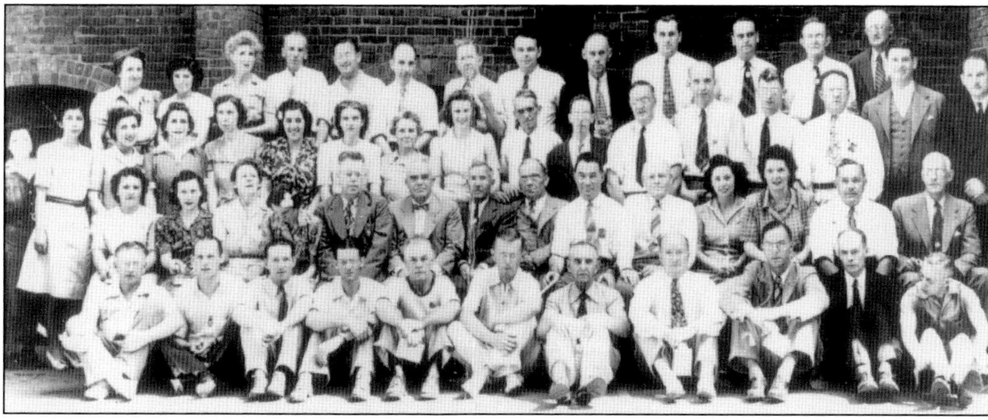

In this 1943 image, the remaining 55 employees of Raytheon Manufacturing Company who had been on the payroll in 1929 assemble for a group photograph. From left to right are the following: (first row) Clayton Stone Jr., John Carroll, Edward Hayes, Jack Soucy, Harry Leonard, Arthur Smith, Carl Schroeder, James Larsen, W. M. Thompson, Waldo Saul, and William Egan; (second row) Vivian Mathieson, Adeline Boutin, Anna McLaskey, Lillian Driscoll, Percy Spencer (Waltham plant manager), Laurence K. Marshall (president), C. G. Smith, John Spencer, David Schultz (vice president), P. T. Weeks (Newton plant manager), Mary Curtin, Beatrice Cormier, Edward Brown, and Stanley Linford; (third row) Flora Fuoco, Catherine Puleio, Anne Mangano, Margaret Crowley, Elizabeth Kane, Rose Ryan, Marion Barry, Lillian MacLean, Grace Jennings, Nat Wright, Brad Reed, Harry Rice, Theodore Burkholder, John McCann, George Nary, J. J. McGilicuddy, and Niles Gowell; (fourth row) Margaret Beals, Frances McDonald, Margaret Lavery, Joseph Rydant, Arthur Short, Walter Goddard, Duncan MacLean, Edwin Thompson, John Day, Leslie Lawrence, and Francis Barry.

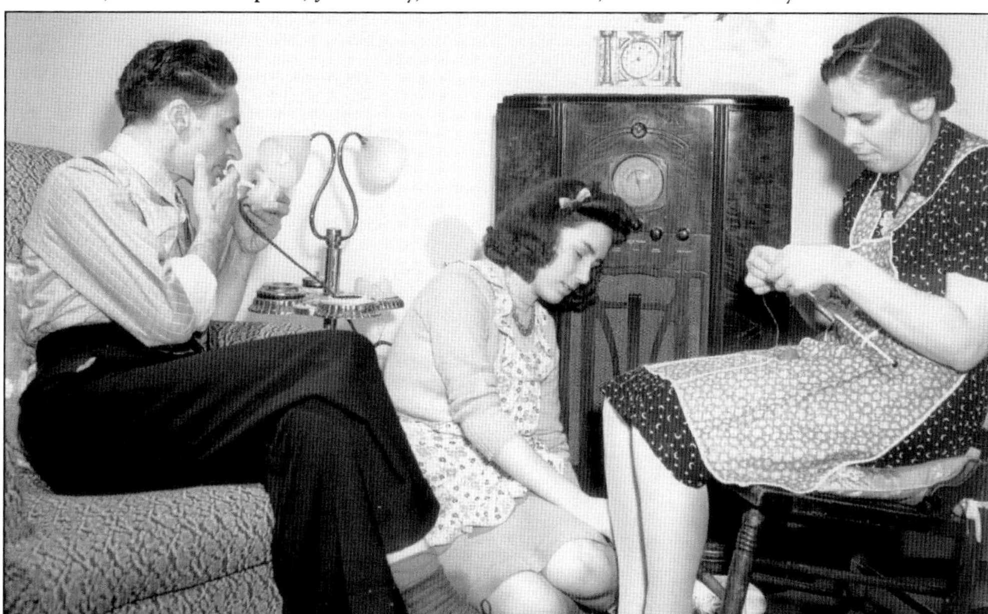

Receiving and transmitting tubes for home radios and radio transmitters constituted Raytheon's main business during the depression years of the 1930s. By the late 1930s, some economic recovery was evident. The family seen here is enjoying the latest technologies, including a console model radio, an electric clock, and even an electric cigarette lighter.

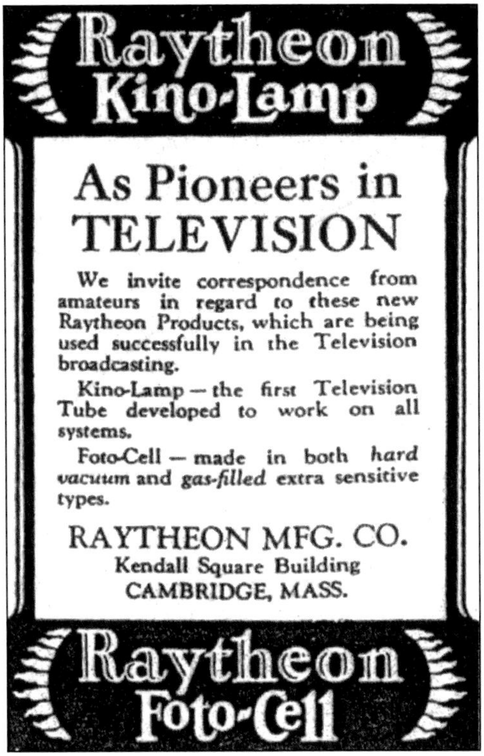

The electronics magazine *QST* published this Raytheon ad in 1926 for the Kino Lamp to be used on "all systems" of television, which were currently in experimental stages at the time. The spinning disc designs, with various versions of spiral hole arrangements through which light was admitted to form a picture, were the only ones in use then.

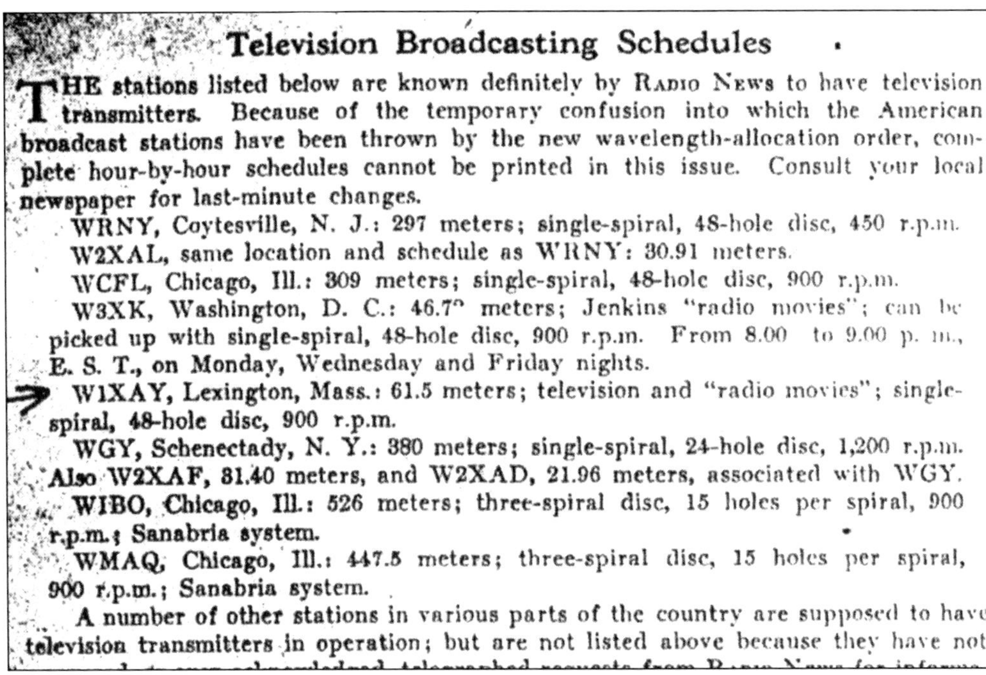

Television Broadcasting Schedules

THE stations listed below are known definitely by RADIO NEWS to have television transmitters. Because of the temporary confusion into which the American broadcast stations have been thrown by the new wavelength-allocation order, complete hour-by-hour schedules cannot be printed in this issue. Consult your local newspaper for last-minute changes.

WRNY, Coytesville, N. J.: 297 meters; single-spiral, 48-hole disc, 450 r.p.m.

W2XAL, same location and schedule as WRNY: 30.91 meters.

WCFL, Chicago, Ill.: 309 meters; single-spiral, 48-hole disc, 900 r.p.m.

W3XK, Washington, D. C.: 46.7° meters; Jenkins "radio movies"; can be picked up with single-spiral, 48-hole disc, 900 r.p.m. From 8.00 to 9.00 p. m., E. S. T., on Monday, Wednesday and Friday nights.

W1XAY, Lexington, Mass.: 61.5 meters; television and "radio movies"; single-spiral, 48-hole disc, 900 r.p.m.

WGY, Schenectady, N. Y.: 380 meters; single-spiral, 24-hole disc, 1,200 r.p.m. Also W2XAF, 31.40 meters, and W2XAD, 21.96 meters, associated with WGY.

WIBO, Chicago, Ill.: 526 meters; three-spiral disc, 15 holes per spiral, 900 r.p.m.; Sanabria system.

WMAQ, Chicago, Ill.: 447.5 meters; three-spiral disc, 15 holes per spiral, 900 r.p.m.; Sanabria system.

A number of other stations in various parts of the country are supposed to have television transmitters in operation; but are not listed above because they have not

Radio News published this roster of working television stations in the late 1920s. Raytheon was a participant in the station listed in Lexington, Massachusetts. That station was licensed in September 1926 and operated until March 1930. All stations listed are of the "spinning disc" design.

Two

THE WORLD WAR II YEARS

As Raytheon emerged from the Great Depression, it was a company with lots of know-how but a tenuous position in the electronics industry. Other companies dominated the field, and Raytheon had to scramble to find its own way to profit. All that changed with the war.

Two key components began the company's rejuvenation and contributed mightily to the Allied victory. One was the cavity magnetron tube. In England, at war already for more than two years, the military had been using low-frequency air defense radars of limited capability. English scientists pushed the state of the art and developed powerful, accurate microwave radars using a revolutionary tube called the magnetron. The development was critical. Nazi bombing of England was decimating the country's defenses and industries; better night and day radar detection of attacking planes was desperately needed.

Fearing it could not produce enough of the magnetrons, which had to be laboriously machined from solid copper blocks, a British delegation called the Tizard Commission sought manufacturing help from large U.S. companies. Although excluded from the earliest discussions, Raytheon's leaders, with help from backers at MIT, were eventually able to get involved. Percy Spencer, in particular, impressed the British with a design suggestion, conceived overnight, that led to a manufacturing breakthrough and an order for a few experimental magnetrons from MIT. Spencer's insight dramatically simplified production by brazing together a laminate of stamped sections of copper to make a finished magnetron, eliminating most of the expensive and time-consuming machining processes.

This innovation was met with skepticism by the government, but company president Marshall made a bet-the-company decision to invest in a new building and the special equipment—including a hydrogen oven—required for the process. The money for the project was diverted from other Raytheon resources several months before the actual military order was received. As a result, Raytheon was eventually able to dramatically out-produce its competitors, making as many as 2,600 magnetrons a day at its peak. By the end of the war, 80 percent of all magnetrons in use by the Allies had been manufactured by Raytheon.

But those were only part of Raytheon's war efforts. Another Percy Spencer innovation also proved vital to the Allied victory. Prior to the war, he had experimented with developing subminiature tubes so that he could make a radio-controlled airplane model for his sons. These tubes ended up playing a crucial role in the development of a proximity fuse (detonator) for artillery shells, a project undertaken by the Carnegie Institute. Existing fuses relied on a timer or on impact with an object to detonate. The goal of the proximity fuse was to make an artillery shell that would burst in the air just prior to impact, potentially increasing its lethality. The work was later extended to include antiaircraft ammunition that would automatically explode when it reached the vicinity of an enemy aircraft. Accomplishing this goal required the creation of a tiny, extremely rugged radarlike transmitter and receiver. The call went out to Spencer at

Raytheon, who with Norman Krim helped set up the mass production of the subminiature tubes that made the proximity fuse a reality. These tubes were an important technical monopoly for the Allied forces, one later declared by military authorities as a key technological factor in winning World War II.

Building on its magnetron triumphs, Raytheon made another great achievement in the war: graduating from component supplier to system supplier. Led by Fritz Gross, the company created a series of radars, including the famous SG series, that were placed on thousands of American and British ships and smaller craft. These systems acquired a reputation for great reliability and were well designed and manufactured. Raytheon provided its own service force for the radars and was quick to make necessary upgrades and design modifications.

Raytheon ended the war a vastly larger company than it had been just a few years earlier. It was now a company that had attracted recognition from top leadership as well as from rank-and-file military people. Production had increased 40 times above the level of 1940, and employment had rocketed to 16,000. The company would never be the same.

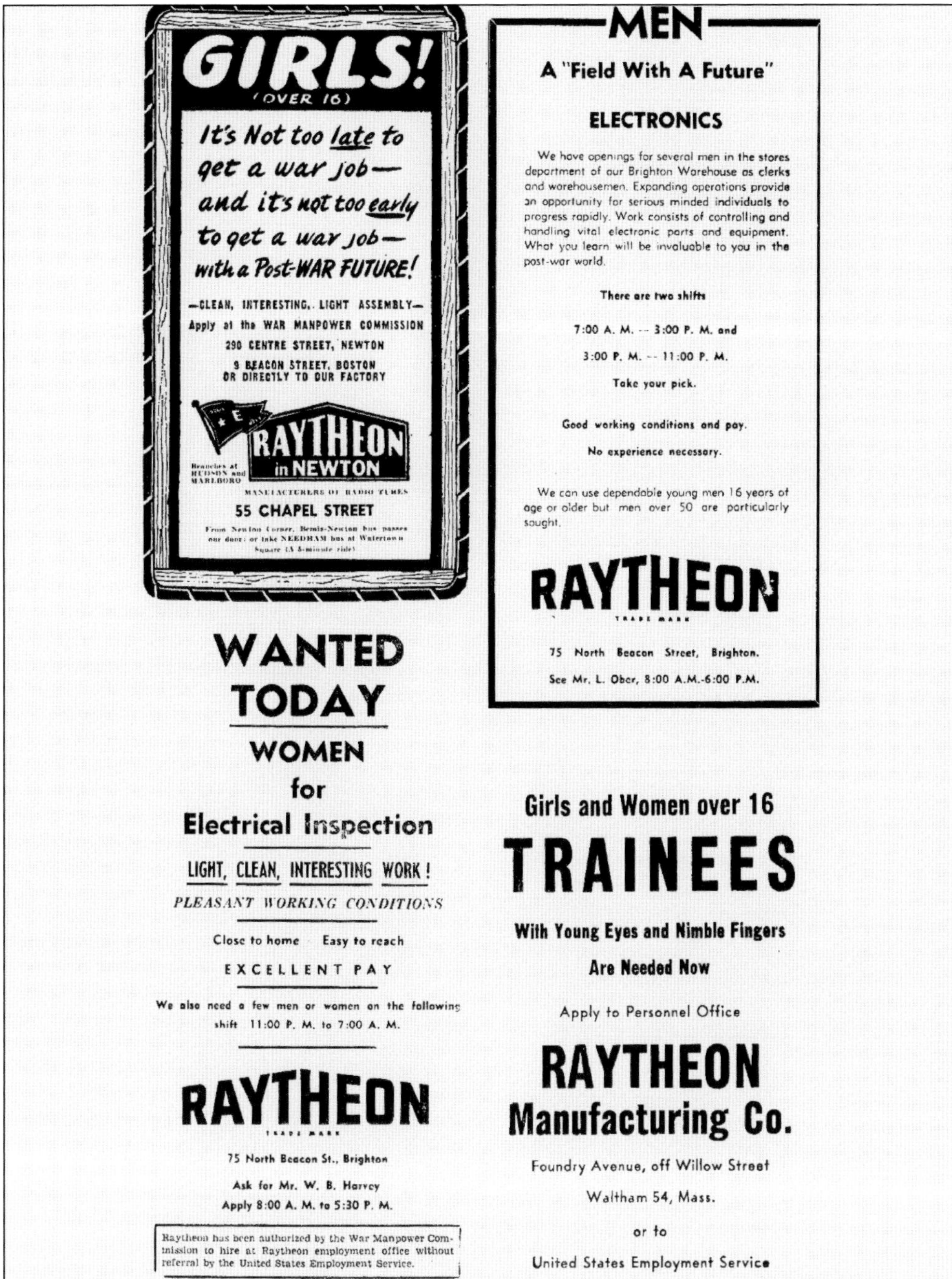

During World War II, Raytheon expanded greatly to handle orders for magnetron tubes and other products for radar, ultimately including entire radar systems. These newspaper advertisements from the early 1940s invite workers to apply to plants at North Beacon Street in Brighton, Chapel Street in Newton, and Foundry Avenue in Waltham (the building that currently houses the Raytheon archive). The advertisement at the upper left includes a small replica of the Army-Navy E for excellence, an award that was granted to four Raytheon divisions simultaneously on May 14, 1943.

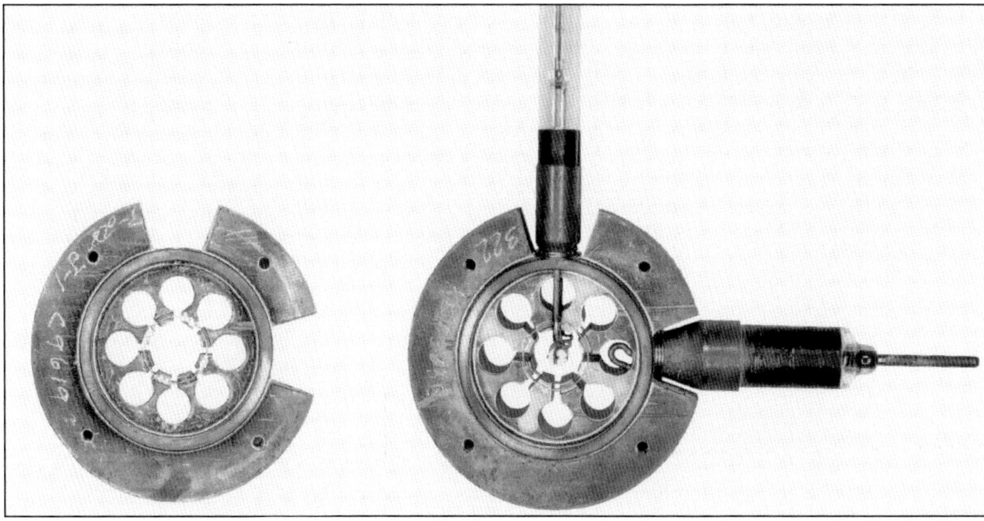

Magnetron tubes, which could generate high power at microwave frequencies, were first made practical by British scientists J. T. Randall and J. A. Boot in February 1940. The devices were critical in building accurate radars, but they were so difficult to build that the British sought American help in August 1940. Shown here is the internal structure of a very early magnetron as built by Raytheon, displaying the eight microwave resonant cavities (the positive electrode) and central suspended cathode (the negative electrode). The output loop is seen in one of the anode cavities. The magnetic circuit was mounted externally in the radar and is not in the photograph.

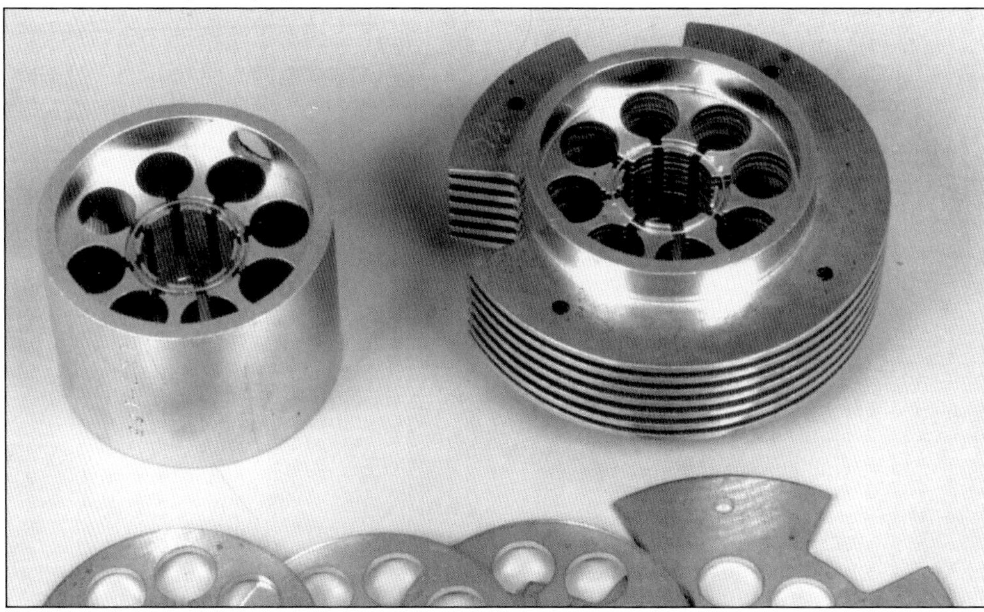

Having established a reputation for ingenuity and quick response, Raytheon was approached in 1940 by the Tizard Commission to help accelerate magnetron tube production for wartime defensive radars. Percy Spencer devised several innovations that broke the manufacturing bottleneck. One of the main improvements was the lamination method, replacing the slow drilling of the critical copper anodes. Production soon rose to 2,600 tubes per day. Raytheon supplied over 80 percent of the magnetrons for Allied radars in World War II.

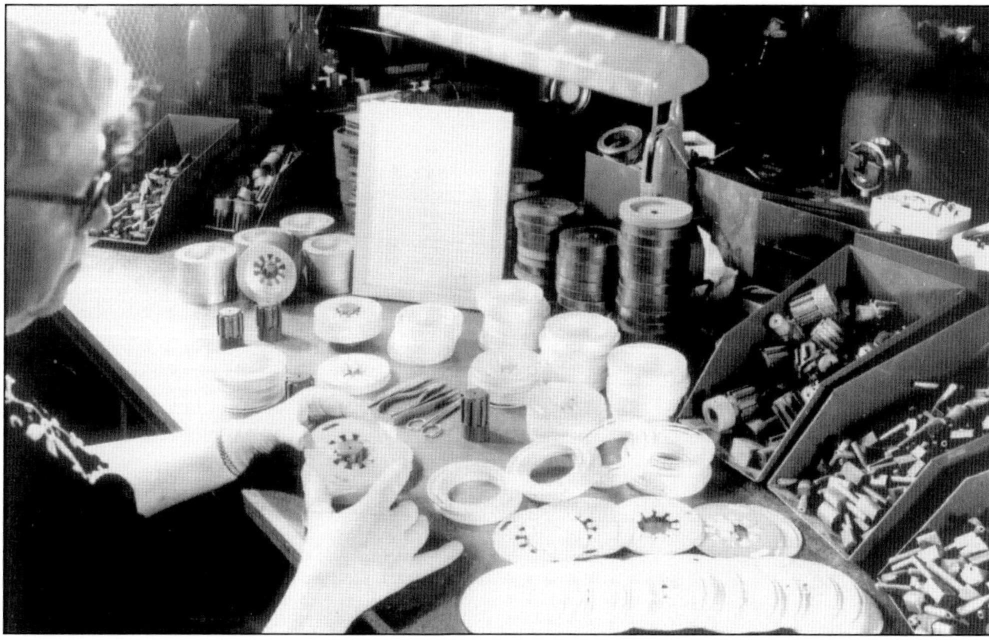

This photograph from the late 1950s shows the process—invented during the war by Percy Spencer—by which stacked copper laminations are used to make the anode structure for magnetrons. This example is a five-megawatt high-power magnetron for use in an air force height-finding radar (FPS-6).

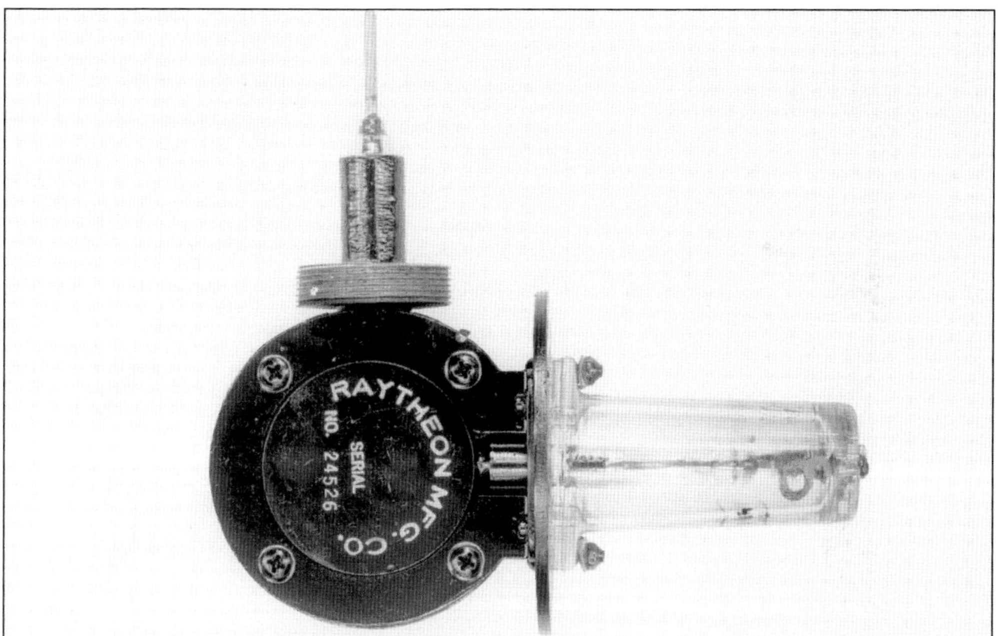

The typical World War II magnetron is illustrated by this Raytheon type 2J37 model. In the early wartime period, the magnets were mounted externally in the radar system. In later years, the development of compact, higher-powered alnico magnets allowed them to be packaged directly on each tube, assuring better control of the magnetic field and better tube performance.

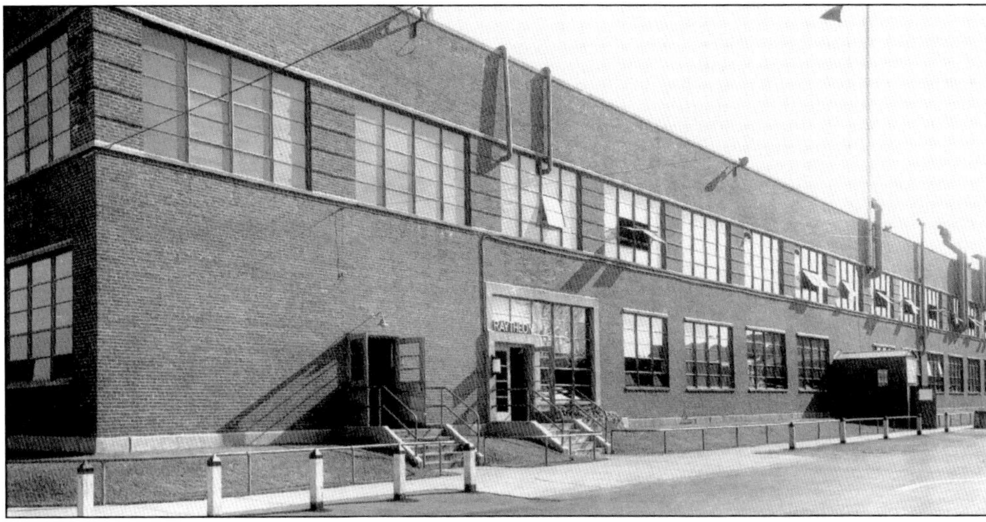

Building 41 in Waltham was Raytheon's headquarters through 1950, when a larger and more modern annex was built. Norman Krim, Raytheon's former vice president and currently its chief archivist, participated in an informal inspection, walking along the top of the steel beams of this building with company president Laurence K. Marshall, who had developed his skills as a construction engineer in the construction industry as a youth. Raytheon produced over 80 percent of the magnetron tubes for World War II Allied radars in this building, supplemented by satellite machine shops and small parts vendors. This wartime contribution was a major factor in building Raytheon into a multimillion-dollar company.

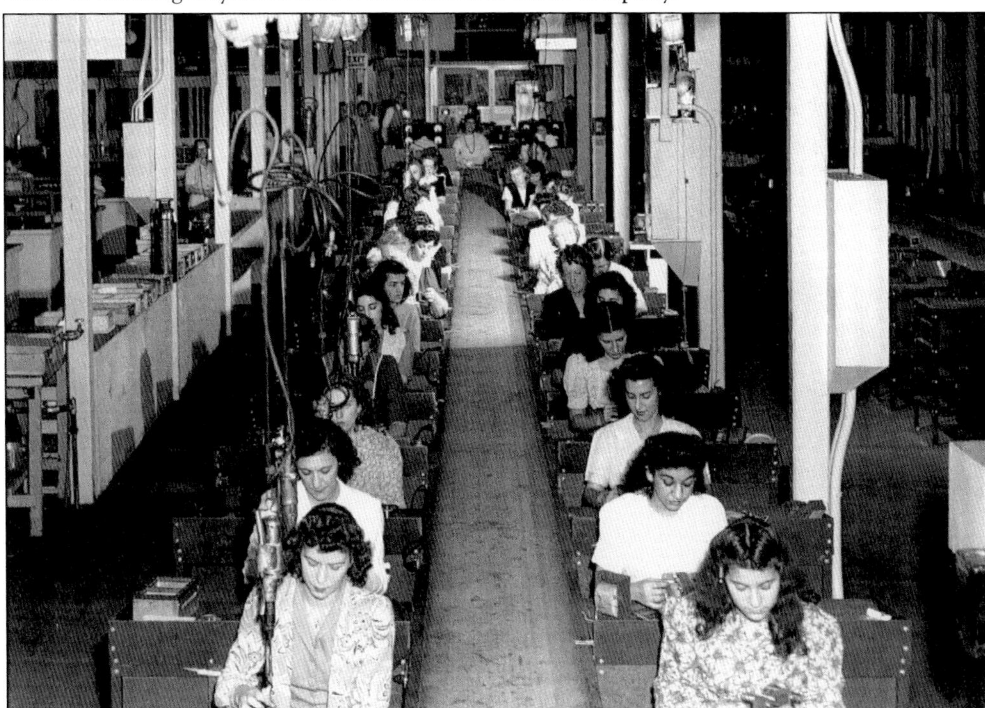

In this image, a wartime assembly line at Raytheon produces transformers, chokes, regulators, and rectifiers.

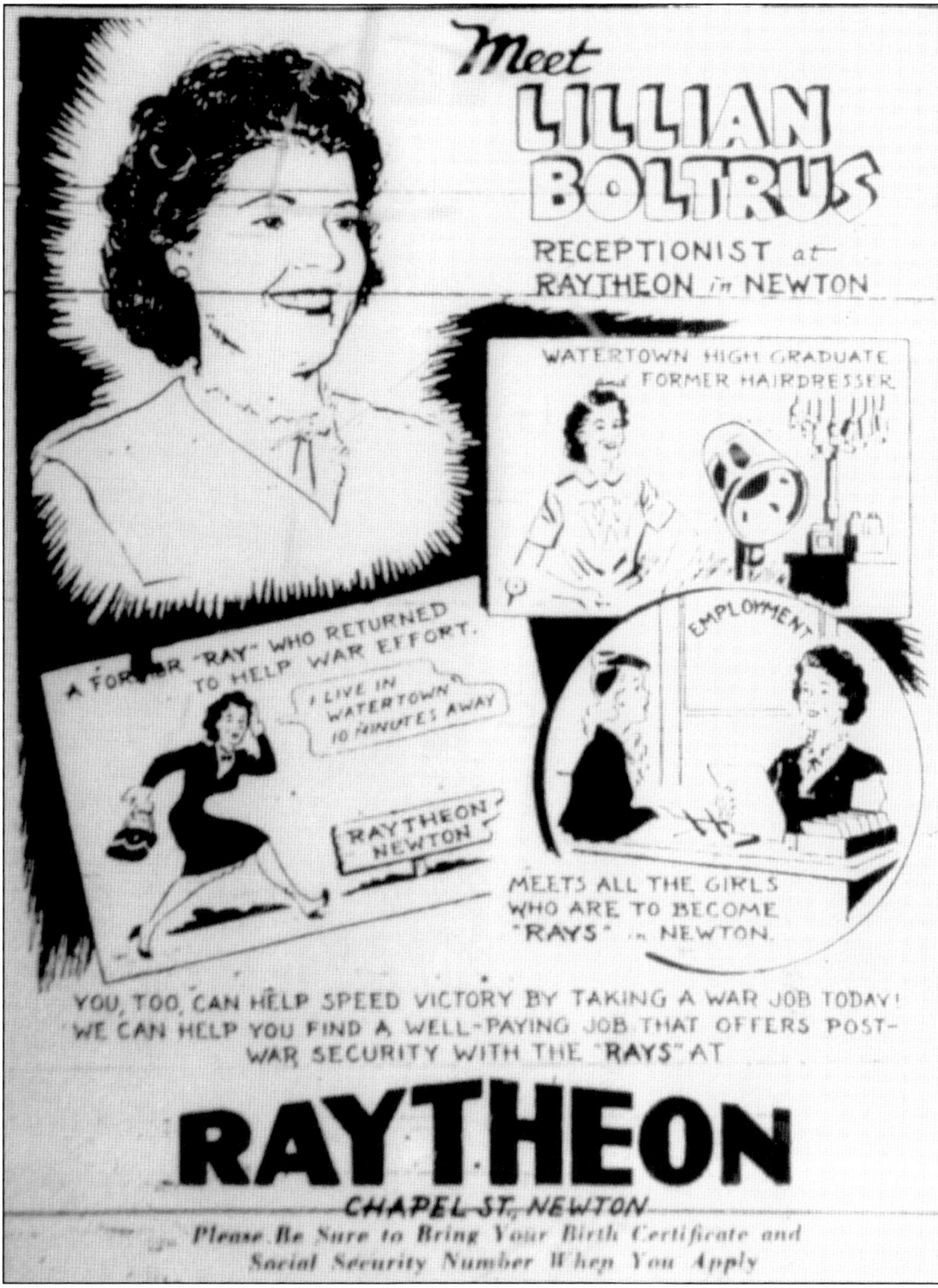

In this recruiting poster, Lillian Boltrus, a former hairdresser, tells her story of joining Raytheon to help in the war effort. She was employed at the Newton plant, where tubes were manufactured for radio and radar applications.

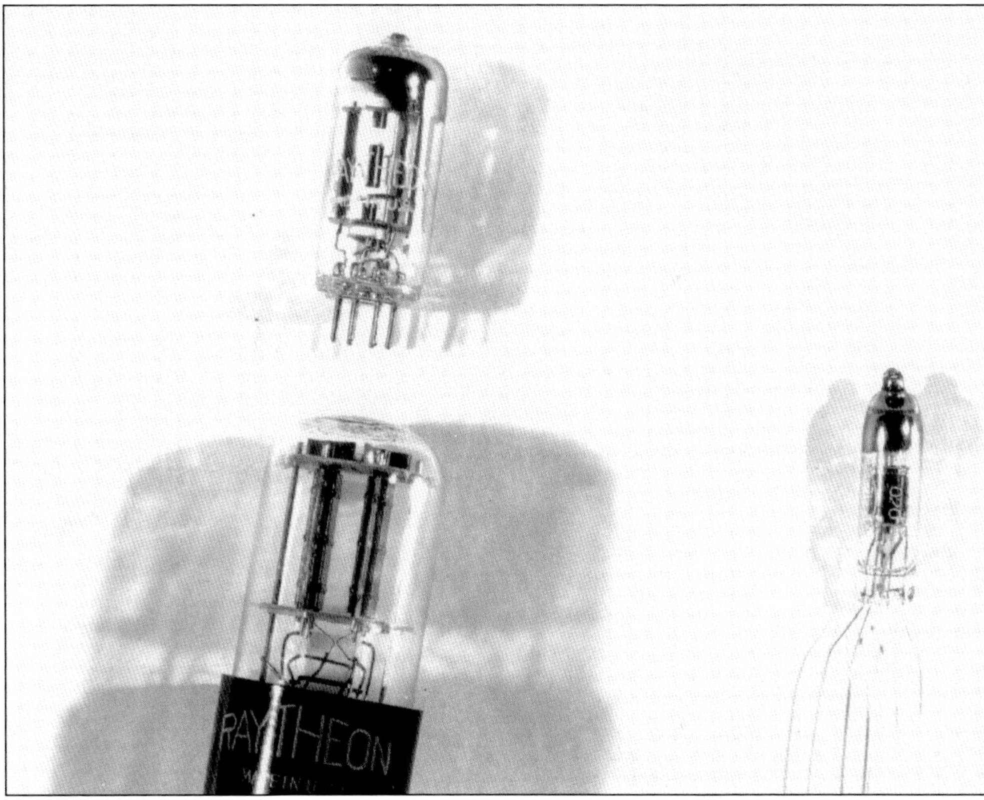

The receiving and transmitting tube business sustained Raytheon from the 1920s through the 1930s and into the wartime years. However, the company was barely profitable through the depression years of the 1930s, not only because of the economy but also due to severe competition from larger tube producers such as General Electric, RCA, and Sylvania. Shown here are a few samples of the many varieties of tubes being produced by Raytheon in the early 1940s. The subminiature type at the right eventually found application in military systems and hearing aids.

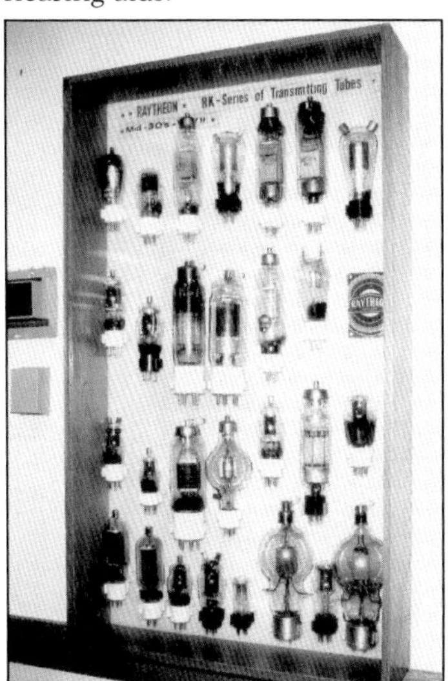

By developing a series of low-power radio transmitting tubes, as shown in this display, Percy Spencer helped sustain the company through the depression years of the 1930s. This work formed the technological basis that carried Raytheon into the microwave and radar business during the war.

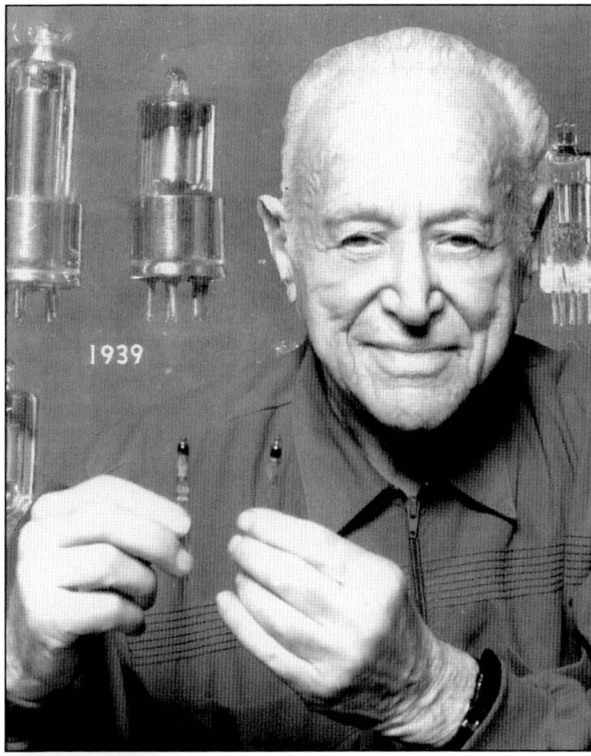

Norman Krim helped develop subminiature tubes between 1938 and 1941, first for use in hearing aids and later for proximity fuse radars used in U.S. mortar shells. Here he holds two examples of subminiature tubes. The proximity fuse, one of the most closely guarded secrets of the war, could accurately detonate an artillery shell just above the ground or an antiaircraft shell when it reached the vicinity of an enemy airplane. Krim was made assistant vice president and general manager of the Receiving Tube Division in 1948 and was promoted to vice president of the division in 1950. This photograph dates from 2003.

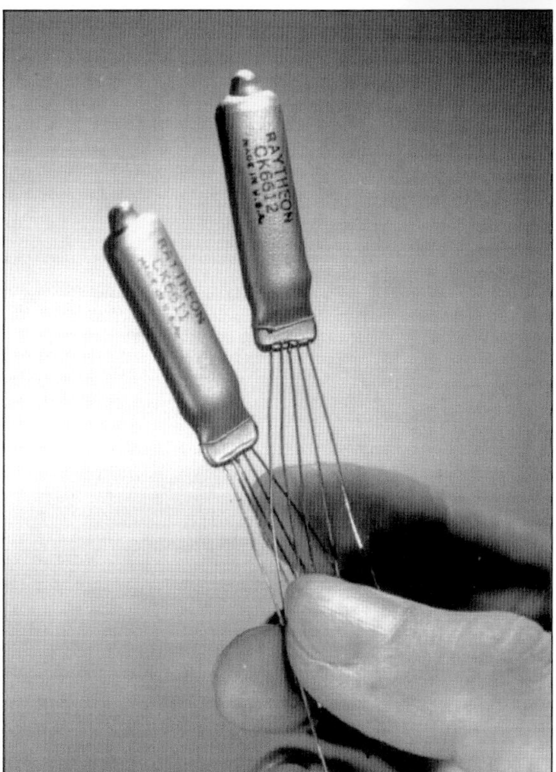

This closeup view shows two of Raytheon's subminiature tubes. Even before the advent of transistors, these tubes made possible remarkable feats of miniaturization. For use in proximity fuses, the tubes went through extensive development to enable them to withstand the extremely high forces—up to 20,000 times normal gravity—of being fired from an artillery piece. The proximity-fused artillery shell, which saved countless Allied lives, so impressed Gen. George S. Patton that he declared, "When all armies get this shell we will have to devise some new method of warfare."

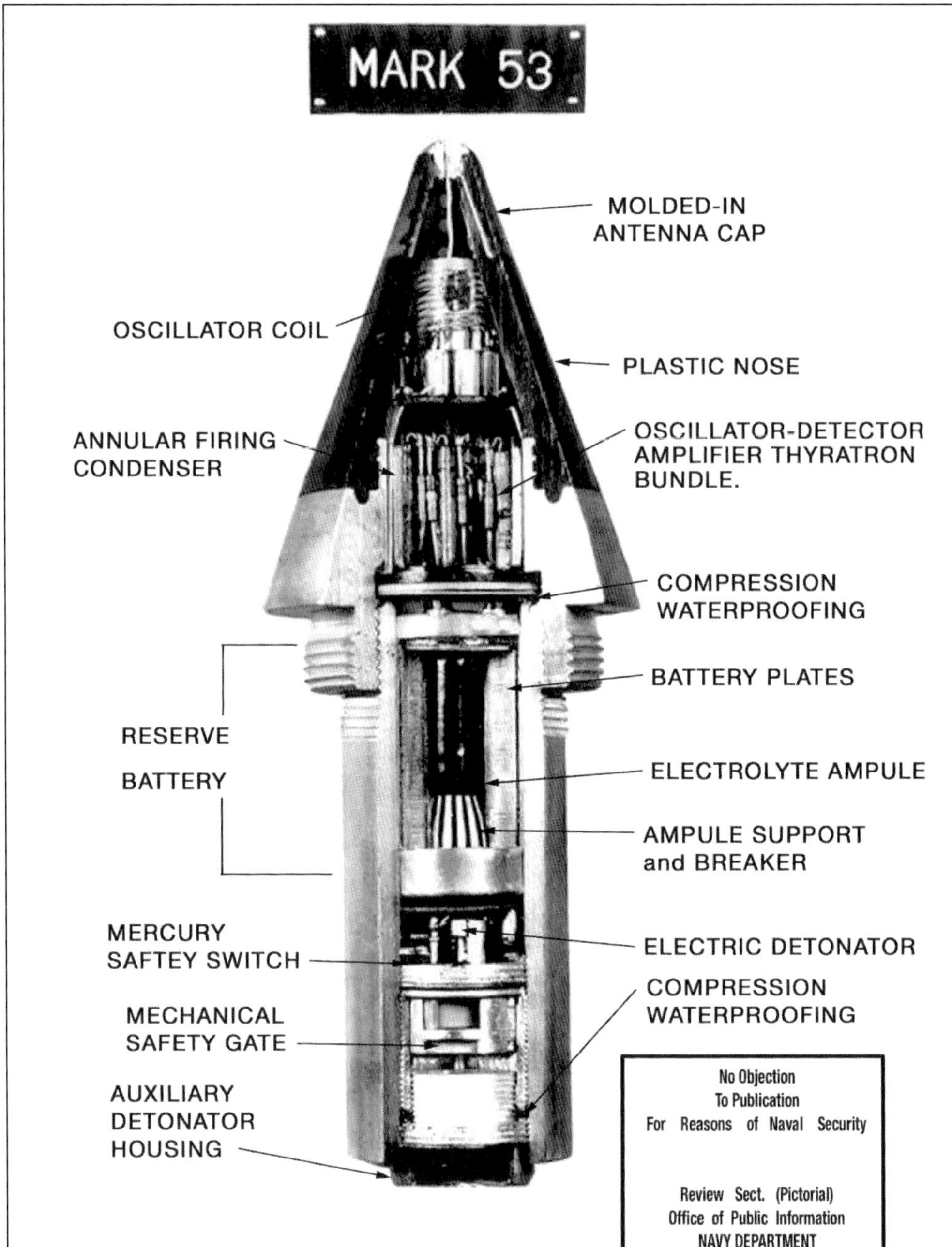

This cross section of the Mark 53 proximity fuse shows its intricacy. This particular unit used a subminiature tube from Sylvania, but it is similar to units built using Raytheon tubes. The tube is located in the oscillator-detector-amplifier-thyratron bundle at the upper right. During the Battle of the Bulge, German forces captured some stocks of U.S. ammunition that included proximity fuses. This prompted a crash program to develop jammers in case the Germans learned the secret of the fuse and tried to copy it. Thankfully, the secret remained a secret until after the war. (Courtesy Department of the Navy, Naval Historical Center Web site.)

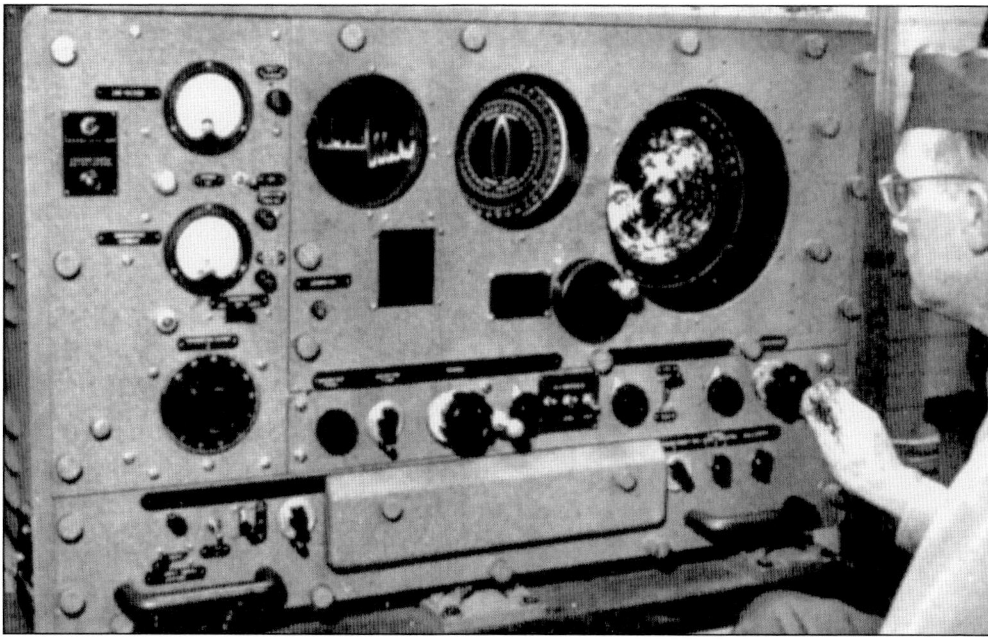

Raytheon's Fritz Gross designed the company's first successful radar, the SG, in 1942. It was widely used on larger Allied ships and was praised for its outstanding performance in pinpointing enemy ships and targets. It often continued to function in the heat of battle when other systems had failed. Sales of the SG grew dramatically during the war, and employment soared to keep up with demand.

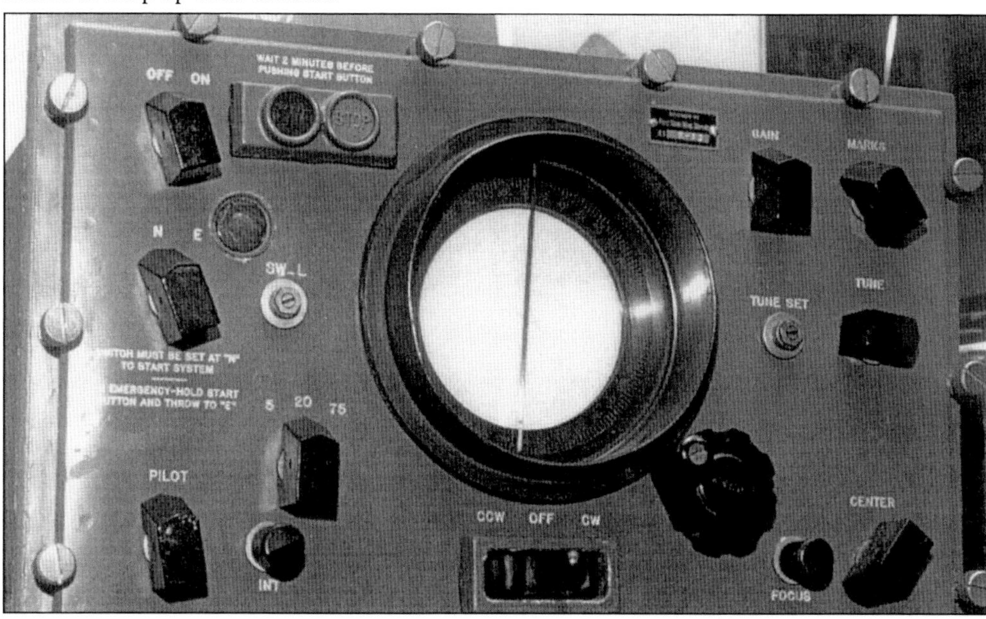

The SG began to reach fighting units in quantity by 1943. The smaller SO radar shown here followed soon afterward. This model was used primarily on smaller warships, such as PT boats. Future president John F. Kennedy's PT-109 was not yet equipped with radar of this type when it was destroyed in a nighttime collision with a Japanese destroyer. While serving in the navy at the end of World War II, coauthor Bob Edwards worked on both SG and SO radars.

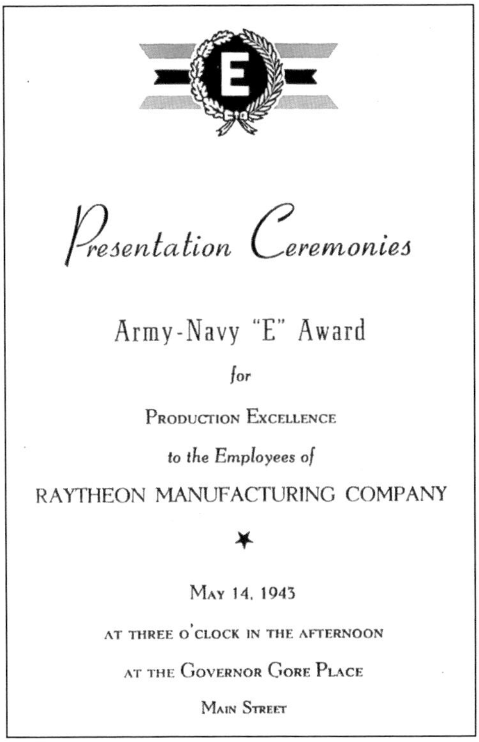

Presentation Ceremonies

Army-Navy "E" Award

for

PRODUCTION EXCELLENCE

to the Employees of

RAYTHEON MANUFACTURING COMPANY

★

MAY 14, 1943

AT THREE O'CLOCK IN THE AFTERNOON

AT THE GOVERNOR GORE PLACE

MAIN STREET

The simultaneous presentation of Army-Navy E Awards to four divisions of Raytheon on May 14, 1943, was a major event held on the grounds of the Gore estate in Waltham.

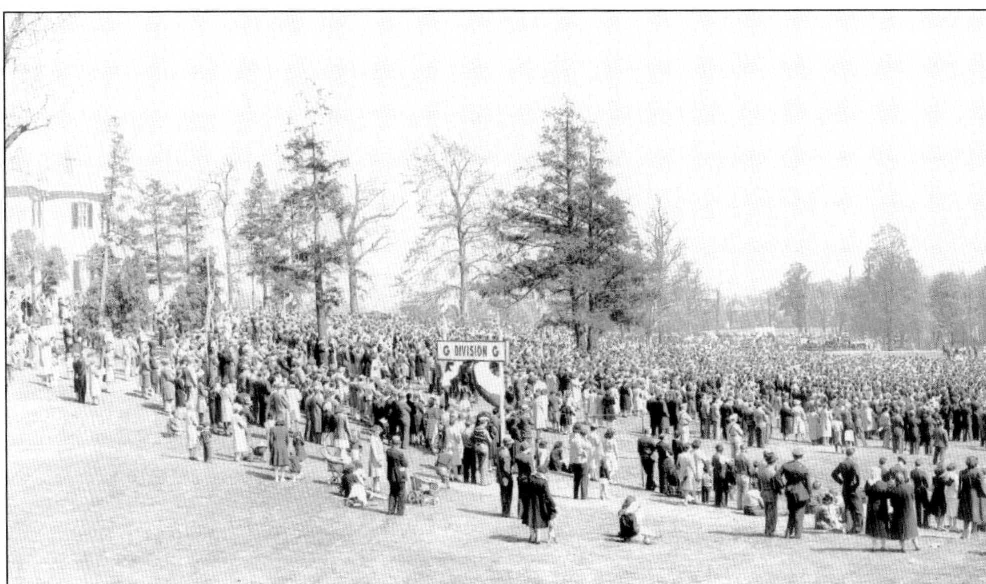

Many Raytheon workers walked miles from their job locations to participate in the Army-Navy E Award ceremony. More than 4,000 E pennants were awarded to defense contractors during the war. The awards were given to individual plants rather than to entire companies. Each employee of an honored plant received an E lapel pin.

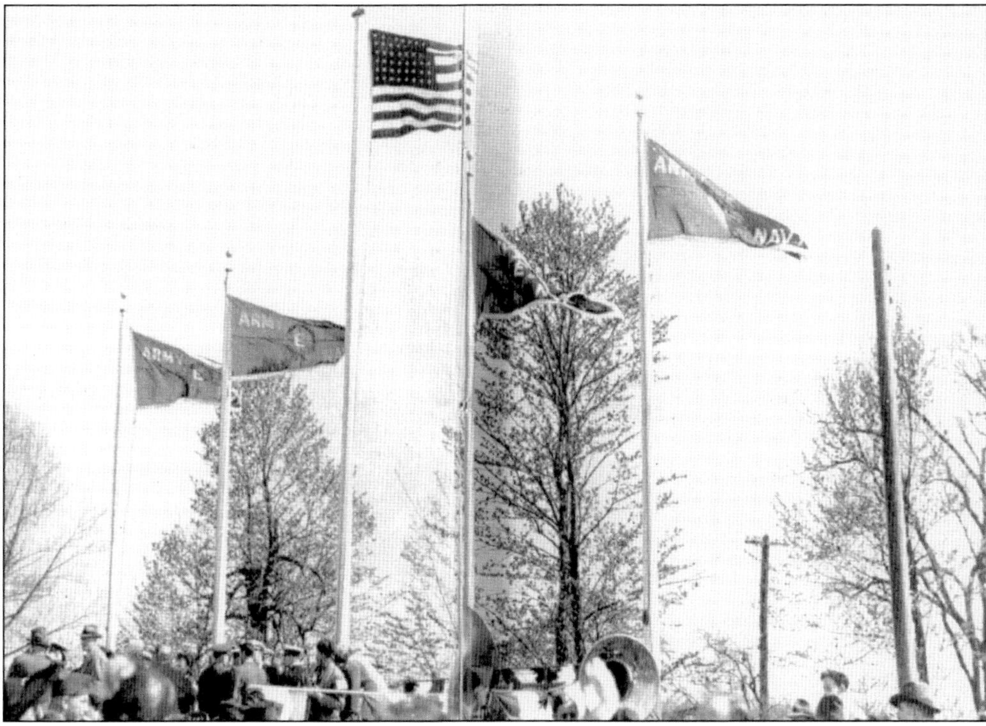

In this view, the Army-Navy E flags fly alongside the American flag.

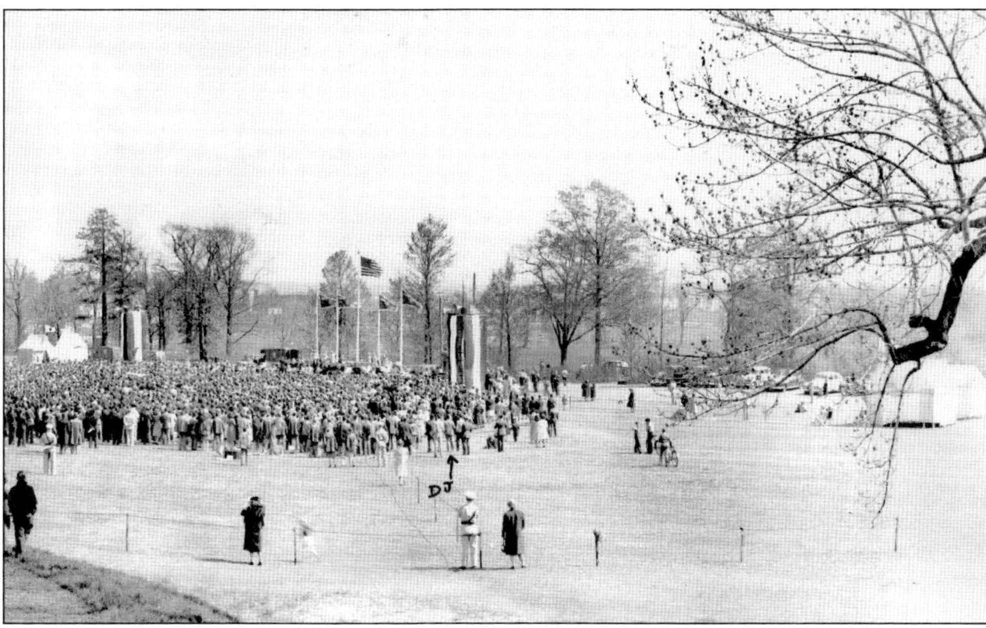

The Army-Navy E Awards ceremony was attended by thousands of Raytheon employees. A potential tragedy was avoided that day. A powerful wind gust blew over two very tall loudspeaker towers, but thankfully the ceremony had already ended and the crowd had dispersed.

RAYTHEON NEWS

VOL. 3 — NO. 13 AUGUST 24, 1945

RAYTHEON NEWS IS PUBLISHED BY AND FOR THE EMPLOYEES OF RAYTHEON

Reveal Raytheon's Radar Feats

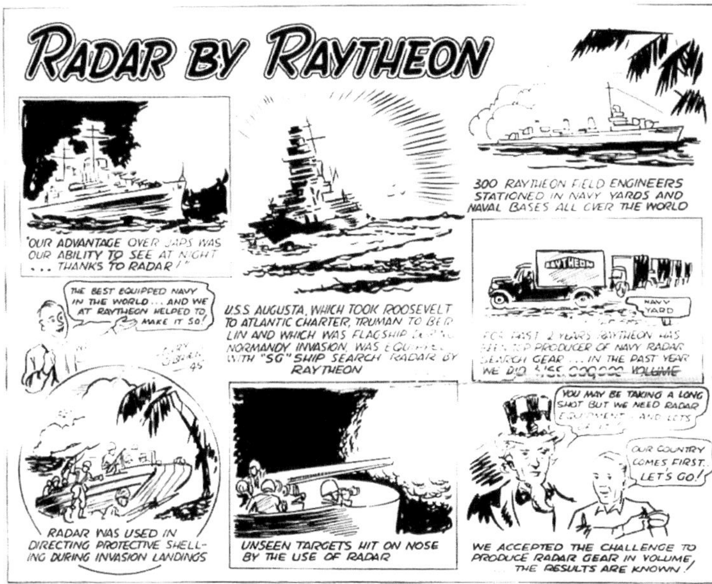

Mr. Marshall Explains Role Plant Played

Designer, Sole Producer Of Ship Search Type (SG)

This entire release has been approved for publication by the Review Section, Office of Public Relations, U. S. Navy.

Following the recent official radar news release by the Navy Department, Mr. Marshall revealed the major role which Raytheon has taken in the development and manufacture of radar equipment.

Under the direction of the Navy Department's expert Bureau of Ships, Raytheon designed and is the sole producer of the ship search radar type known as SG, which was the first commercial microwave equipment made in America and today is in use on every combatant ship of the U. S. Navy. More recently Raytheon also designed and is the exclusive supplier of a compact type to be found on thousands of landing craft, PT boats and other small craft used in amphibious operations.

Throughout the past two years Raytheon has been the country's top producer of Navy radar search gear, and its production of microwave tubes has equalled that of all others combined. Its volume for the year ending May 31, 1945, was 168 million dollars.

Recalling the simultaneous rapid growth of the radar industry and Raytheon's annual volume, Mr. Marshall stated that during the emergency period, prior to the war, Raytheon made a fundamental policy decision that has controlled its operations since that time.

"Prior to the war," Mr Marshall said, "Raytheon manufactured vacuum tubes in substantial quantities and conducted experimental work on electronic equipment. It was evident not only that the demand for tubes would be very great, but that a conventional expansion of this business would be easy, safe, and profitable."

"At this time," Mr. Marshall continued, "an alternative choice was presented: It involved development of electronic devices employing microwave tubes and components for radar — then in the laboratory stage — for military purposes. Although not possessing certainty of

See RAYTHEON'S RADAR, Page 2, Col. 1

Congratulations

My sincere congratulations to all at Raytheon who have contributed to the great victory.

I am sure that we all consider the problem of peace a small price to pay for its blessings.

Let us turn the energy and intelligence that helped win the war to the building of a peace that we can all enjoy.

JOHN H. BEEDLE.

Announcement

No person or industry has been left untouched by our sudden victory. We have reached the goal for which we have been striving and must make the adjustment we have known would come when the war was over.

On Aug. 17, after a two-day holiday, the 3 to 11 shift was dispensed with, and the remainder of the personnel was put on a 40-hour week. This was done to enable as many employees as possible to work. Naturally, many day-shift people will return to their peacetime occupations, housewives will return to their homes, and many of the war brides will now go housekeeping.

As these people sever their connections with Raytheon, people from the 3 to 11 shift who desire to work will replace them.

The 3 to 11 people were at work when news of victory was announced, and within a short time were evacuated from the building. These people are to be paid for Aug. 14, 15, 16, and 17. The day shift will be paid for the two holidays. For the present we are to have one shift, 8 to 5.

You have done your job well.

A Message From Mr. Marshall To His Fellow Workers

To my fellow workers: August 17, 1945.

This edition of the *Raytheon News* carries the Raytheon radar story as released nationally to the press.

While the story only scratches the surface, it does enable you to get some idea of just what we have done at Raytheon throughout the war.

We have been the country's top producer of Navy radar search gear and we have made more tubes for radar than all other manufacturers in the world combined. . . . Raytheon transformers have been used on all the critical Navy radar equipment. . . . There is not a piece of radar gear that does not use some Raytheon equipment.

The introduction of our SG ship search radar marked the turning point in the Pacific, and many Naval Officers have claimed that the SG radar was the advantage held by our Fleet over the Japs.

During the past three years we have received from the Navy Department and Naval bases everywhere the highest commendations on the performance and excellence of our equipments. They have been instrumental in saving countless lives and ships. They helped materially in hastening the end of the war.

All in all, every man and woman at Raytheon can be proud of the achievements accomplished during the world's most terrible conflict in all history.

Permit me to thank each and every one of you for the unstinting services which you have rendered both to your country and the company. In Navy parlance, Well Done!

LAURENCE K. MARSHALL, *President.*

With the war over, the August 24, 1945, issue of the *Raytheon News* states that the company's vital part in the war effort could finally be disclosed. News of the breakthrough in magnetron tube manufacture for radars and the production of the highly effective SG and SO radar systems, among other accomplishments, had not been previously published.

Three

Postwar Survival and Redirection

After completely transforming itself to meet the national crisis, Raytheon faced a daunting challenge in the months following the war's end. The first need was reducing costs and getting the company stable financially. Then there was the question of which opportunities would best employ the capital, equipment, and talents of the Waltham-based firm.

While cognizant of the need to trim sail, Marshall, ever the entrepreneur, saw a vast range of opportunities ahead. Through a subcontract Raytheon had earned to produce portions of the firing mechanism for the atomic bomb, Marshall had apparently divined enough about the purpose of the Manhattan Project to be able to predict to his astonished subordinates early in 1945 that the war would end in the summer. He had asked them to join in envisioning the company's postwar future.

Marshall took immediate steps to diversify, acquiring the Chicago-based Belmont Radio Company in a stock swap and purchasing the Russell Electric Company, a maker of phonograph parts, for more than $1 million. At the same time, he was rushing to establish a network of microwave relay sites that he hoped would link television broadcasters, FM radio stations, a facsimile transmission system, and even a weather information system.

The ever-inventive Percy Spencer opened another important door for Raytheon when he decided to experiment with the well-known warming capacity of the microwaves emitted by magnetrons. Spencer, intrigued by a candy bar that melted in his pocket when he was near an operating magnetron, decided to see what the waves would do to popcorn kernels and was delighted to find that they quickly popped. The next day he exploded an egg by the same means. With the support of Marshall, a patent application was put in process for microwave cooking, and an employee suggestion put a name to what became one of the company's most famous products: the Radarange, the pioneer appliance in a field that has since produced hundreds of millions of microwave ovens worldwide.

But even for the larger Raytheon that had emerged from the war, the scope of Marshall's ambition was problematic. Enter Charles Francis Adams Jr., newly returned from the U.S. Navy, who had joined the firm of Paine, Webber, Jackson, and Curtis. Adams, who was acquainted with Marshall and with Harold John Warren Fay, the president of the Submarine Signal Company (a maker of sonar and other equipment with roots that predated World War I), saw the potential for the two companies, both facing declines in military business, to join forces. In due time, the merger was arranged, and it was completed in May 1946, at which time Adams was invited to join the expanded board—a step that led to his appointment as president two years later. A further two years saw the departure of Marshall and the opening of a new era in the company's management.

In these years, Raytheon also moved into the promising field of television. A pioneer in electromechanical television as early as 1926, Raytheon sought to ride the expansion of the industry in the 1940s and 1950s. It provided entire broadcasting facilities to the hundreds of stations being set up across the country, manufactured picture tubes and other components, and, through its Belmont unit, even provided television sets to consumers.

When Bell Labs announced the development of the transistor in the summer of 1948, Raytheon was already in the loop. Norman Krim had heard of the breakthrough through personal contacts, and in company with Marshall, he made a visit to Murray Hill, New Jersey, to learn more. Upon his return to Waltham, where semiconductor technology had been on the radar screen, so to speak, for years, Krim, whose purview had long included subminiature tubes, saw to it that Raytheon not only got into the transistor business but did so before anyone else. In 1949, the company's point contact germanium transistor, the CK703, was on sale, and by the early 1950s, Raytheon was out-producing the next three largest semiconductor makers and was the world's largest semiconductor manufacturer.

Demand from the military did not disappear after the war; Raytheon's newly won reputation in radar ensured that. Opportunities were also emerging, most notably in the field of guided missiles. Raytheon's Royden Sanders had recognized that existing pulse radar sets did a poor job of detecting low-altitude aircraft because of "clutter" generated by objects on the ground or by ocean waves. He proposed the idea of a continuous wave radar that would harness the Doppler effect to identify and track moving objects, such as aircraft or missiles. This type of radar would be ideal for the high-speed, continuous feedback needed for a target-seeking missile.

Even before the war's end, this work had gotten the attention of the navy, and before long, Raytheon found itself developing the radar seeker guidance for a first-generation antiaircraft missile called Lark. This program continued until 1950 and culminated with the first-ever direct hit on an airborne target drone by a guided missile. According to an account in the *Creative Ordeal*, it was not long after, as Raytheon was on the brink of winning more work on a successor project, the Sparrow missile, that Sanders and several of his subordinates decided to leave the company. They eventually launched Sanders Associates (now BAE Systems Information and Electronic Systems Integration Inc.) and focused on developing military electronic countermeasures.

Those left behind to carry on, almost all of them junior members of the team, included engineer Thomas Phillips. Although less experienced, the team members took a do-or-die, around-the-clock approach to their work and proved to the navy that they were up to the challenge, winning the company a contract to develop a version of the Sparrow air-to-air missile. From that accomplishment by Phillips and other Raytheon loyalists came the demand for a host of missile products—including contracts for the Hawk missile and, later, the Patriot missile—that shaped the company's future for decades to come.

While some of the products of this period—including missiles, radar, and the Radarange—were business successes, others were not. For instance, Raytheon's forays into consumer electronics remained noteworthy but modest footnotes in an industry that measured success in millions of units. Clearly, Raytheon could succeed technically almost anywhere it chose, but achieving solid financial results was not so certain. These facts laid the groundwork for the further clarification of the company's structure and focus in the 1960s and beyond.

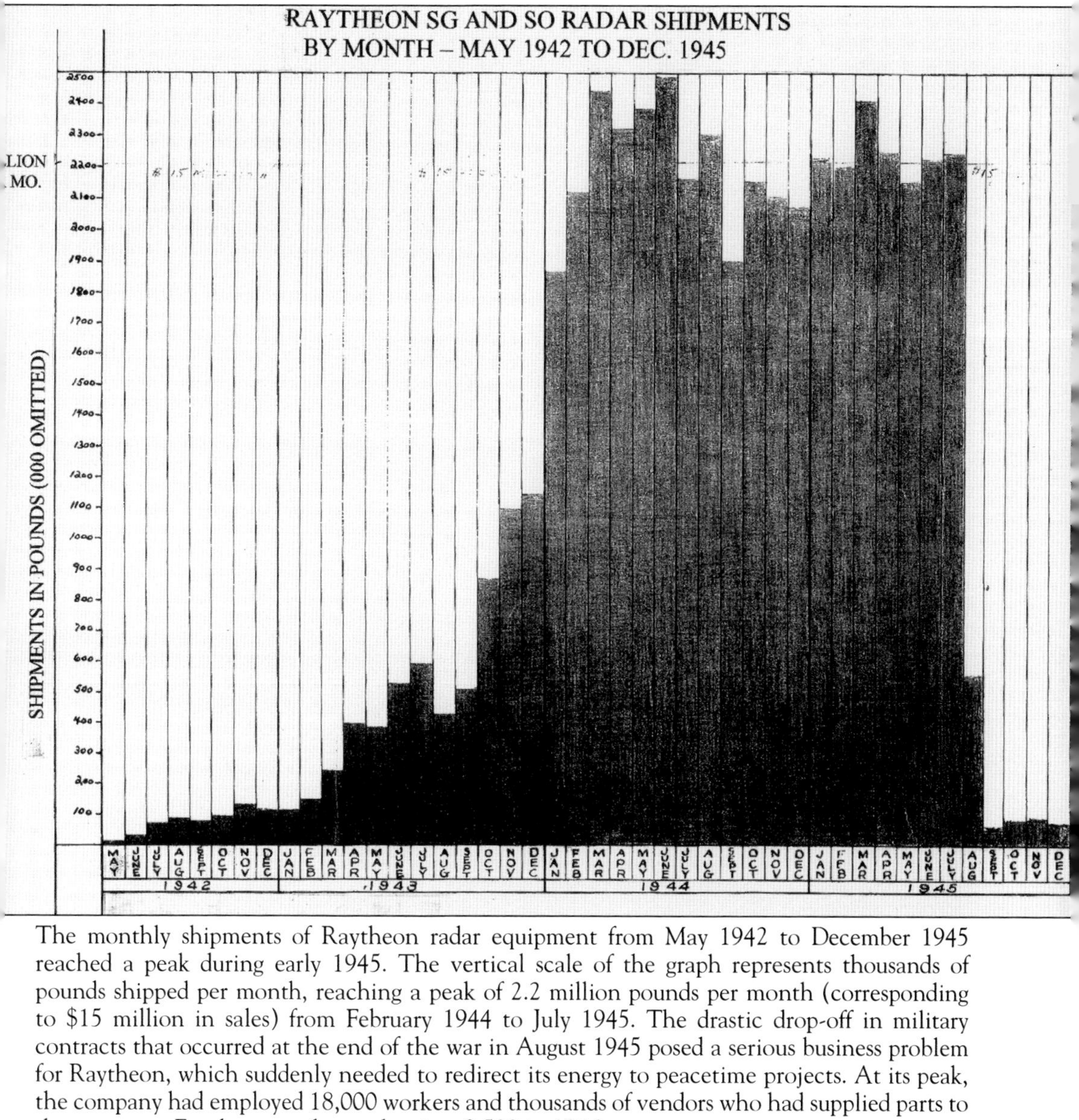

The monthly shipments of Raytheon radar equipment from May 1942 to December 1945 reached a peak during early 1945. The vertical scale of the graph represents thousands of pounds shipped per month, reaching a peak of 2.2 million pounds per month (corresponding to $15 million in sales) from February 1944 to July 1945. The drastic drop-off in military contracts that occurred at the end of the war in August 1945 posed a serious business problem for Raytheon, which suddenly needed to redirect its energy to peacetime projects. At its peak, the company had employed 18,000 workers and thousands of vendors who had supplied parts to the company. Employment dropped to just 3,500 in 1946.

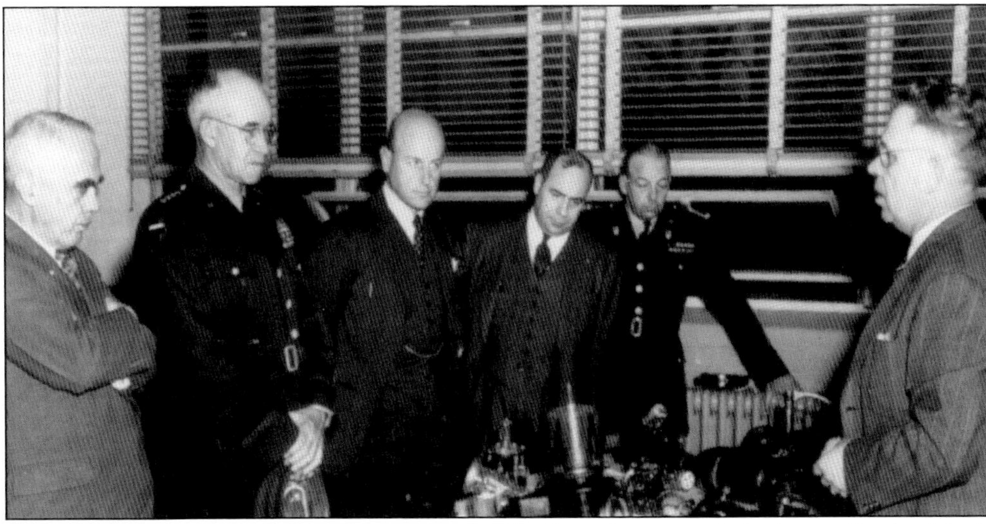

On his 1949 visit to Raytheon, Gen. Omar N. Bradley, chairman of the Joint Chiefs of Staff, received information on a variety of magnetron programs from Percy Spencer. Pictured are, from left to right, Raytheon chairman Laurence K. Marshall, General Bradley, Charles F. Adams, Raytheon consultant Dr. Edward Bowles, Col. Willis Mathews, and Percy Spencer. Marshall and Spencer had a long working relationship that occasionally showed signs of fraying. One Raytheon executive remembers a dinner with customers at the famous Locke-Ober's restaurant in Boston. The dinner was interrupted by commotion from an adjoining private dining area, where Marshall and Spencer were engaged in a wrestling match on the floor!

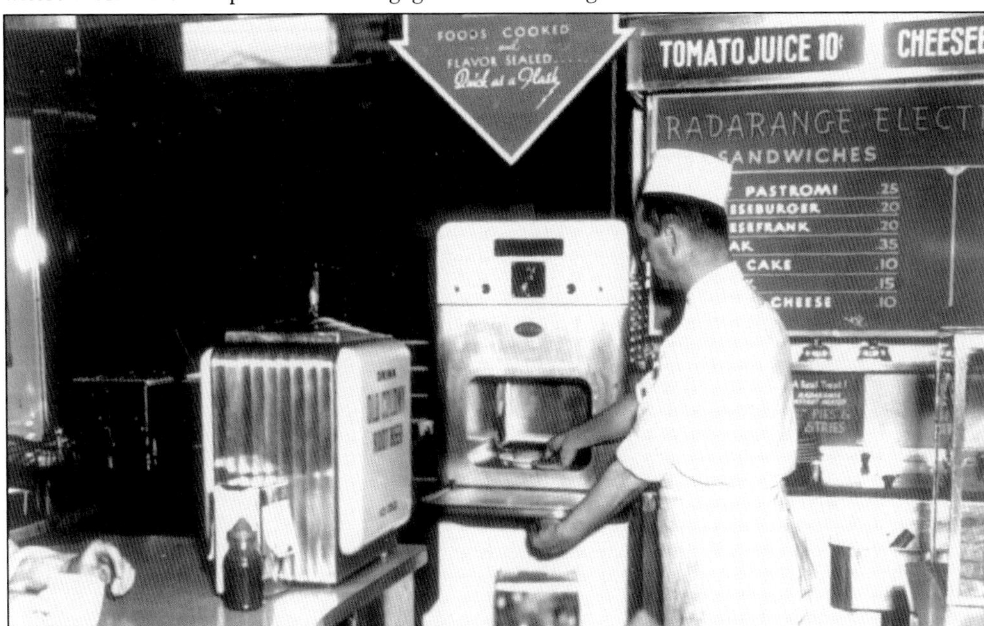

Raytheon began a revolution in food preparation. Here, a restaurant worker uses the 1947 model Raytheon Radarange microwave oven. Note that the price of either a cheeseburger or a cheese frankfurter was only 20¢, and tomato juice was 10¢ a glass. During the war, Percy Spencer noticed a candy bar melting in his pocket when he was standing near a magnetron processing station, leading him to conceive the idea of microwave cooking.

A caption with this early-1960s photograph touts the advantages of upgraded design features "for easy maintenance," not usually a consideration in today's microwave ovens. One area resident recalls that a Raytheon Radarange once held crowds spellbound at the now defunct Norumbega Park in Newton with its ability to convert cellophane bags of corn into popped corn in a matter of seconds.

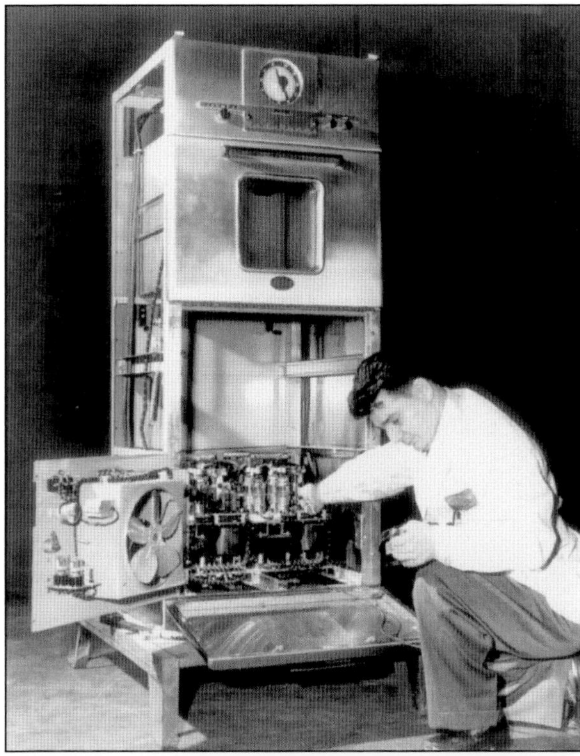

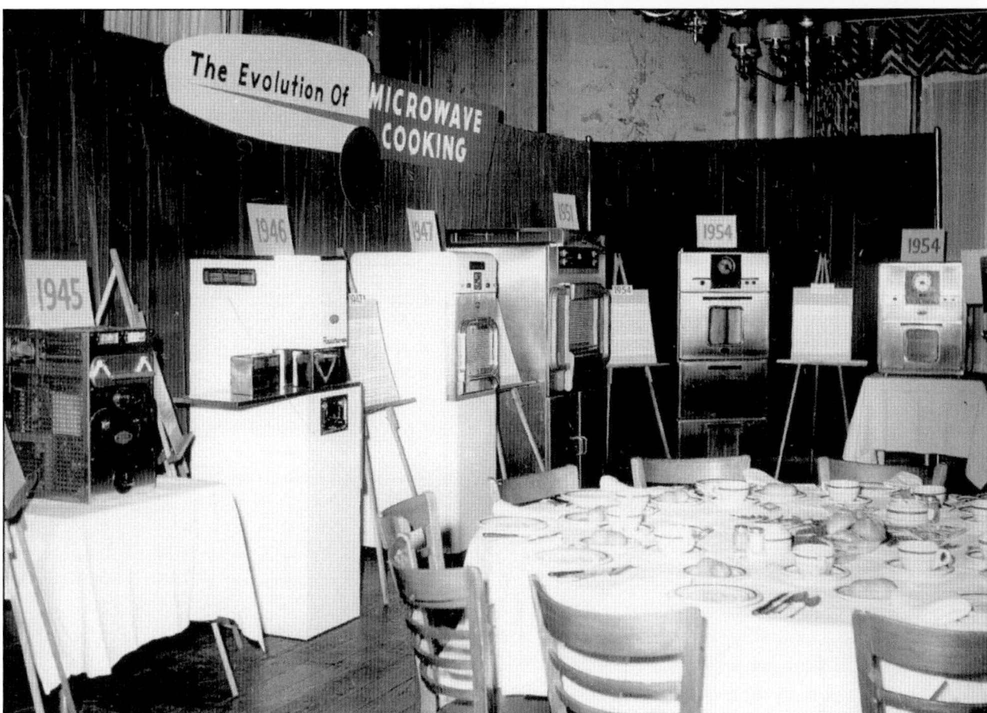

A Raytheon display from the mid-1950s has ovens dating from a 1945 experimental model (left) to the latest 1954 tabletop version (right).

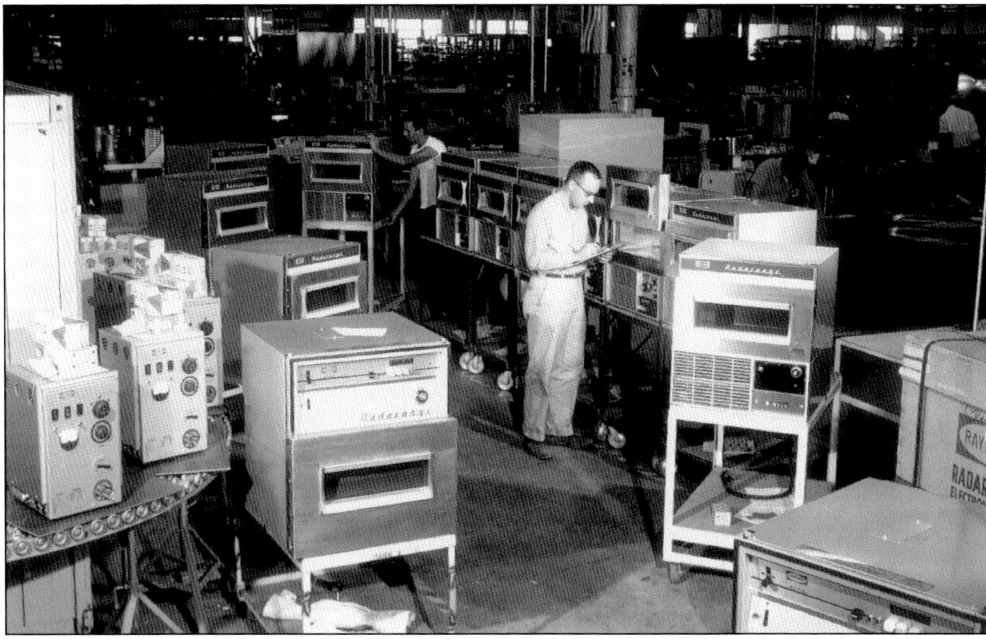

The Raytheon Radarange oven-production line is shown here, with various 1963 models being readied for shipment. With the acquisition of Amana about two years later, Raytheon undertook a redesign of the product and launched a renewed marketing effort that inaugurated the era of widespread home use of microwave ovens.

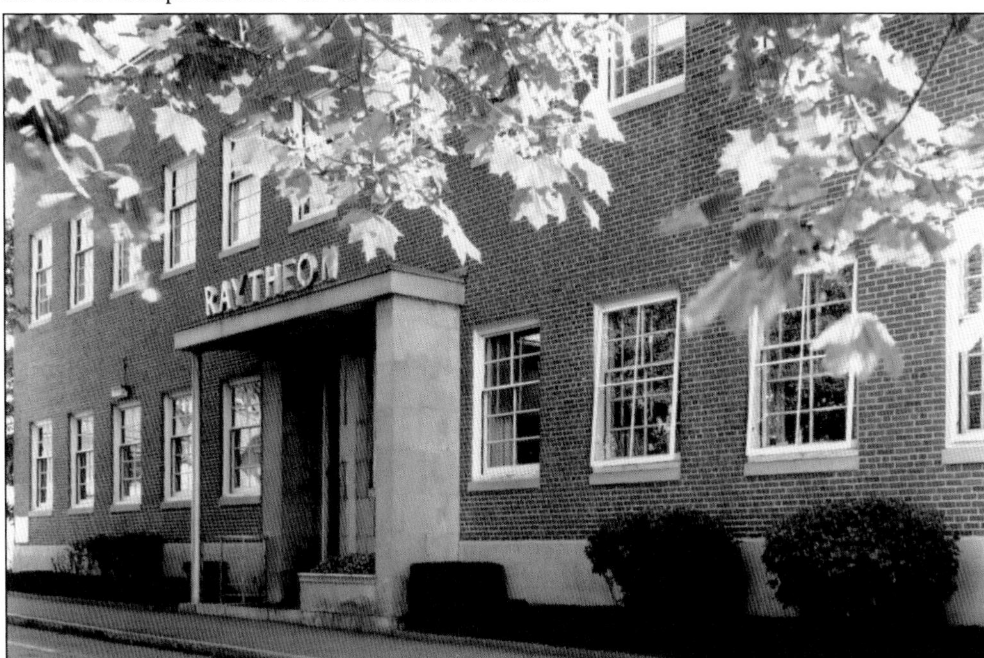

In 1950, Building 50 was constructed as an addition to the Waltham plant. It became the company's new headquarters, accommodating administrative and marketing functions, development and manufacture of a variety of microwave tubes and transformers, and work on microwave ovens.

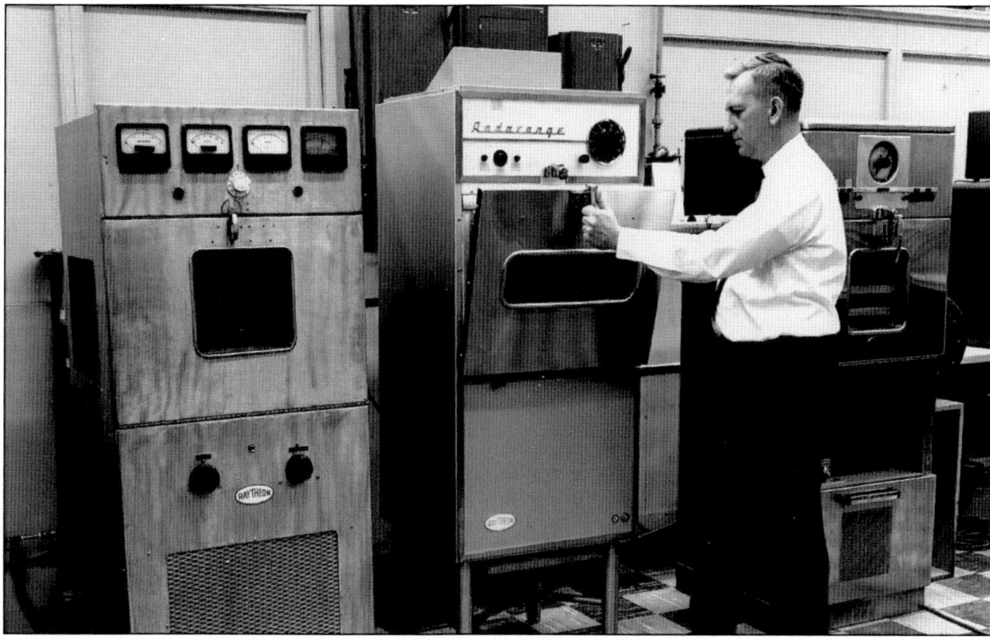

Applications engineer Bob Peterson displays the 1946 microwave oven (center) surrounded by other ovens from the late 1940s and early 1950s. These went mostly into restaurants, hospitals, and other commercial establishments where the oven's requirements for a 220-volt input and water cooling, along with its size, weight, and cost, were not prohibitive.

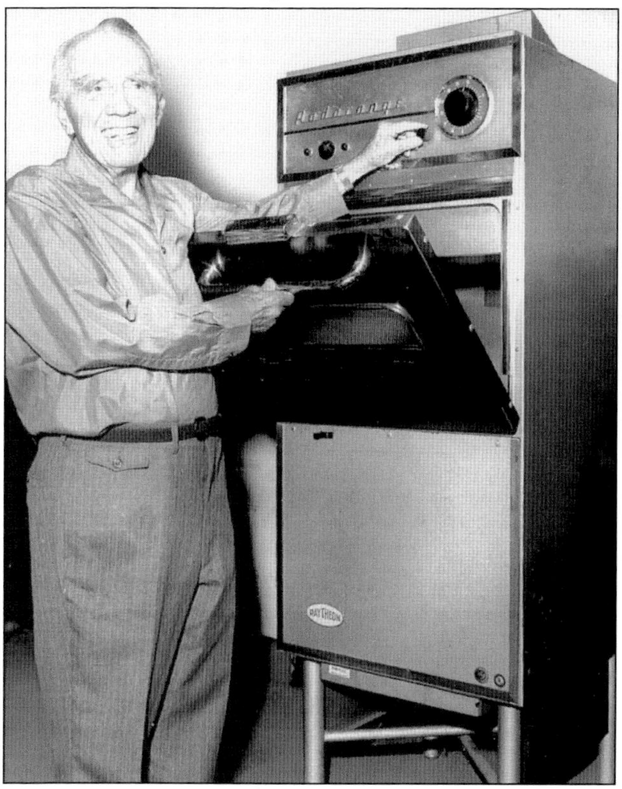

Laurence K. Marshall, Raytheon founder and its president until 1948, is shown at age 90 with an original 1946 microwave oven that he used in his home for many decades before donating it for display at the Raytheon archives. The cost of this oven, including development, is often quoted at $100,000. For contrast, a new home microwave oven costing $27 was recently placed next to this one in the archives.

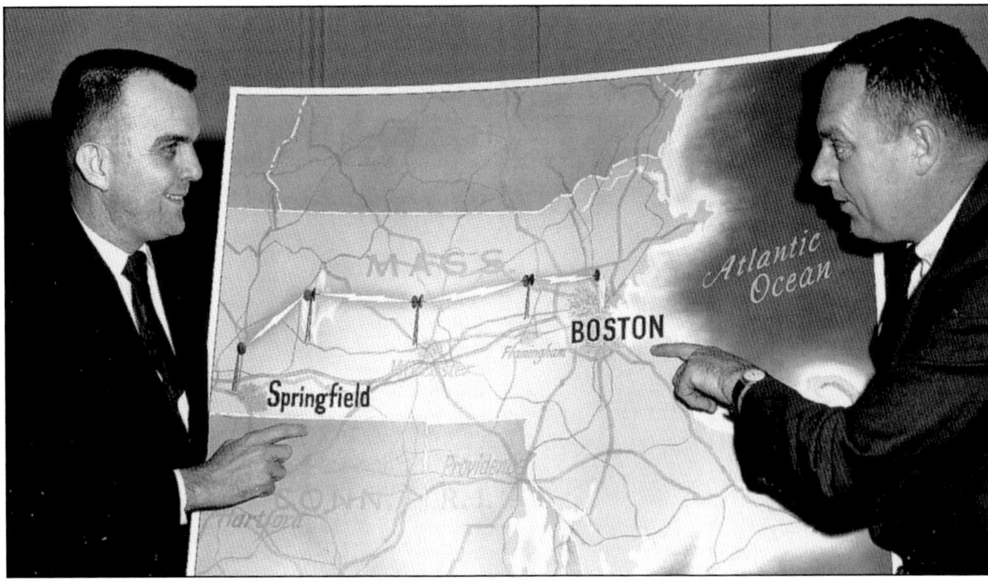

In the 1950s, Raytheon began work on a microwave relay link to join Boston and Worcester with an express telephone system. C. William Anderson of New England Telephone Company examines the plan with Raytheon's Bill Welsh, manager of communications and data processing. The speed of the system was accelerated to handle 1,200 voice conversations simultaneously.

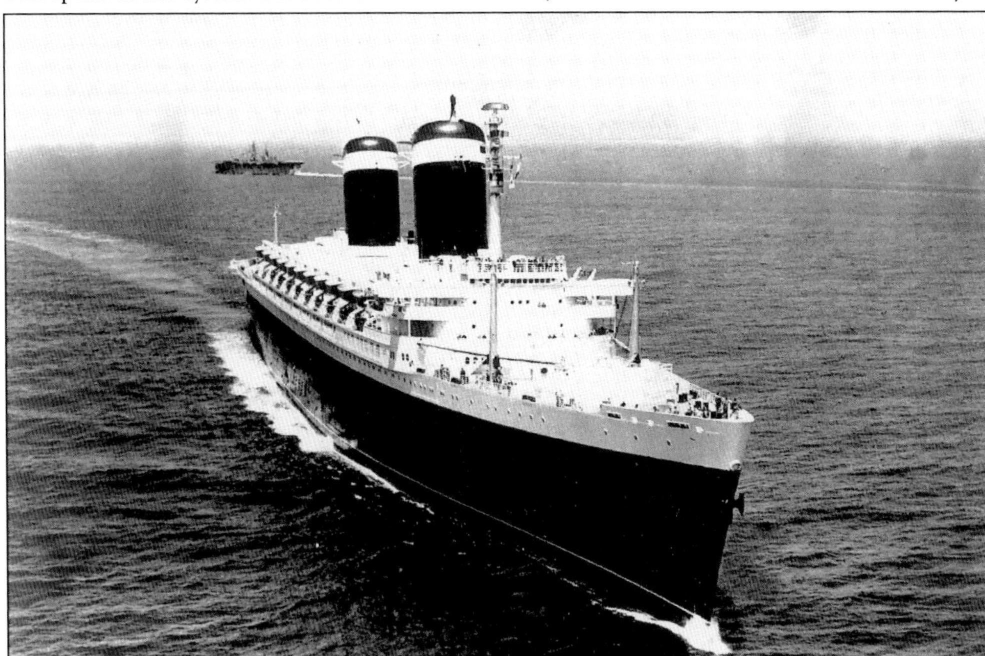

Raytheon's 1952 annual report contains information on the 1,000th Mariner's Pathfinder Radar and Submarine Signal Division Fathometer (Raytheon-SubSig trademark). Both were used as navigational aids on the ocean liner *United States*, the pride of the American merchant marine. Several Raytheon Radarange microwave ovens were also being employed in the ship's food-preparation areas. The ship's commander emphasized that the Mariner's Pathfinder was "indispensable in maintaining the ship's schedule in all kinds of weather."

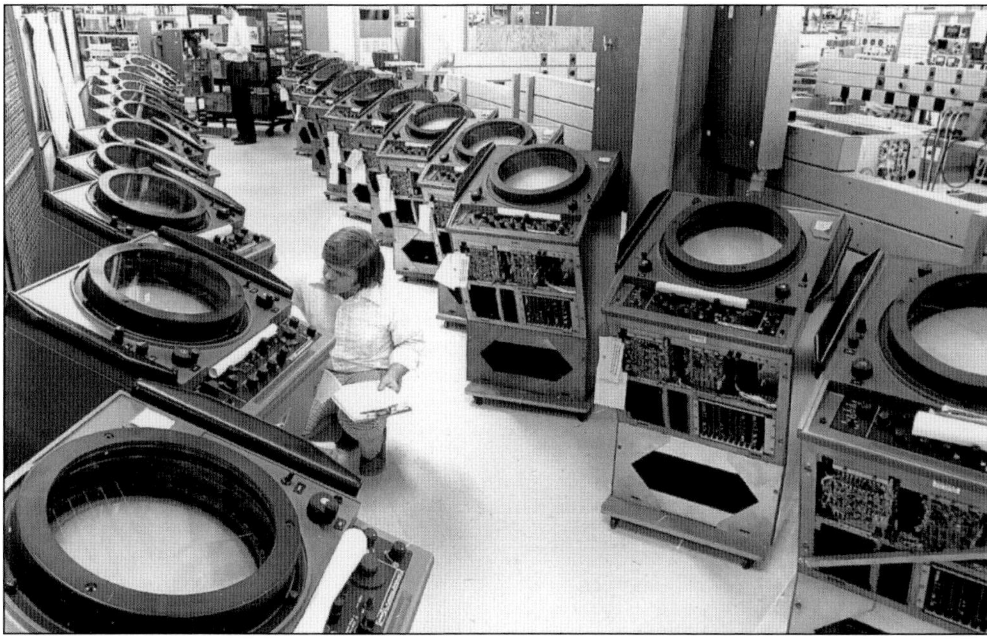

Commercial shipboard radars became a significant business area in the postwar years. They are an example of the application of military technology to beneficial peacetime uses. Here, inspectors at Raytheon Marine Company are conducting final checks on a shipment to the U.S. Coast Guard of radars based on the Mariner's Pathfinder system.

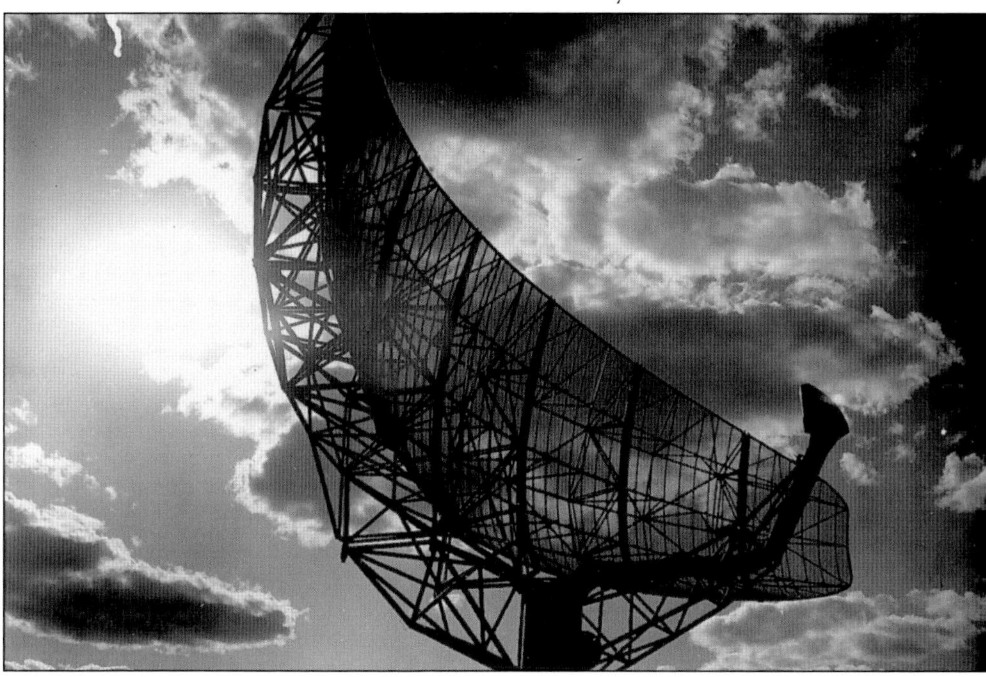

A leading effort in the company's postwar ventures was the application of its military radar experience to various commercial radar applications, such as marine, aircraft, and weather systems. This antenna for an air-traffic control radar is representative of the transfer of technology to meet important peacetime needs.

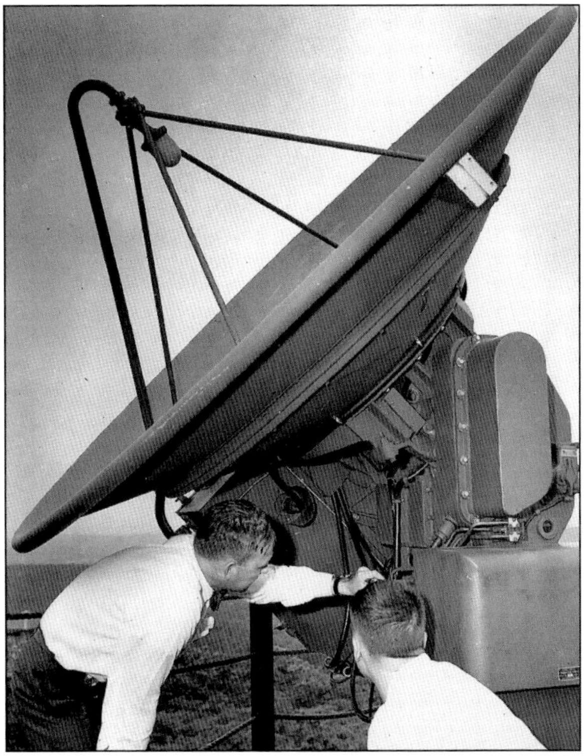

These two engineers are examining the antenna system for an early weather radar built by the Raytheon Equipment Division. Weather radars contributed to the great improvements in forecasting in the last half-century and have saved many lives by providing timely notice of severe weather conditions, such as tornadoes, torrential rains, and snowstorms.

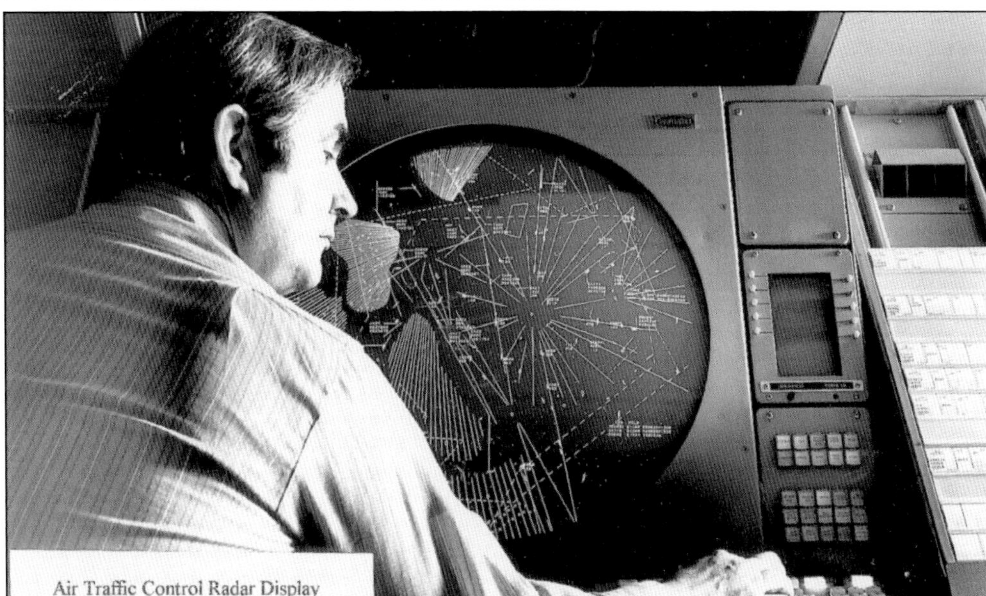

The display console for the air-traffic control radar illustrates the complexity of the traffic controller's task in guiding scores of airplanes at various speeds, directions, and altitudes. Raytheon has been and continues to be an important contributor to improving air-traffic control technology. For example, in Indianapolis in May 1946, the Civil Aeronautics Administration demonstrated the first radar-equipped control tower for civilian flying, which used Raytheon-built radar equipment.

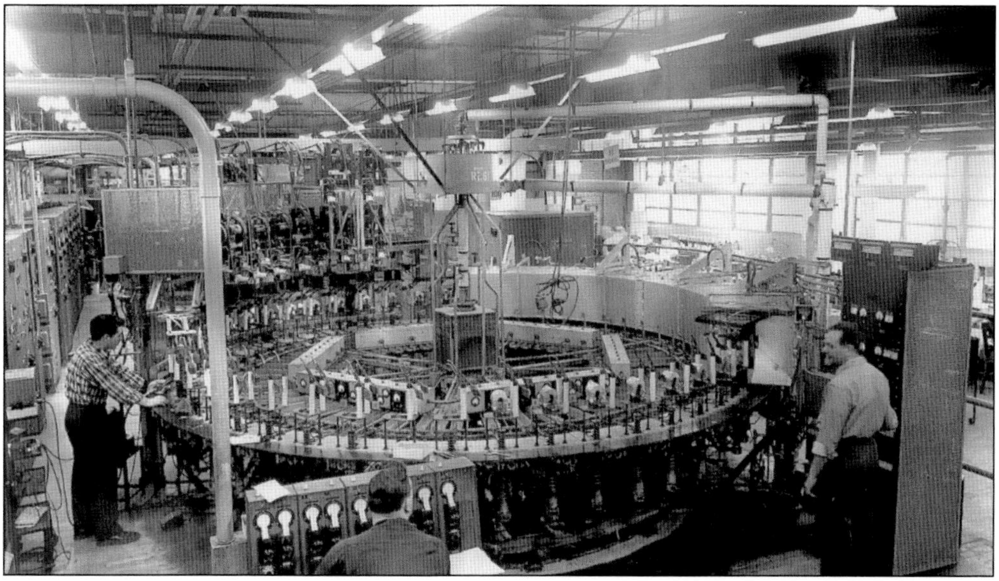

From the 1950s through the 1990s, the top floor of Building 50 in Waltham was home to three of these large rotary exhaust systems, used for processing magnetron tubes. Multiple exhaust pumps were used for removing gas from the tubes while they were baked out at high temperatures to achieve good vacuum quality. The tubes were then subjected to high-power operation before being sealed off from the pumps. Using this equipment, many tubes could be processed simultaneously. A typical cycle was about 12 hours per tube for high-power models.

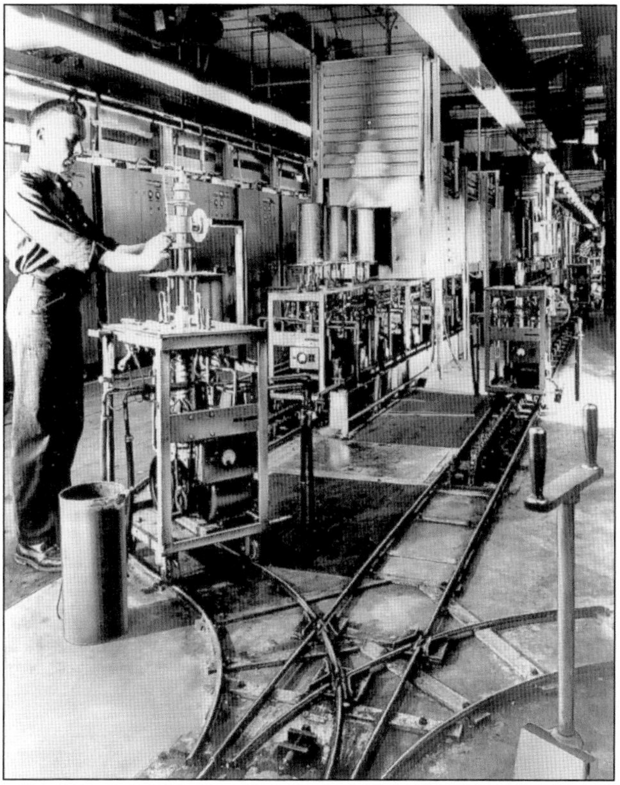

Another means of processing magnetron tubes was this in-line "trolley" exhaust system. Tubes were sealed onto individual vacuum pump dollies, then slowly run through bakeout ovens and operating stations for "aging" to full power.

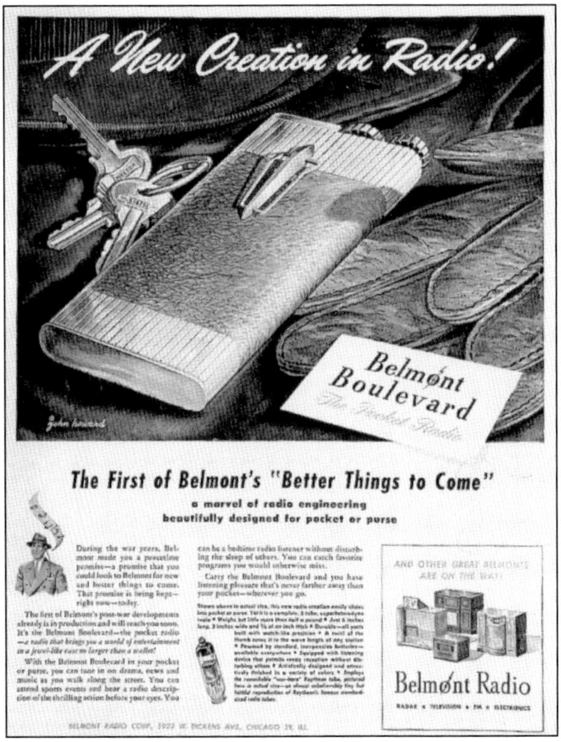

The Raytheon-Belmont pocket radio was based on the subminiature tubes developed during World War II. It appeared *c.* 1945 and was an early forerunner of the Sony Walkman and similar pocket radios.

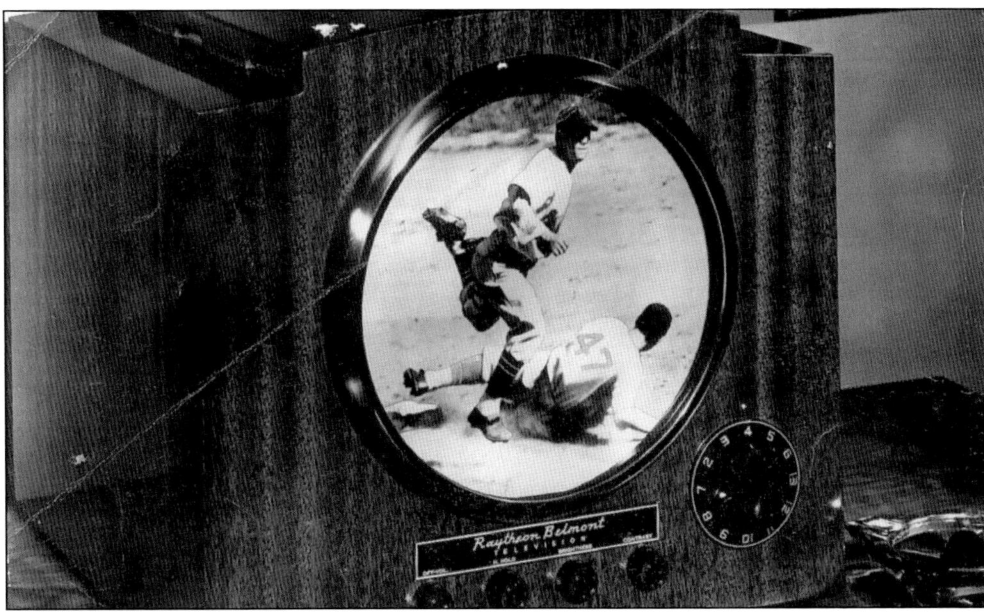

By acquiring the Belmont Radio Company of Chicago, an experienced marketer and manufacturer, Raytheon found a way to quickly enter the civilian radio market and the new market for television sets. Although the field was extremely competitive, products marketed under either the Raytheon or Belmont brands found favor with many consumers. There are three excellent examples of Raytheon-Belmont television sets and several radios from the mid-1950s on display in the company archives in Waltham.

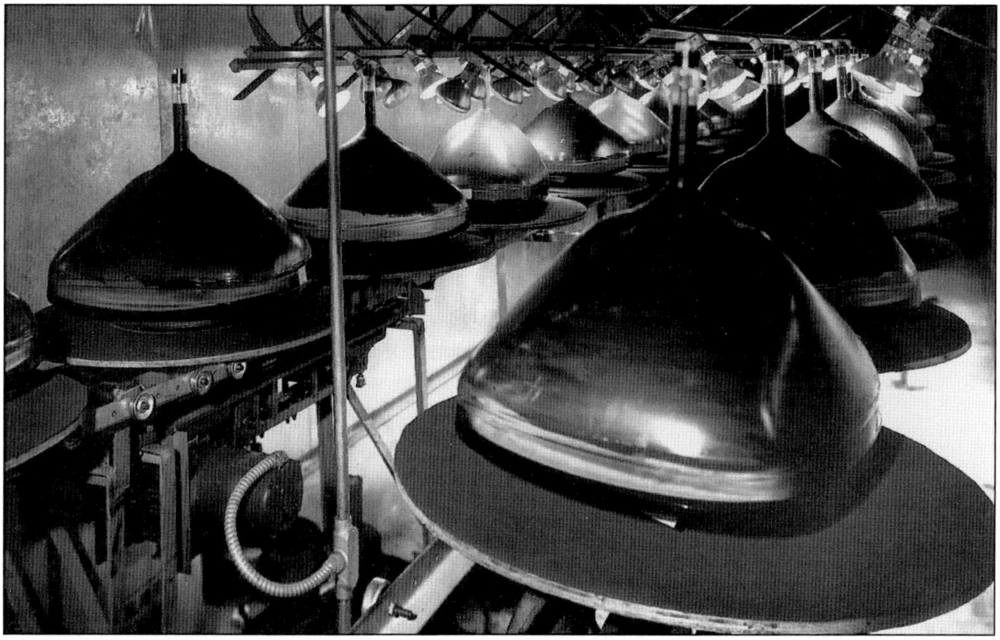

The company's background in developing and manufacturing a variety of vacuum tubes provided an excellent foundation for making television picture tubes. Television tube production, which continued through the 1950s and 1960s, started in Waltham and later moved to Quincy. The facilities later produced specialized display tubes into the 1990s.

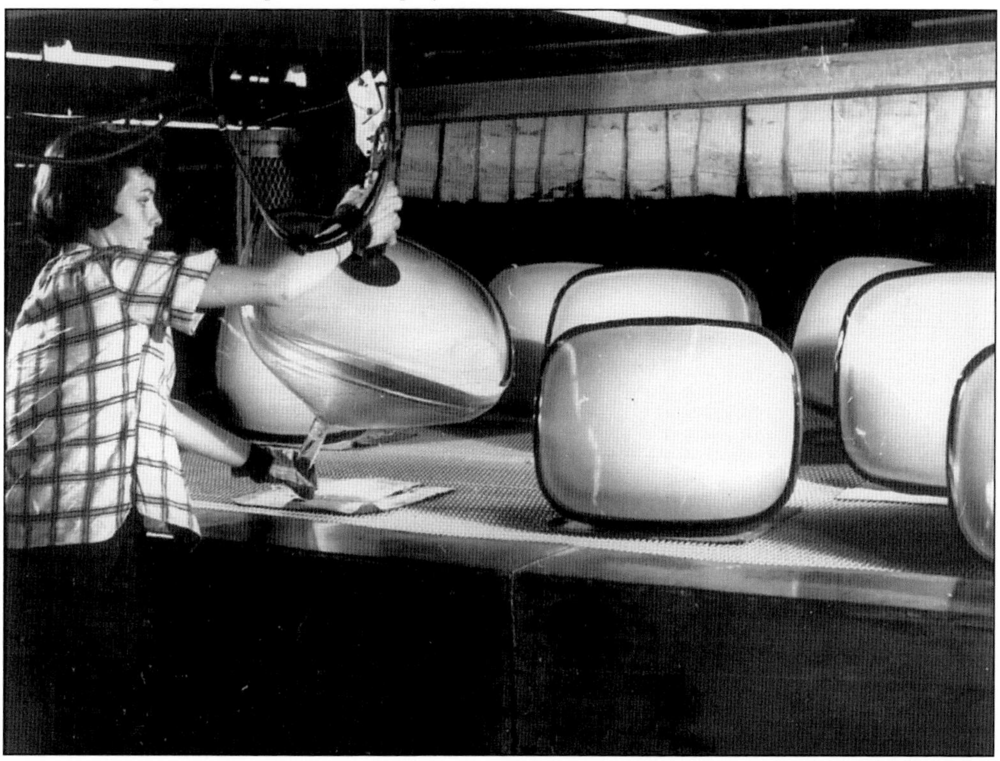

Here, a worker handles a picture tube with the help of a vacuum grip and an overhead trolley.

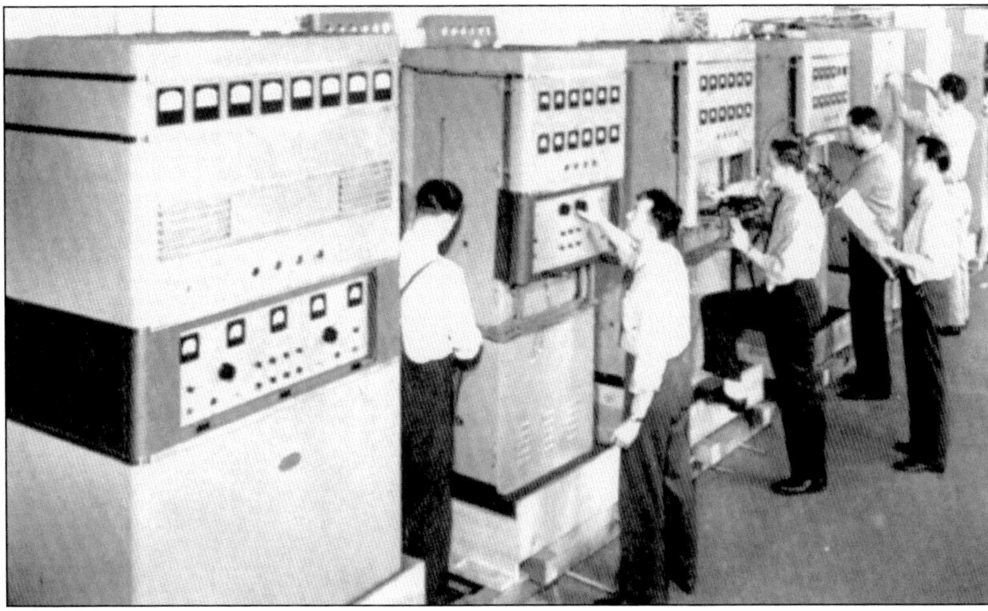

Emerging from World War II with a reputation for building complex, high-quality electronic systems such as the SG and SO radars, Raytheon turned its talents to the production of these one-kilowatt AM radio broadcast transmitters for the civilian market. These units were built at the Waltham facility.

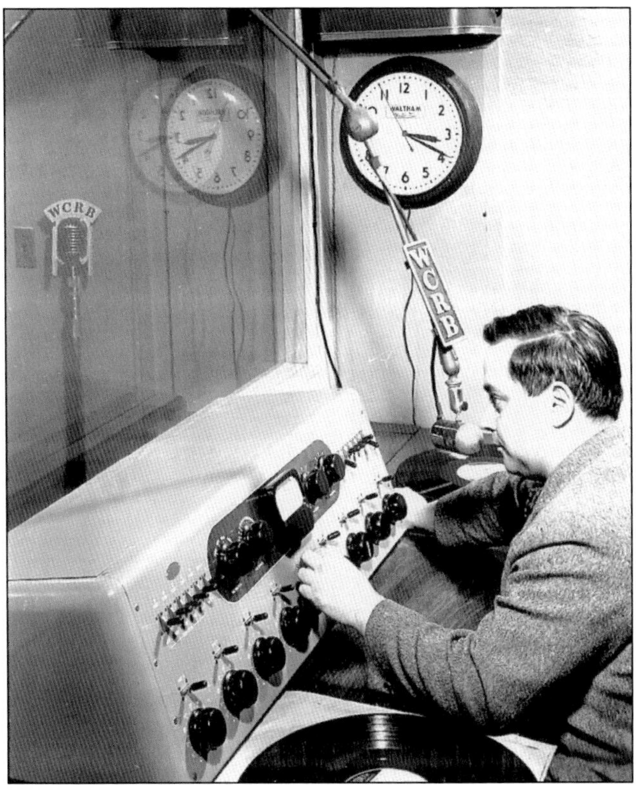

The popular WCRB radio station in Waltham employed the Raytheon equipment seen in this photograph. Raytheon has often been a sponsor for this station over the years. Since its early years, WCRB has achieved a unique position as one of only a handful of commercial broadcasters of classical music in the country.

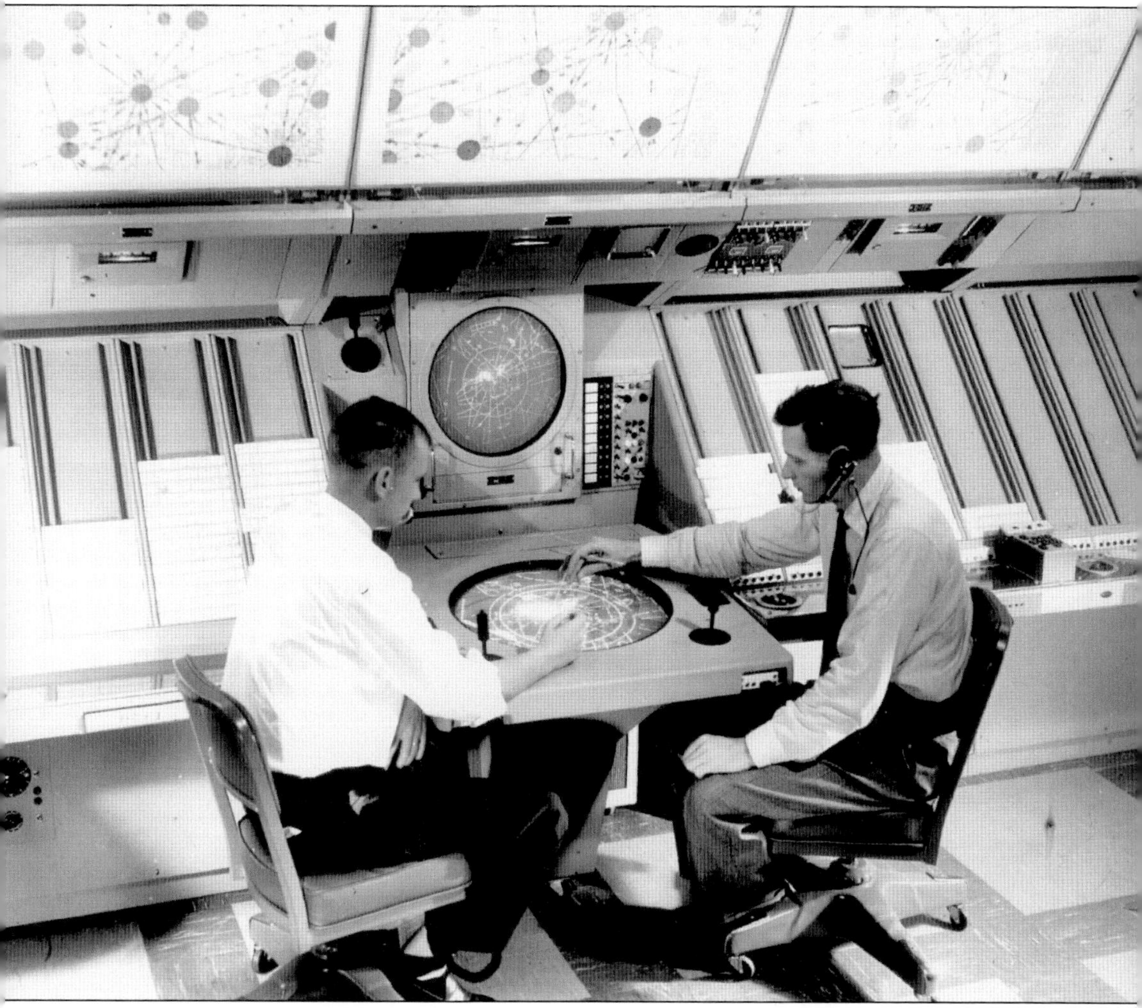

This image of air-traffic control radar (also seen on the cover of this book) underscores the pioneer role played by Raytheon in this field. The new "bright display" presentation allowed viewing of aircraft radar traffic data without the necessity for a darkened room. In 1967, the Federal Aviation Administration awarded Raytheon a large contract for the first computer display channels for the National Airspace System En Route Stage A, the agency's automation program for its air route traffic-control centers. Then, in the 1980s, Raytheon produced DARC (direct access radar channel) as a backup system to fill in when the primary system was down for any reason.

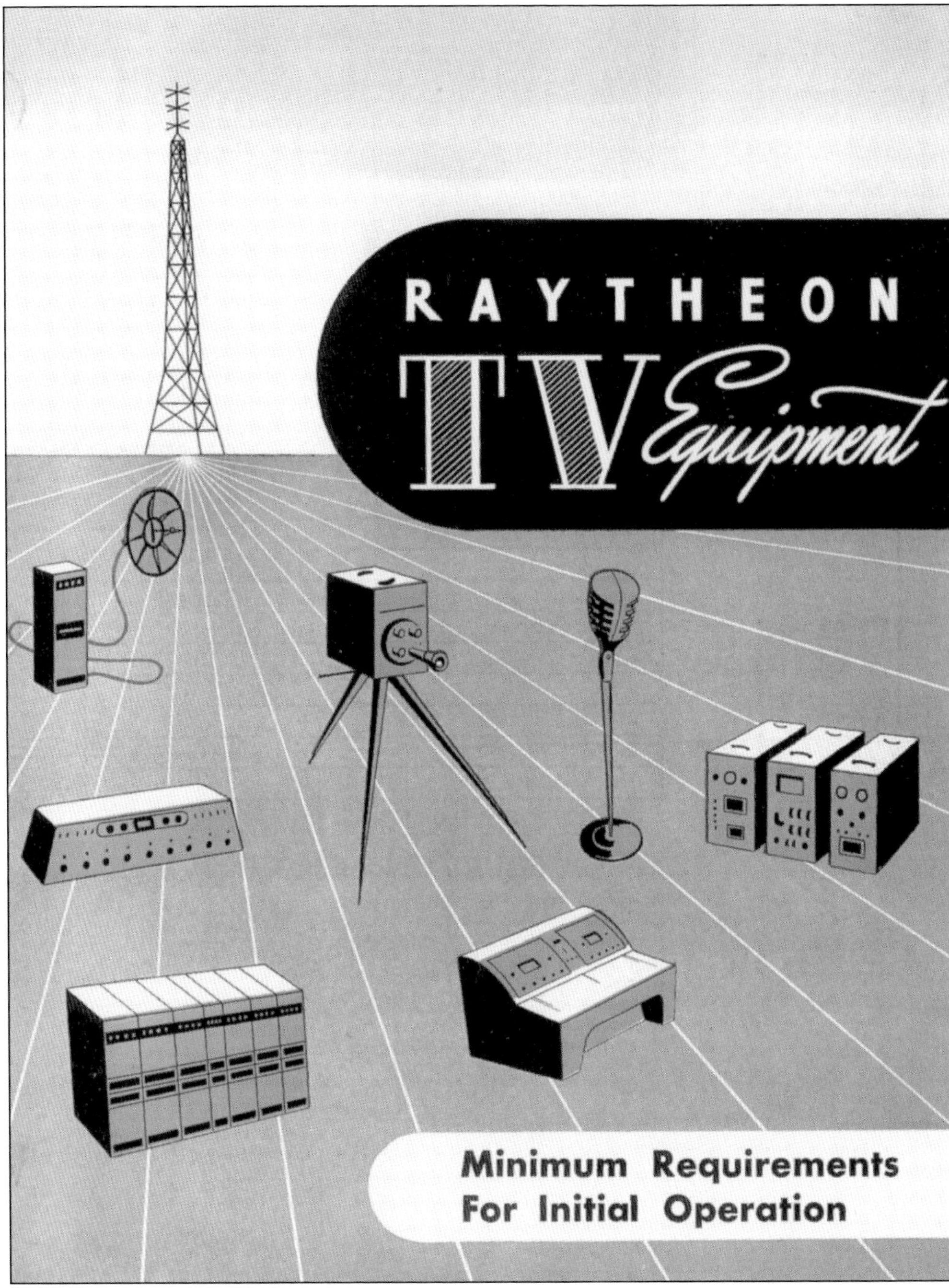

In addition to providing AM radio broadcasting equipment, Raytheon also offered all of the electronic equipment needed to set up a television broadcast station. According to this brochure, equipment was available for stations ranging in size from 500 watts up to 5,000 watts.

RAYTHEON

Excellence in Electronics

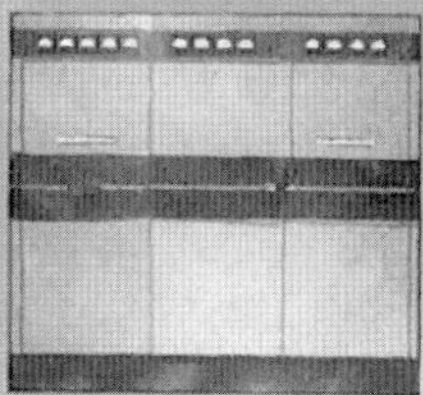

RTV 500 TRANSMITTER
500-watt peak *visual* power; modulation at medium power level; requires no external side band filter. 250-watt FM *aural* power with Raytheon Cascade Phase-Shift Modulation. RTV 500 may be used later as a driver for power amplifiers.

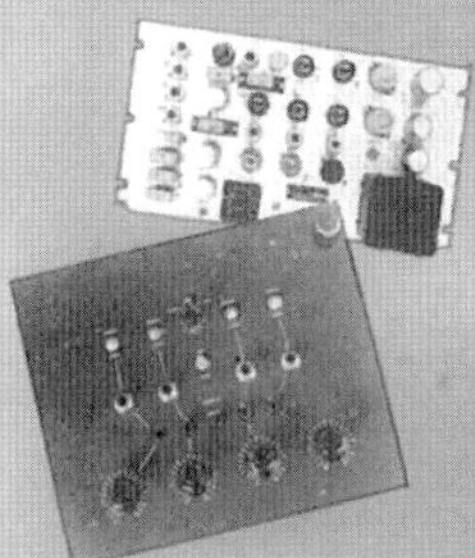

VIDEO LINE AMPLIFIER AND SWITCHING UNIT
A line amplifier for selecting or mixing video channels by push-button switching with automatic lap-fade effects. Provides all necessary controls for up to four channels.

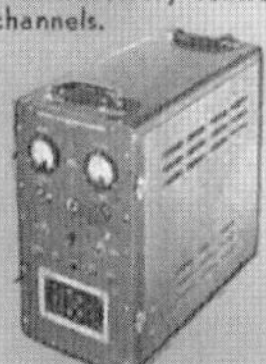

SYNC GENERATOR
Provides standard RMA blanking, synchronous and driving pulses.

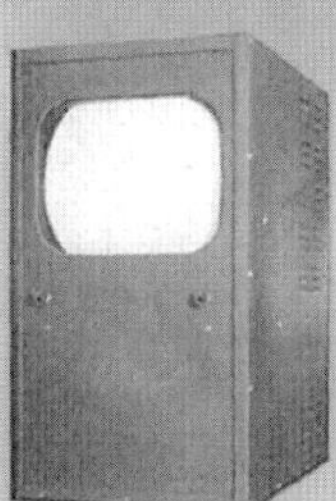

Minimum Requirements For A LOW POWER NETWORK OUTLET

This "stripped down" package is presented chiefly to indicate the bare minimum required for low power non-originating television broadcasting. It is presumed that a network link exists in the form of a coaxial cable, microwave relay or direct receiving equipment and that the originating station would be used as the source of all program material. It is presumed also that the local station would be content with *aural* identification and announcement only.

PROGRAM LIMITATIONS

The following chart shows the limitations of a television station with minimum equipment for telecasting network-originated programs.

Network Programs	YES
Station Announcements	SOUND ONLY
Local Commercials	SOUND ONLY
Film Entertainment	NO
Film Commercials	NO
Slide Commercials	NO
Live Talent Shows	NO
Remote Pickups	NO
Test Pattern	NO

EQUIPMENT REQUIRED

- (1) **RTV-500 500-watt Transmitter* and Station Monitors**
- (1) **TF3A or TF6A Antenna**
- (1) **Video Line Amplifier and Switching Unit**
- (1) **Video Distribution Amplifier**
- (1) **Picture Monitor**
- (2) **Microphones**
- (1) **RPC-40 Consolette**
- (1) **RM-10 Speech Monitor Amplifier**

* For 5KW operation, substitute Raytheon RTV-5 5000-watt Transmitter. Note: power amplifiers can be added to an existing RTV-500 installation with minor field modification.

APPROXIMATE COST. All of the equipment listed above is basic equipment required by any television station and will serve as a foundation for future expansion. The investment required for 500-watt operation would be on the order of $50,000 to $55,000.

The component list shown here is for the equipment needed to start a "bare-bones" 500-watt television station, which would be suitable for rebroadcasting programming provided from a network connection. Details of the elements needed are listed, including a control console. The price for such a setup was in the range of $50,000 to $55,000.

RAYTHEON

Excellence in Electronics

Minimum Requirements For A NETWORK OUTLET and LIMITED LOCAL STATION

By adding a camera chain and film and slide projectors to the foundation equipment described on page 2, a small television station can provide the same network outlet service plus limited local program origination. Local activities would be restricted by the limitations of minimum equipment to film entertainment and commercials, slide commercials, simple live talent spots, local publicity and TV promotion. Major reliance would still be placed on network program sources.

PROGRAM POSSIBILITIES

With only one camera available, local programming will be restricted and inflexible. In most cases, it will be necessary to confine local programs to intervals between network telecasts to provide time for changing camera position, film changes, studio set-ups, etc.

Network Programs	YES
Station Announcements	YES
Local Commercials	YES
Film Telecasts	YES (16-mm.)
Slide Projection	YES
Local Talent	LIMITED
Remote Pickups	VERY LIMITED
Test Pattern	YES

EQUIPMENT REQUIRED

(1) RTV-500 500-watt Transmitter* and Station Monitors
(1) TF3A or TF6A TV Antenna
(1) RTC 10 Single Image Orthicon Camera Chain
(1) RTF16 16-mm. Film Projector, Prism and Screen
(1) 2" x 2" Slide Projector
(1) Video Line Amplifier and Switching Unit
(1) Video Distribution Amplifier
(5) Microphones
(1) Picture Monitor
(1) RPC-40 Consolette
(1) RR-30 Remote Amplifier
(1) RM-10 Speech Monitor Amplifiers

* For 5KW operation, substitute Raytheon RTV-5 5000-watt Transmitter. Note: power amplifiers can be added to an existing RTV-500 installation with minor field modification.

APPROXIMATE COST. The minimum equipment required for a limited 500-watt station of this type depends upon the plans and opportunities for local program origination. Since this will affect the extent of the camera, video and other equipment required, the cost can be stated only very approximately as on the order of $75,000 to $80,000.

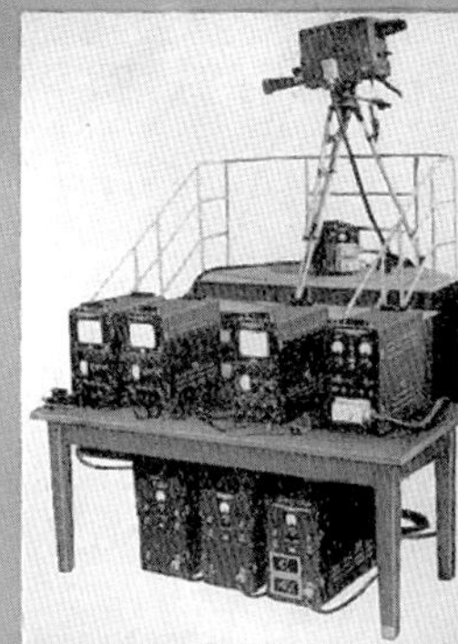

IMAGE ORTHICON CHAIN

Available as single or dual chain of cameras and associated equipment. Camera features four-lens turret, electronic view finder, rear control of focus and iris adjustment. Power, synchronizing, amplifying and monitoring supplied by compact, portable, matched units through single cable connection.

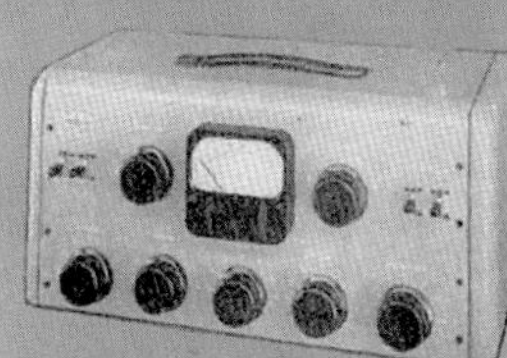

RPC-40 CONSOLETTE

Ideally suited for programs originating at the transmitter as well as remote pick-ups. Four channels of high level mixing.

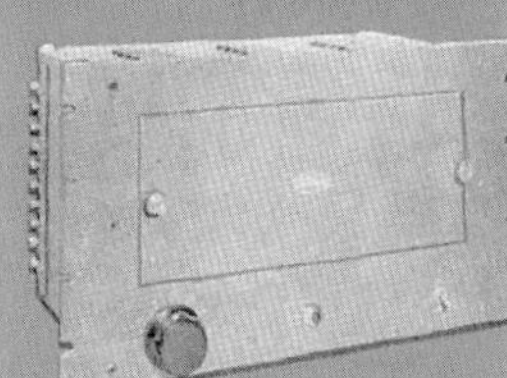

RM-10 SPEECH MONITOR AMPLIFIER

A high-fidelity, high-level audio amplifier for monitoring purposes.

For a 500-watt television station with its own studio and the added capability of generating local programming, the price rose up to $80,000.

EQUIPMENT REQUIRED

(1) RTV-5 Transmitter and Control Console
(1) TF3A or TF6A Antenna Equipment
(2) RTC 20 Dual Image Orthicon Camera Chains
(2) Camera Dollies
(1) RTF 16 16-mm. Film Projector, Prism and Screen
(1) 2″ x 2″ Slide Projector
(1) Rack, including Distribution Amplifier, Line Amplifier, Sync Phasing Unit, Patch Panels
(1) Control Console (Includes Picture Monitor, Wave Form Monitor, Switching Unit, Level Control)
(3) Picture Monitors
Complete Speech Equipment (Includes: 6 Microphones, 1 RC-11 Console, 3 RM10 Monitors, R40 Limiter, RR30 Remote Amplifier, 2 RTT20 Turntables, Speakers, Jacks and Panels, Plugs and Connectors, Racks, Traveling Boom Stand)
(1) 2000 MC Microwave Relay System for Video Channel

and a 5KW class B linear power amplifier for the visual channel. No vestigial side band filter required. *NOTE: Where an RTV 500 installation exists, a power amplifier can be added with minor field alterations for 5KW operation.*

RTC 20 Dual Image Orthicon Camera Chains. Two dual camera chains are recommended to provide the flexibility needed for efficient studio operations and studio-remote continuity. Standardization on a dual camera chain for both studio work and remote assignments makes for more effective camera coverage and uniform operation procedure. The availability of additional pick-up facilities also provides for adequate maintenance and emergency spares.

Master Control Console. The single position Master Console serves as the control center for the entire station. Studio productions, film and slide continuity and remote events picked up by either camera chain as well as programs from network sources are channeled to the Control Console, where they are monitored and mixed for transmission and/or distribution within the station. The Console, together with its associated rack equipment, includes: 12″ Picture Monitor, 5″ Waveform Monitor, Switching (automatic or manual), Program Level Control, Sync Phasing Unit and Picture Distribution Amplifier.

Microwave Relay System. This equipment may be used for remote video pickups, as a studio-transmitter link when the studio and transmitting facilities are separated, or as equipment in a point-to-point multiple hop relay system. The equipment may be either rack mounted or portable and provides 50 watts output in the 2000 MC band.

APPROXIMATE COST. The equipment for an intermediate television station as suggested above, while broadly applicable, cannot be applied to specific cases without considering individual needs and requirements. Some modification would undoubtedly be made to allow for variation in the opportunities, plans, and aspirations of any specific station. The cost, therefore, can be stated only approximately as on the order of $190,000.

RAYTHEON
Excellence in Electronics

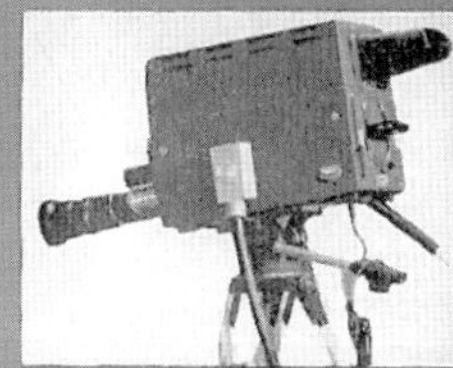

IMAGE ORTHICON CAMERA
Combines camera pickup and electronic view finder. Camera features four-position lens turret, rear control of focus and iris adjustment. Illumination levels may be from 1 to 1000 foot candle. Only one cable required to connect camera to associated equipment.

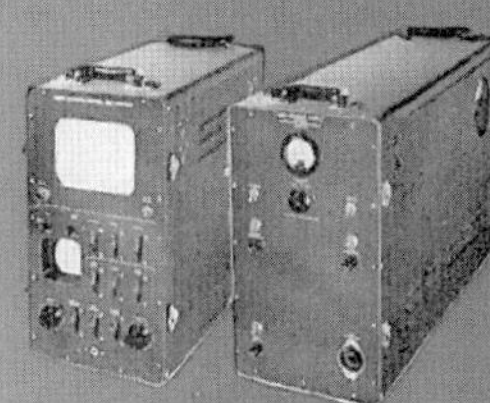

CAMERA CONTROL UNIT AND LV POWER SUPPLY
Camera Control and Monitor (left) provides visual monitoring and control of brightness, contrast, focus, program channel, etc. Low Voltage Supply (right) provides DC power for the pickup, view finder, camera auxiliary, monitor, etc.

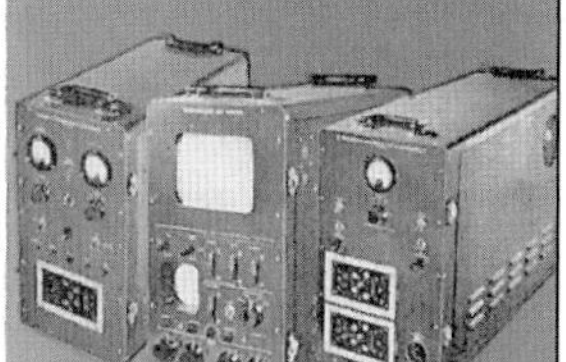

CAMERA CHAIN UNITS
Typical packaged units include: left, Portable Sync Generator (supplies standard RMA blanking, synchronous and driving pulses to all camera chain units) center, Mixer Amplifier and Monitor (serves as master control and monitor for two or more cameras) right, Distribution Amplifier and Low Voltage Supply (supplies power for the mixer and master control).

A larger 5,000-watt television station with full network and local programming capabilities was priced at about $190,000, which included two Raytheon television cameras with dollies, control consoles with picture displays, and a 16-millimeter movie projector.

April, 1953

Raytheon Cited as Largest Producer of Junction Transistors by *Fortune* Magazine

Fortune Magazine calls 1953 "The Year of the Transistor."

In its March issue, *Fortune* told how the transistor, "the pea-sized time bomb," is revolutionizing the electronics industry. Since the beginning of the year when mass production of transistors got under way, Raytheon is leading as the biggest producer of junction transistors. Production of transistors at Raytheon is at the rate of tens of thousands per month.

"In the transistor," *Fortune* said, "man may hope to find a brain to match atomic energy's muscles." One of electronic's wonder devices, transistors free electronics from the limitations of vacuum tubes by providing compactness and low power consumption.

The first small commercial returns of transistors are now coming in through the immediate practical application of the hearing aid trade. Over ten concerns are now manufacturing tubeless hearing aids using three Raytheon junction transistors. Many other manufacturers have purchased small quantities since tors in September, 1952, to the hearing aid trade.

Fortune's report outlined the history of the development of the transistor. It pointed out that the transistor, far from being an accidental discovery, proves the importance of fundamental research.

Until now, most proposed uses of transistors have been concentrated on military equipment. Applications still have to be worked out, but *Fortune* reports that the greatest value of transistors lies in computers and communications systems — radio, television, telephone — in many home instruments, memory tubes, automobile headlights and countless other uses undreamt of at present.

Photographs and colored diagrams were included in *Fortune's* comprehensive study on the transistor. A picture was shown comparing two hearing aids: a vacuum-tube set and a new set made by Maico Co., which uses three Raytheon transistors. The transistorized set is almost half the size of the old-

The April 1953 issue of *Raytheon News* reports that the company was the largest producer of junction transistors, turning out tens of thousands per month. Raytheon first introduced the transistor in September 1952 for use in hearing aids. The March 1953 issue of *Fortune* magazine, quoted in this article, predicted widespread use of the transistor in computers, radios, and televisions because of its small size and its low power consumption compared to vacuum tubes. Although vacuum tubes remained important for Raytheon, the company was quick to seize the lead in producing these solid-state devices.

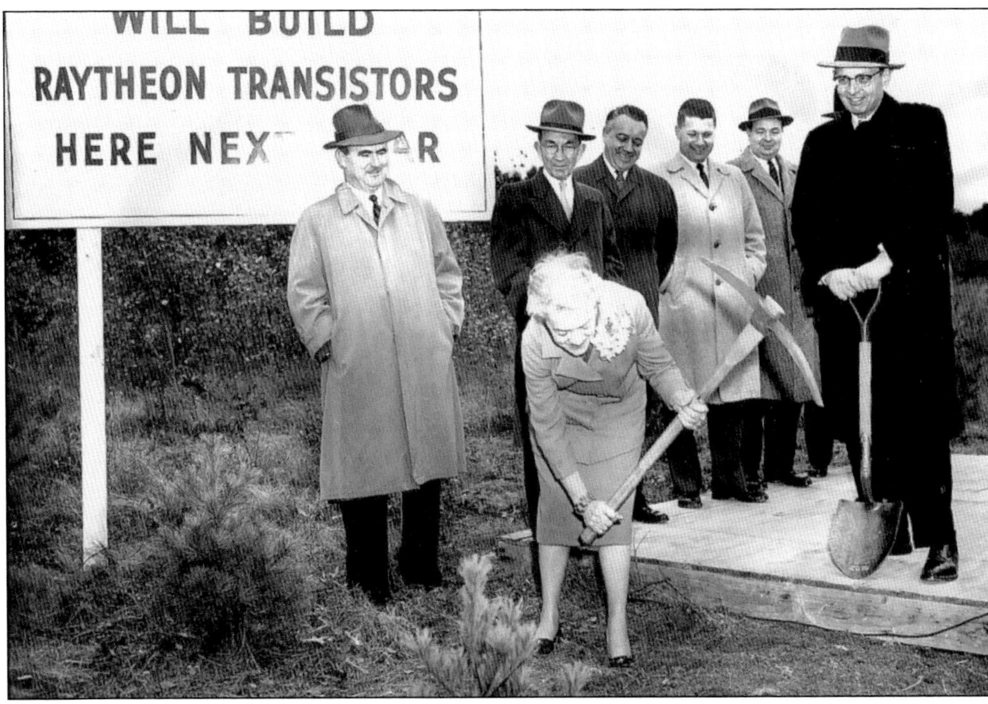

In this view from the early 1950s, Sen. Margaret Chase Smith participates with various Raytheon and local officials in the groundbreaking ceremony for a new transistor plant in Maine.

Although transistors were originally developed at Bell Labs, Raytheon was the country's largest producer of transistors between 1952 and 1956. Here are a handful of examples of Raytheon's production of this revolutionary new product, which completely changed the design of radios and televisions and made computers practical.

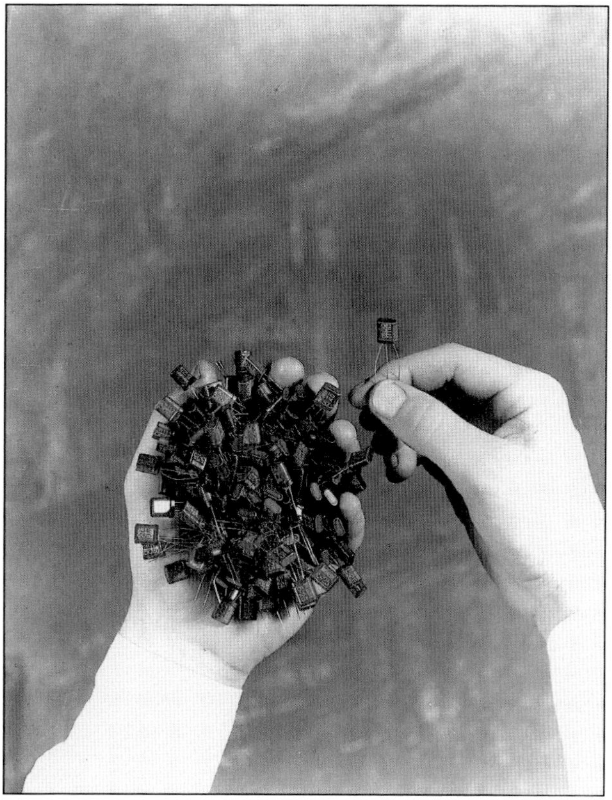

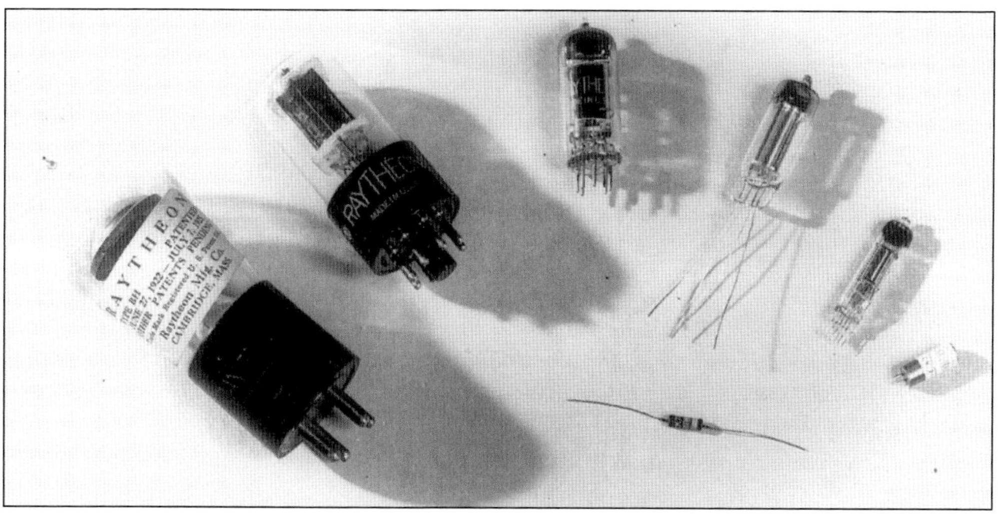

This photograph shows a size comparison of Raytheon electronic devices over the years. To the left is the Percy Spencer 1920s BH tube. Next are receiving tubes of the 1930s and 1940s, followed by the subminiature tubes. At the right and bottom are transistors from the 1950s.

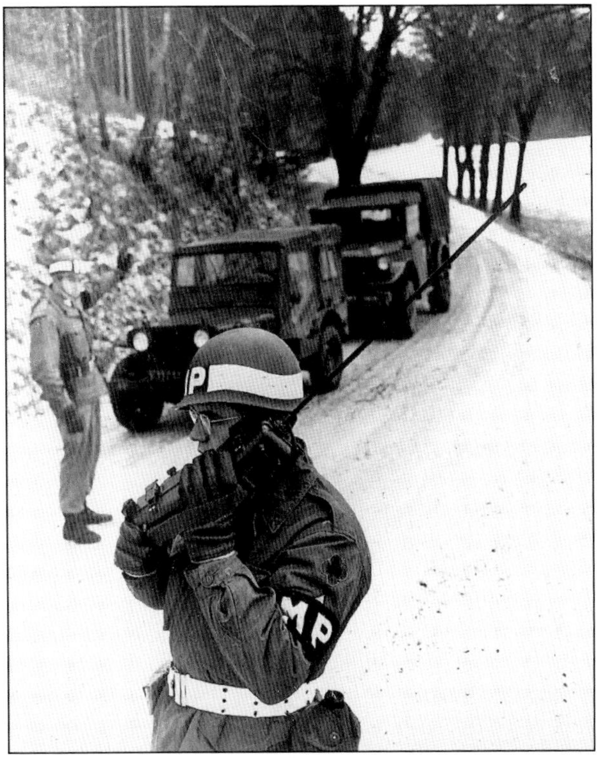

The first portable two-way radios (often called walkie talkies) were developed in the early 1940s, most notably by Motorola. Raytheon, drawing upon the knowledge of subminiature tube technology that it had gained in World War II, also began to produce portable radio transceivers. This photograph shows the radios in use in the field at the time of the Korean War in the early 1950s.

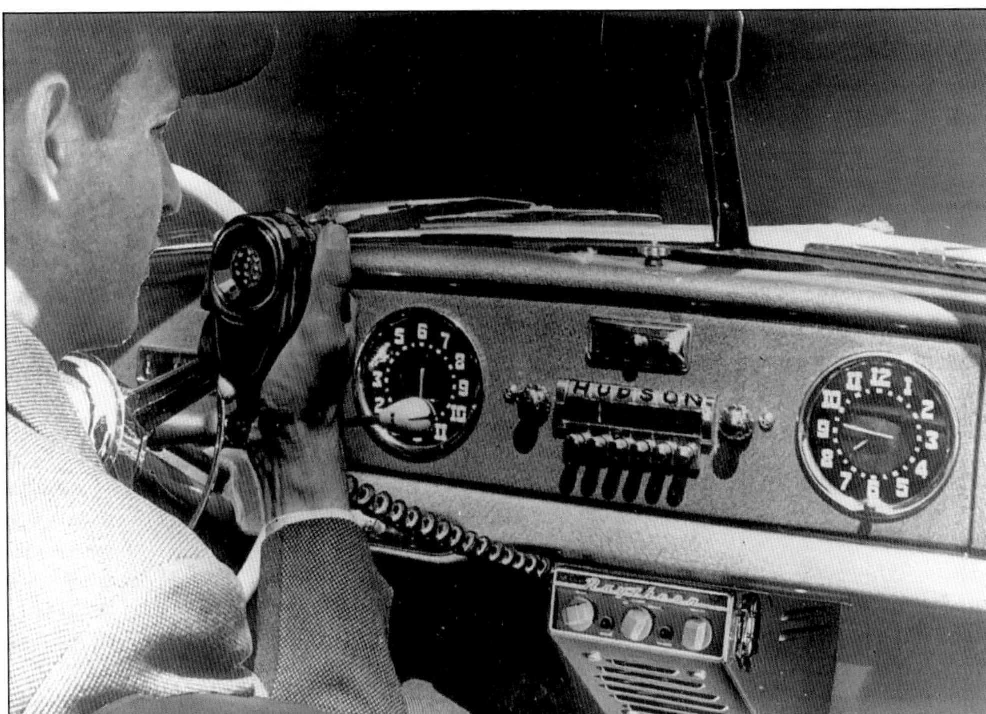

A Raytheon two-way car radio, useful for police and for public service workers, is seen here mounted in a Hudson car.

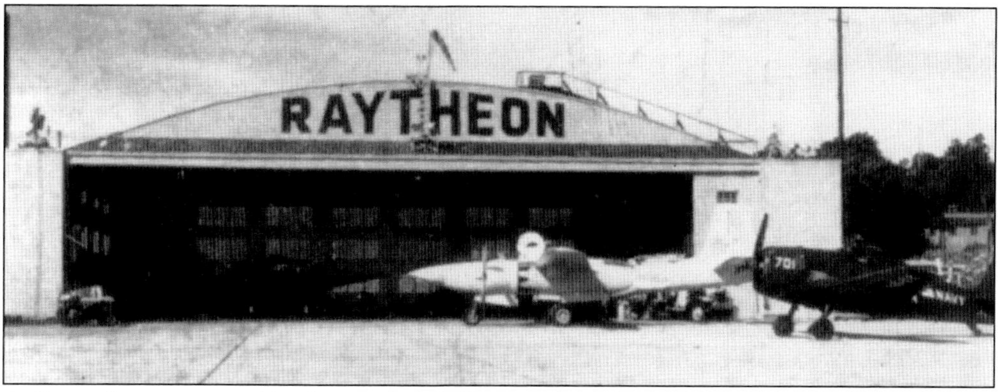

A fleet of up to seven Raytheon-owned planes was kept at Hanscom Field in Bedford for business flights to visit military and commercial customers. One of them was a converted B-26 bomber that was adapted for commercial use. On one trip, coauthor Bob Edwards recalls crawling under the wing (which passed through the center of the fuselage) and coming up to sit in a jump seat behind the pilots to watch flight activities at close range.

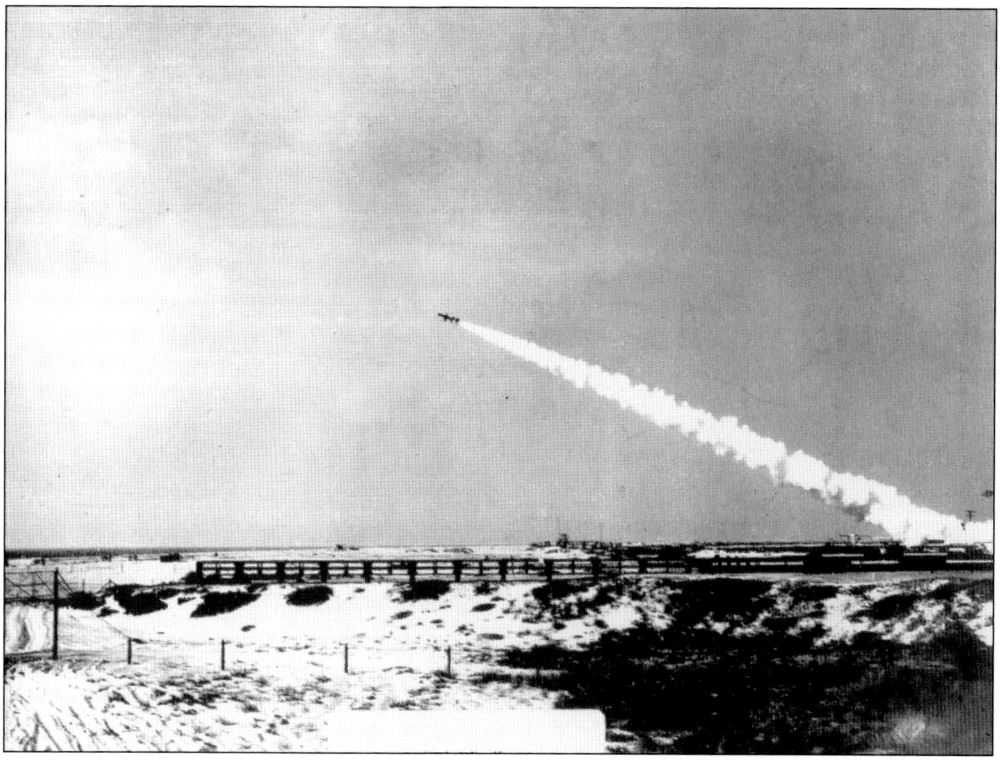

Raytheon engineers began investigations into missile-guidance systems as early as 1944. The Lark missile was Raytheon's first product in the new field. In 1950, the Lark successfully destroyed a test drone airplane, achieving the first intercept of a plane by a missile.

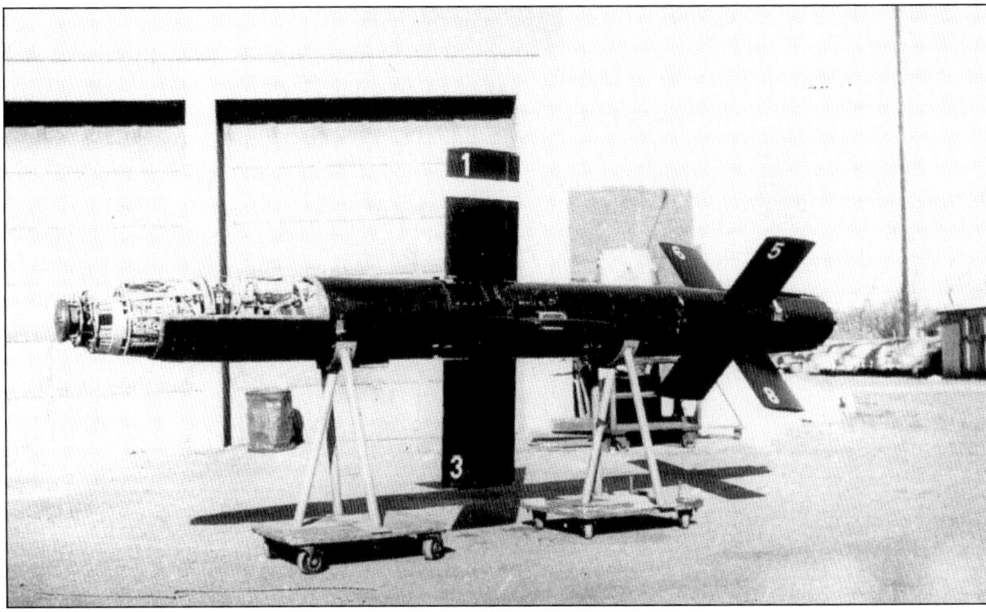

This is a closeup view of Raytheon's first missile, the Lark.

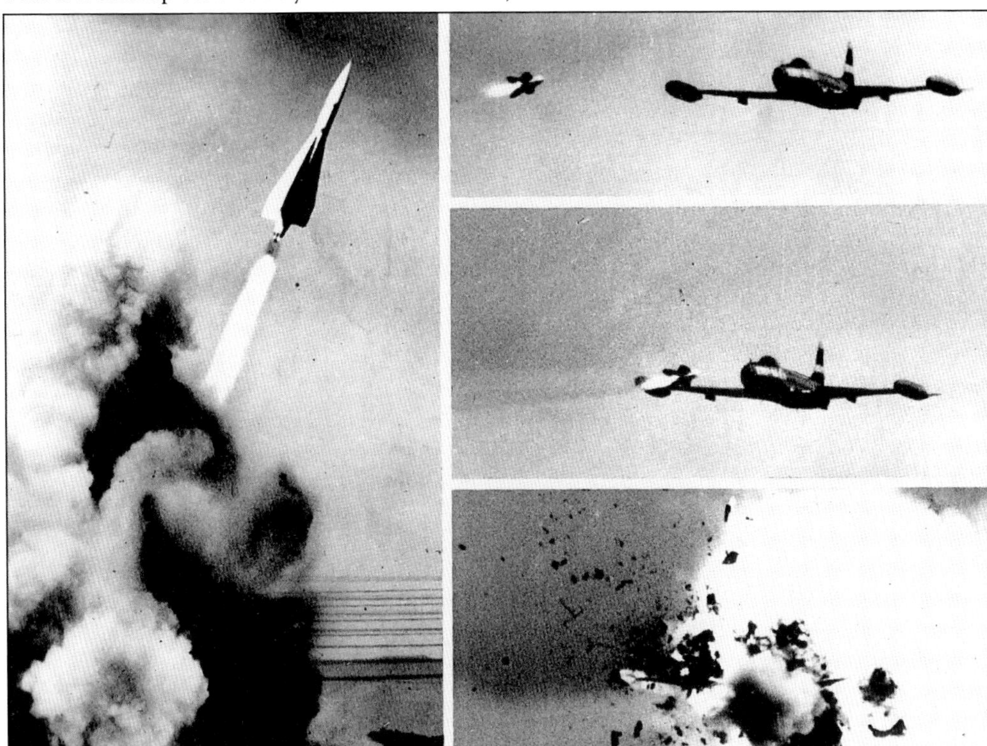

In the 1950s, soon after the achievements of its Lark guided missile, Raytheon earned major contracts for the Sparrow and Hawk missile systems. The photographs show a Hawk intercepting an F-80 target drone plane. Raytheon's news release about this intercept declared the target "blown to smithereens." Tom Phillips worked some 35-hour days as a young engineer to develop initial models of the Hawk system and to assure landing the prime contract.

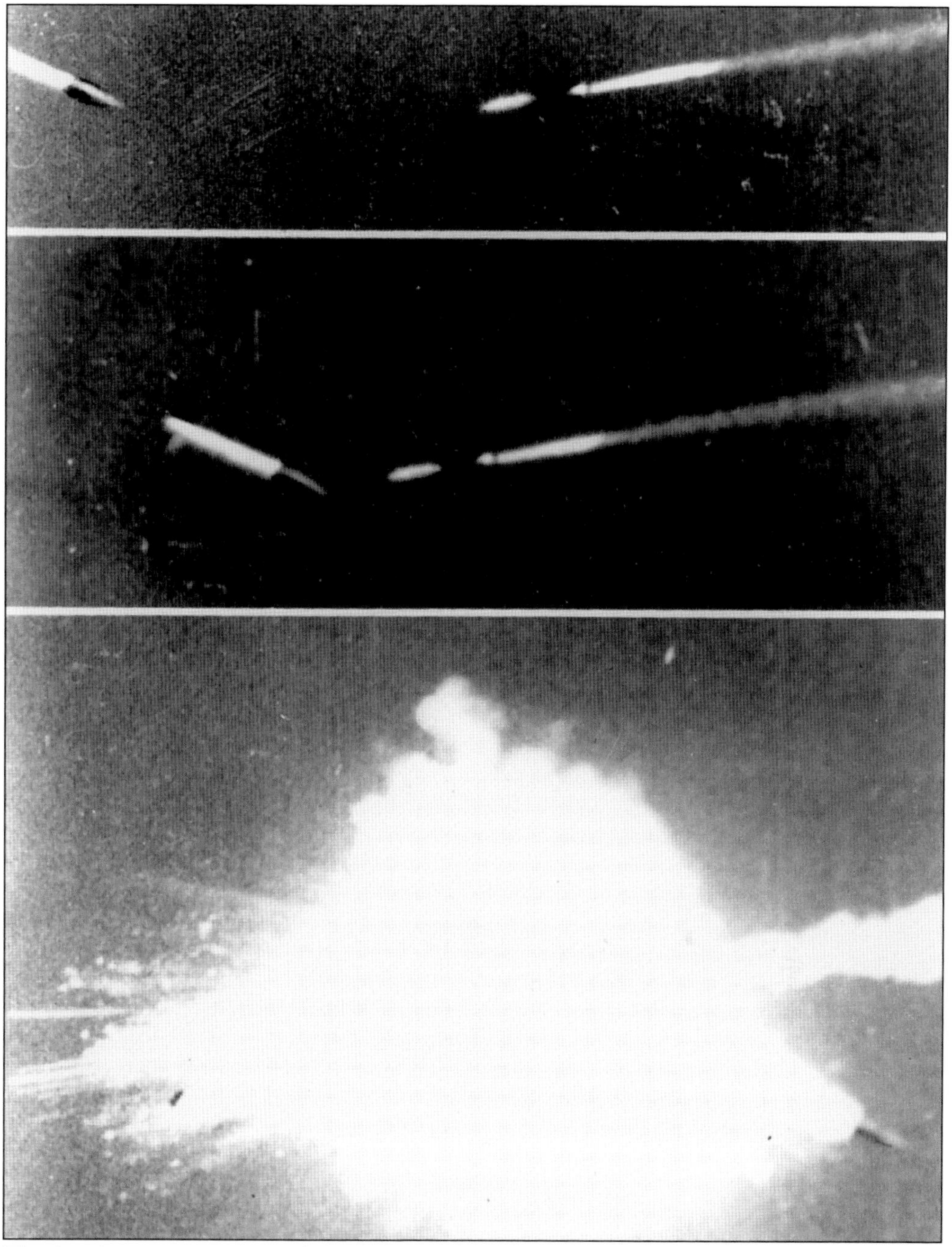

The first known intercept and destruction of a ballistic missile by another missile, performed at supersonic speed, was scored in 1960 by a Raytheon-Army Hawk (right) against an Honest John (left) at the missile range in White Sands, New Mexico. The continuous wave radar concept pursued by Raytheon was largely responsible for the Hawk's unique ability to track low-flying targets.

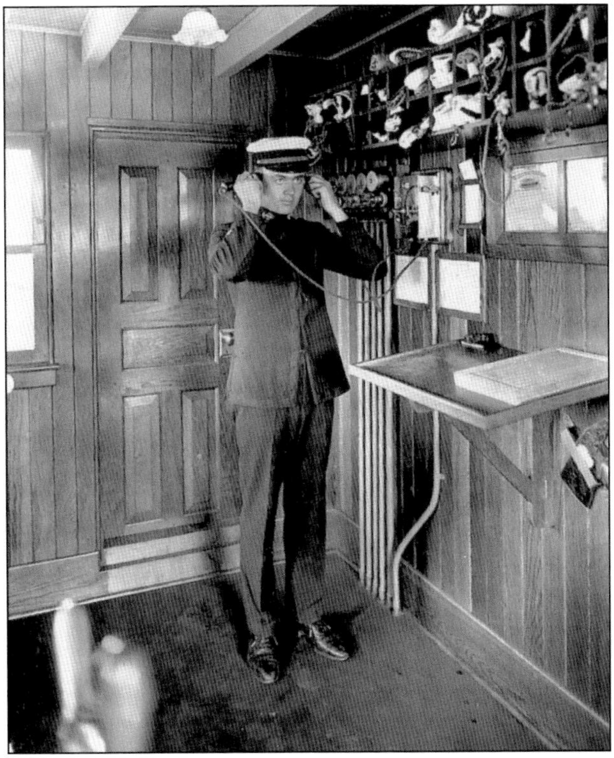

In 1946, Raytheon acquired an important pioneer in marine electronics, the Submarine Signal Company. In early underwater sound tests, illustrated here, a pair of microphones (one on each side of the ship's bow, underwater) picked up the sound of a bell, which was fed into each earphone of the listener. By rotating the direction of the ship until the two sounds were equal, the operator could determine the bearing of the source.

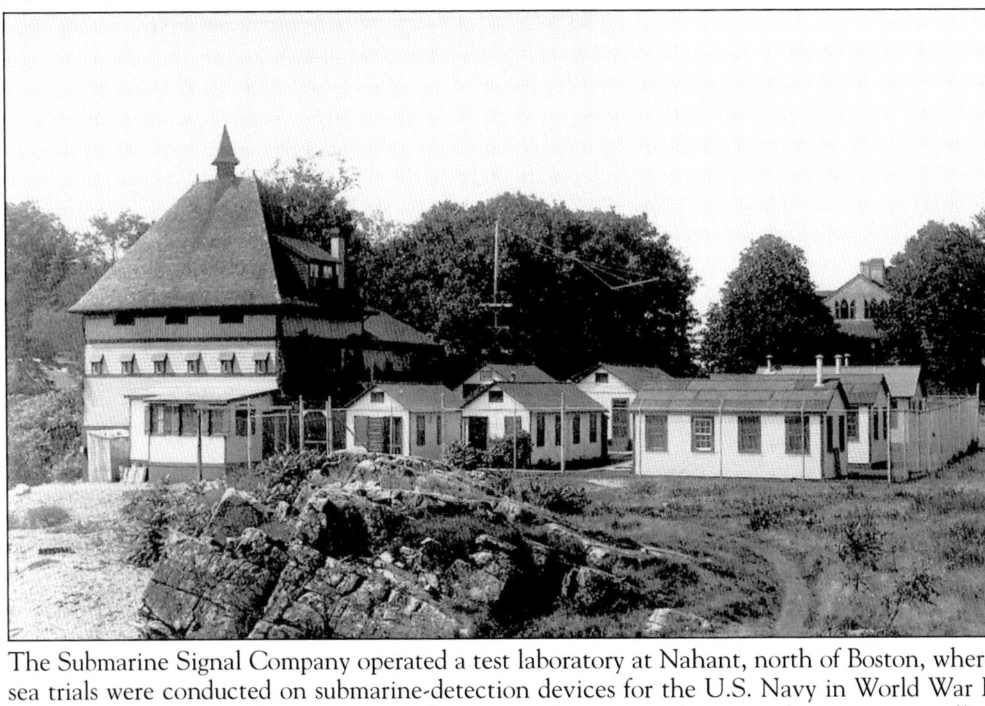

The Submarine Signal Company operated a test laboratory at Nahant, north of Boston, where sea trials were conducted on submarine-detection devices for the U.S. Navy in World War I. The Raytheon archives have extensive data logs and correspondence on these tests, as well as the many design variations tested in 1917 and 1918 using the Coast Guard cutter *Miami*. High-level naval officers were frequent visitors to observe the tests and oversee the program.

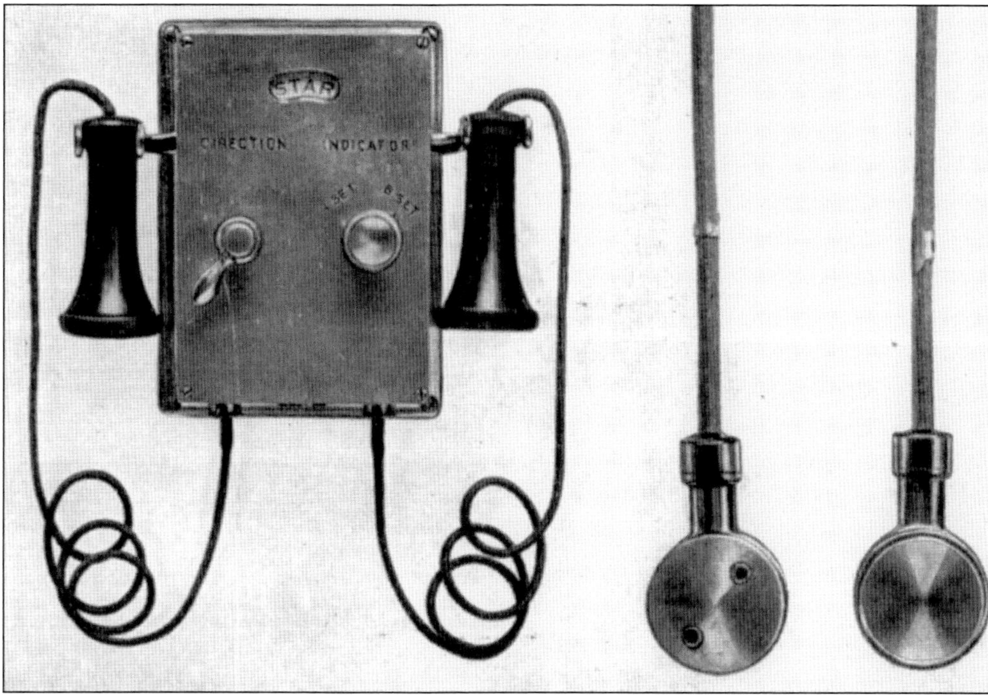

This image shows the microphones, the indicator box, and the earphones for the early underwater sound location device.

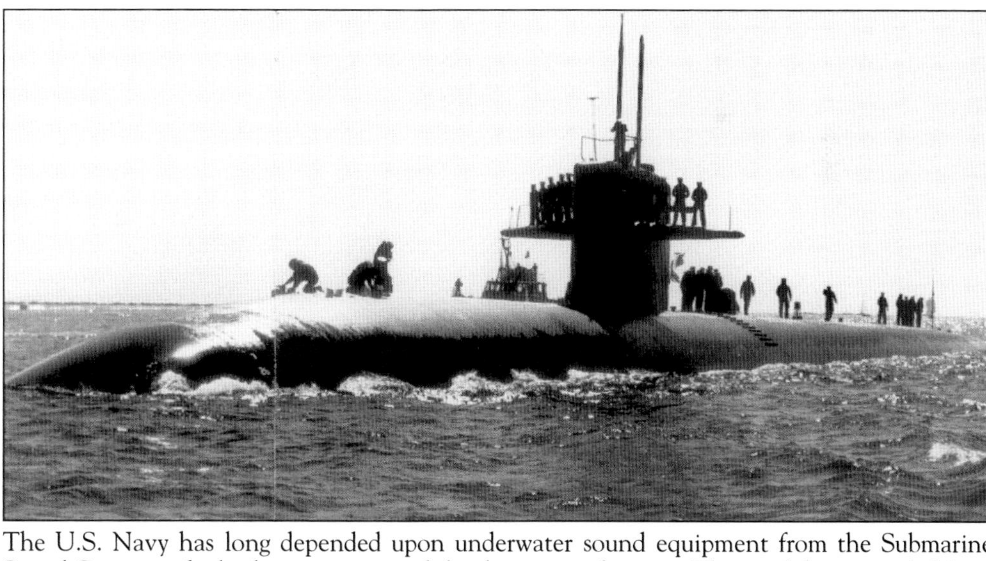

The U.S. Navy has long depended upon underwater sound equipment from the Submarine Signal Company for both navigation and the detection of targets. This work has extended from the days of World War I up to the present nuclear submarine era. The Raytheon archives house documents dating back to 1917, when submarine detection was in its infancy, including data logs from Submarine Signal Company sea tests held for the navy off the New England coast.

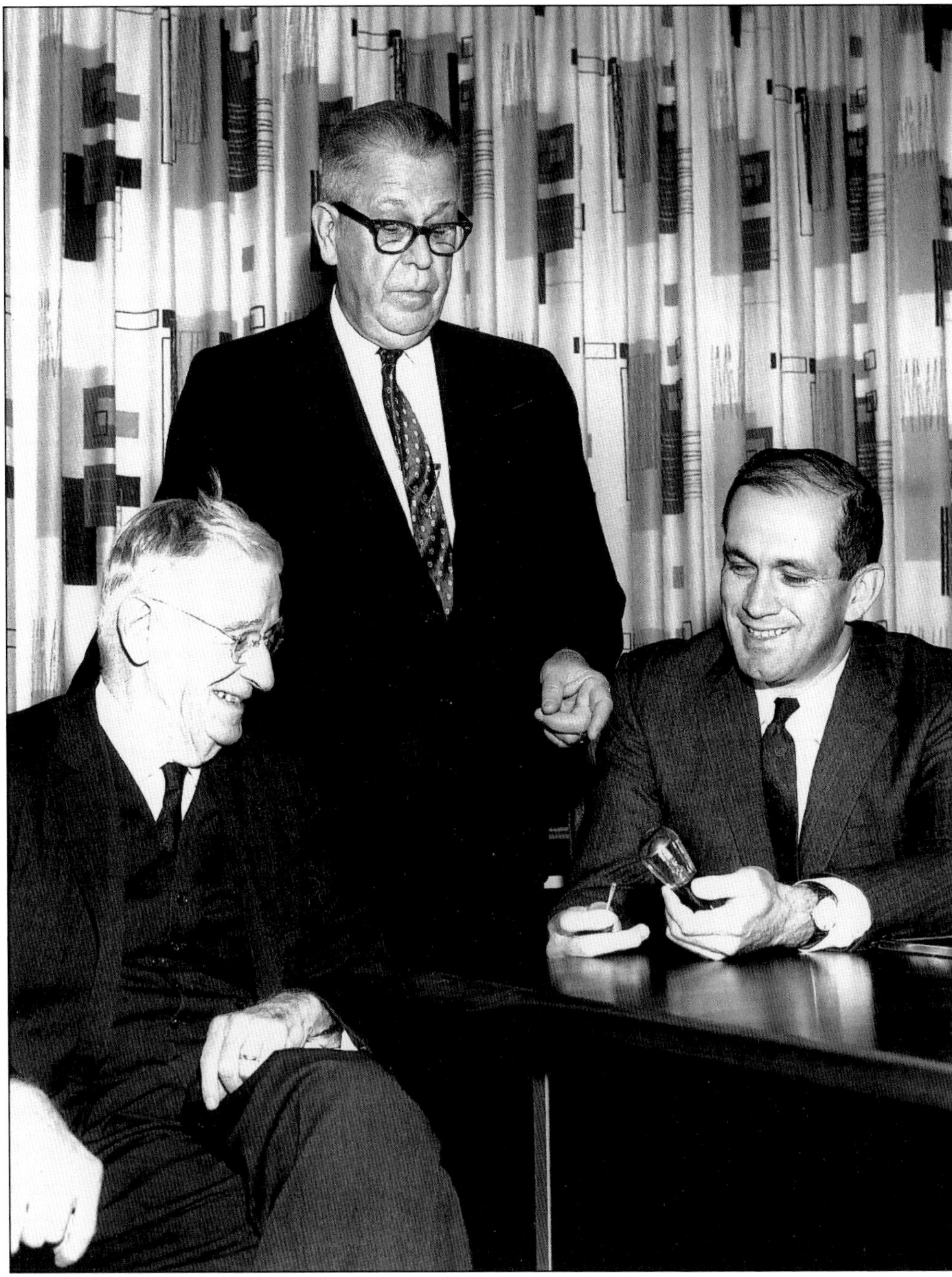

Unlike companies that have suffered from complete shifts in direction and management philosophy, Raytheon evolved gradually and with a strong sense of continuity. Here, three of Raytheon's most influential figures are seen discussing one of Percy L. Spencer's BH rectifier tubes, probably in the early 1960s. They are, from left to right, Vannevar Bush (a company founder), Percy Spencer, and Tom Phillips (who joined the company after World War II and rose into management in the 1950s).

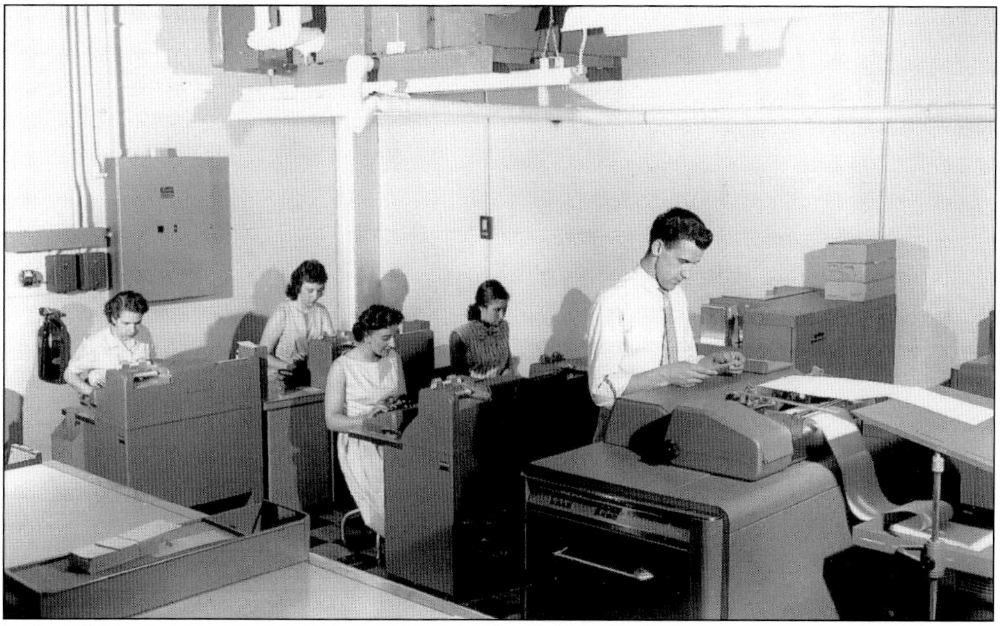

Before there were computers, there were punch cards and tabulation machines. In the 1950s, workers entered test data about microwave tubes, equipment maintenance and calibration, and more onto cards using these machines at the Waltham facility.

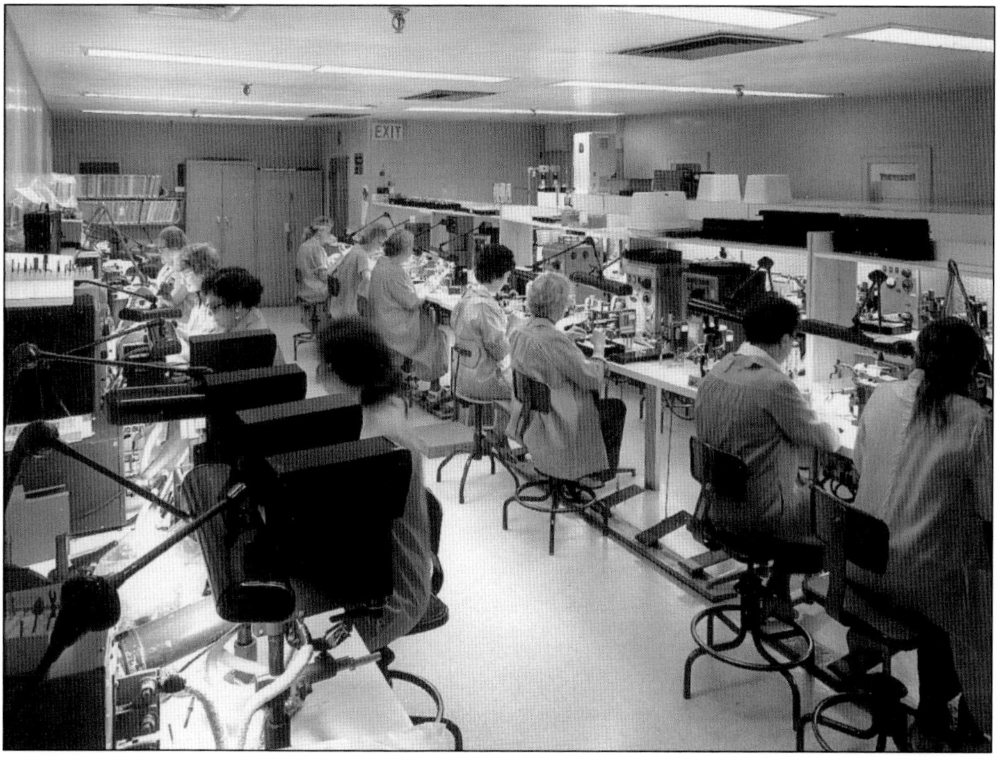

In spite of the improving sophistication of technology, hand operations by skilled workers, as seen in this photograph, remained a very important part of most manufacturing processes.

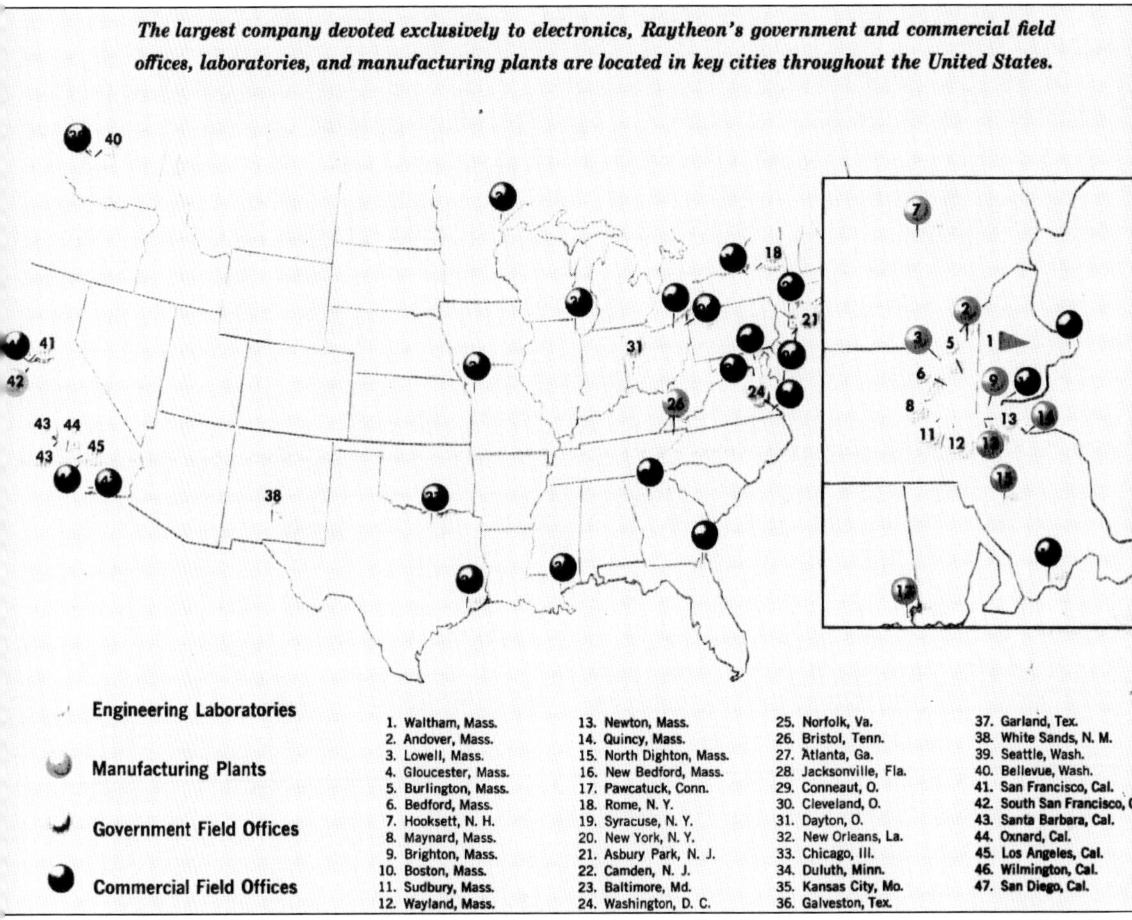

The expansion of the company over the years from a small local operation to a national and, ultimately, international corporation is illustrated by this map showing the locations of the numerous Raytheon installations around 1970. At that time there were distributorships in 83 countries, licensees in 16 countries, and service facilities at 167 global ports.

Four

Growth and Diversification

The years after World War II had transformed Raytheon into a more sleek and manageable organization with clear lines of command and a focus on the bottom line. And while boom and bust remained an inevitable pattern in the government electronics business, factors such as the cold war and the space race seemed to ensure long-range opportunities for Raytheon in fields where it had earned an enviable reputation for quality and competence.

As Raytheon prepared to enter the 1960s with its divisions focused on components and on more complex systems such as missiles and radars, it also began to look for acquisition opportunities. In 1959, the company took over Apelco Applied Electronics, a maker of marine electronic equipment, and Machlett Laboratories, a maker of medical equipment. A few years later, with a nod to the craze for "conglomeration" sweeping American business, company president Phillips sought to add a stable of businesses that would earn their keep and perhaps even prosper in those periods when the government market took a downturn. However, unlike Harold Geneen, the ITT architect and former member of the Raytheon management team who was famous for his sometimes unrelated array of acquisitions and personnel, Phillips insisted on finding synergies between Raytheon's core capabilities and the operations of the firms it acquired. Caloric, a maker of kitchen ranges, was made part of the Raytheon family, as were D. C. Heath, an educational textbook publisher, and Seismograph Service Corporation, a player in the petroleum exploration business.

Intending to take the Radarange, hitherto a commercial and industrial product, into America's kitchens, Phillips also added the Amana Refrigeration Company to the roster. Other acquisitions continued through 1969 and included the Badger Company, a petroleum and petrochemical plant designer, and United Engineers and Constructors.

The company continued its acquisitions, albeit at a slower pace, through the 1970s and 1980s. Companies joining the Raytheon fold included Iowa Manufacturing Company (renamed Cedar Rapids), which specialized in construction equipment; Data Logic, a software company; Speed Queen, a maker of washers and dryers; Seiscor Technologies, a maker of telephone equipment; and Beech Aircraft.

In its business dealings with the government, Raytheon cemented its reputation as a system designer and supplier with continued improvements to the Hawk and a variety of other missile systems, radars, and communication equipment.

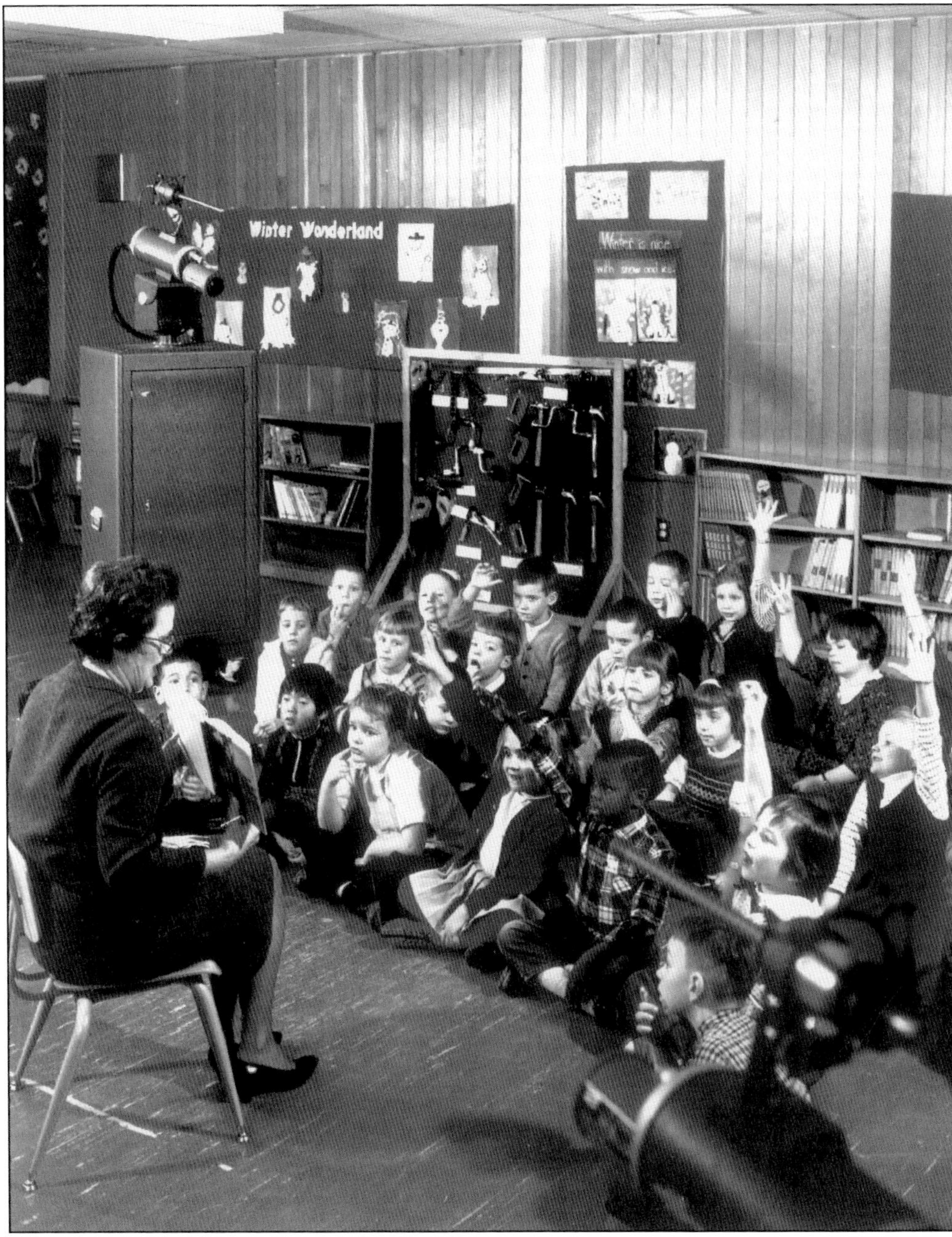

A good example of Raytheon's diversification into new areas is shown in this image from the cover of the 1965 annual report. A training session for a preschool class at University Schools, Bloomington, Indiana, is being televised for a closed-circuit broadcast to be viewed by student teachers at the Indiana University School of Education. The closed-circuit system was designed and engineered by the Dage-Bell Corporation, which was one of three education companies acquired by Raytheon in 1965.

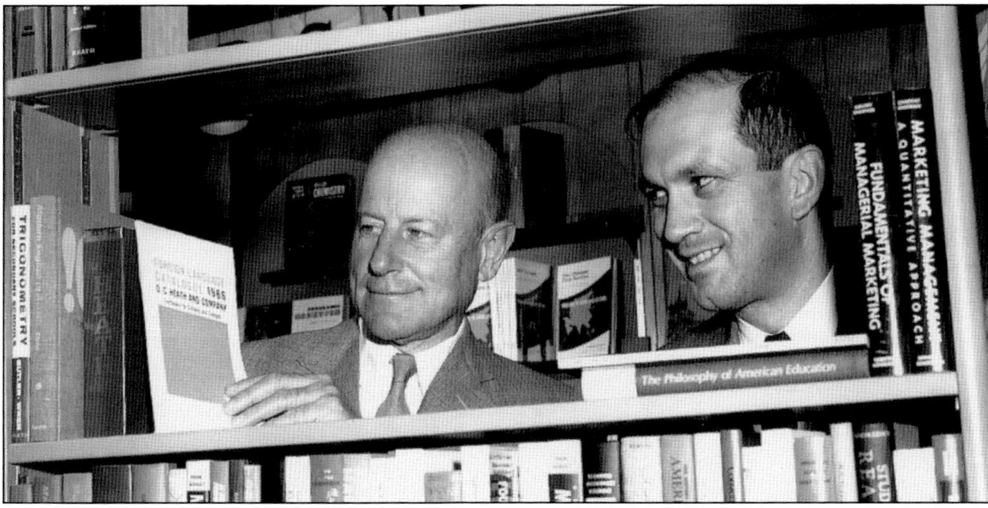

Two of the most crucial men in Raytheon's postwar history were Charles F. Adams and Tom Phillips. Adams brought financial acumen and stabilized the company's outlook after World War II. He worked with Phillips to initiate an enormous variety of new military and commercial ventures, converting Raytheon into a worldwide industrial giant. Phillips was known in the industry for his high standards of ethics and integrity and his insistence upon these characteristics in his employees. This publicity photograph shows the men perusing the products of newly acquired educational publisher D. C. Heath.

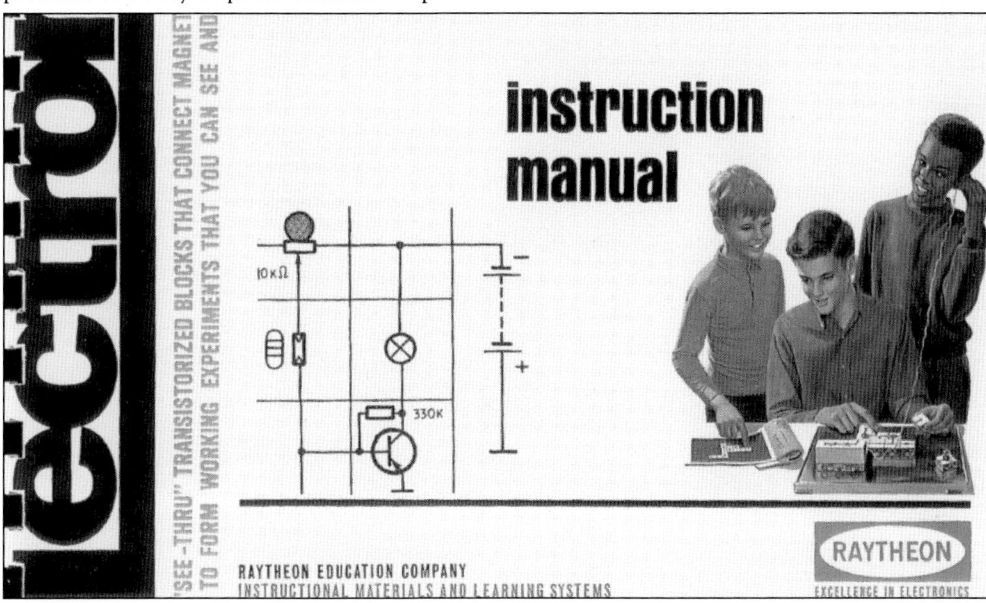

The Raytheon Education Company produced a series of electronic learning kits for school-age children in 1967 and 1968. The Lectron series included complete instructions, explanations of the principles being taught, and all necessary parts (including transistors, capacitors, and a loudspeaker). It even featured add-on kits to expand the number of projects that could be built. The basic model allowed a total of 56 circuits to be constructed, including a Morse code set, a simple electronic organ, a light dimmer, and a two-transistor radio. Electronic devices were enclosed in blocks marked with appropriate schematic symbols and were assembled, without soldering, to form complete circuits.

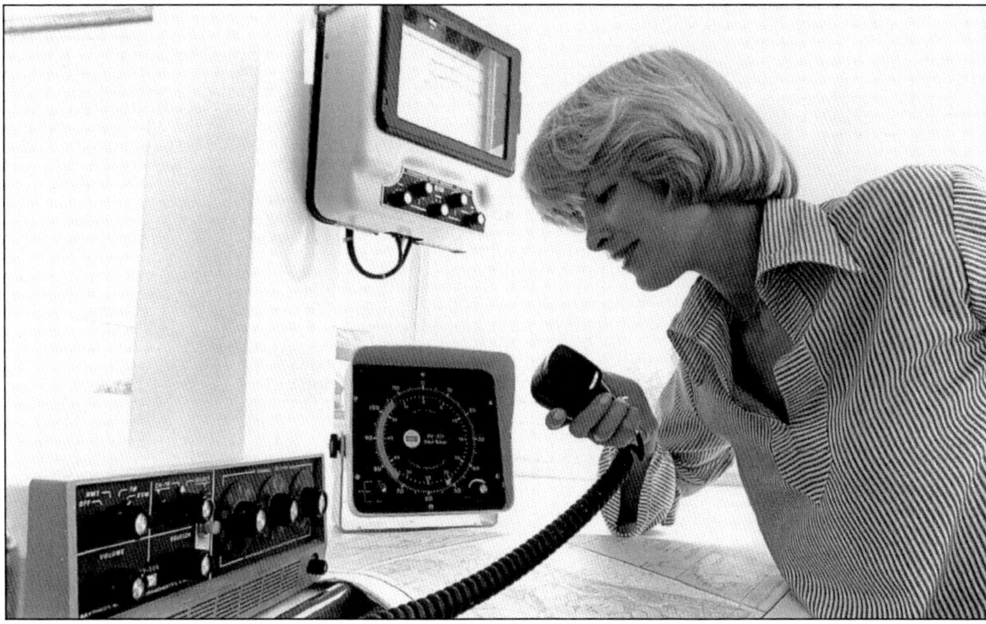

Raytheon's marine products have included such items as radio communications transmitters and receivers, loud-hailers, Fathometers (Raytheon-SubSig trademark), and radars.

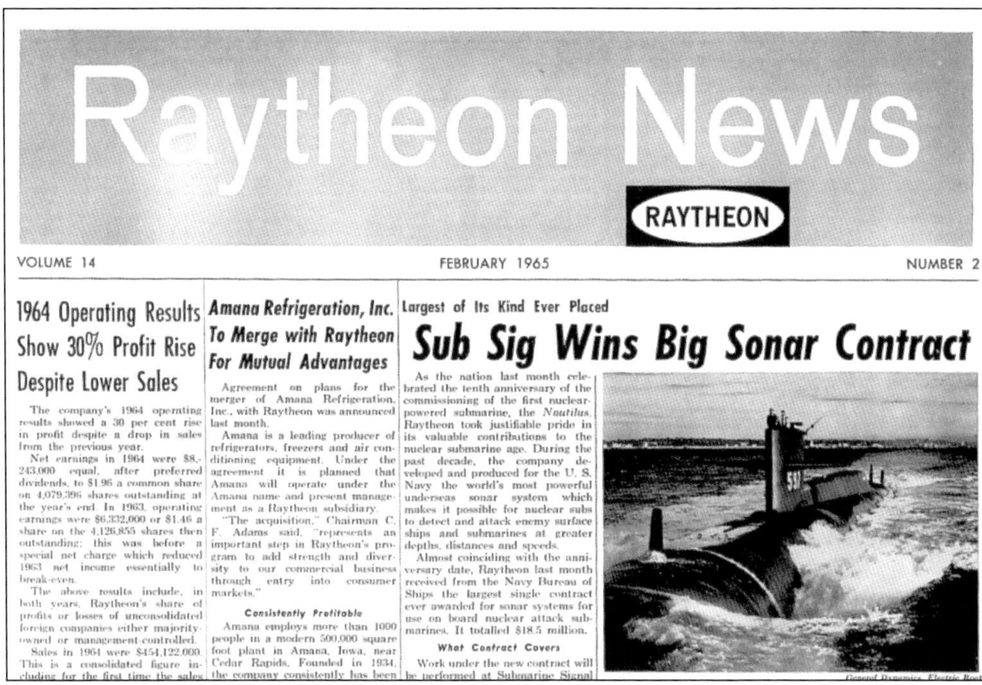

Raytheon News

RAYTHEON

VOLUME 14 FEBRUARY 1965 NUMBER 2

1964 Operating Results Show 30% Profit Rise Despite Lower Sales

The company's 1964 operating results showed a 30 per cent rise in profit despite a drop in sales from the previous year.

Net earnings in 1964 were $8,-243,000 equal, after preferred dividends, to $1.96 a common share on 4,079,396 shares outstanding at the year's end. In 1963, operating earnings were $6,332,000 or $1.46 a share on the 4,126,855 shares then outstanding; this was before a special net charge which reduced 1963 net income essentially to break-even.

The above results include, in both years, Raytheon's share of profits or losses of unconsolidated foreign companies either majority-owned or management-controlled.

Sales in 1964 were $454,122,000. This is a consolidated figure including for the first time the sales

Amana Refrigeration, Inc. To Merge with Raytheon For Mutual Advantages

Agreement on plans for the merger of Amana Refrigeration, Inc., with Raytheon was announced last month.

Amana is a leading producer of refrigerators, freezers and air conditioning equipment. Under the agreement it is planned that Amana will operate under the Amana name and present management as a Raytheon subsidiary.

"The acquisition," Chairman C. F. Adams said, "represents an important step in Raytheon's program to add strength and diversity to our commercial business through entry into consumer markets."

Consistently Profitable

Amana employs more than 1000 people in a modern 500,000 square foot plant in Amana, Iowa, near Cedar Rapids. Founded in 1934, the company consistently has been

Largest of Its Kind Ever Placed

Sub Sig Wins Big Sonar Contract

As the nation last month celebrated the tenth anniversary of the commissioning of the first nuclear-powered submarine, the *Nautilus*, Raytheon took justifiable pride in its valuable contributions to the nuclear submarine age. During the past decade, the company developed and produced for the U. S. Navy the world's most powerful underseas sonar system which makes it possible for nuclear subs to detect and attack enemy surface ships and submarines at greater depths, distances and speeds.

Almost coinciding with the anniversary date, Raytheon last month received from the Navy Bureau of Ships the largest single contract ever awarded for sonar systems for use on board nuclear attack submarines. It totalled $18.5 million.

What Contract Covers

Work under the new contract will be performed at Submarine Signal

In early 1965, *Raytheon News* told of the planned merger of Amana with Raytheon. Amana provided Raytheon with the distribution, service, and marketing capabilities needed to promote home use of its microwave ovens. For its part, Amana gained technological know-how from Raytheon's electronic and microwave experience. Demonstrating the company's commitment to both civilian and military markets, the *Raytheon News* also reported the earning of a large sonar contract by Raytheon subsidiary SubSig.

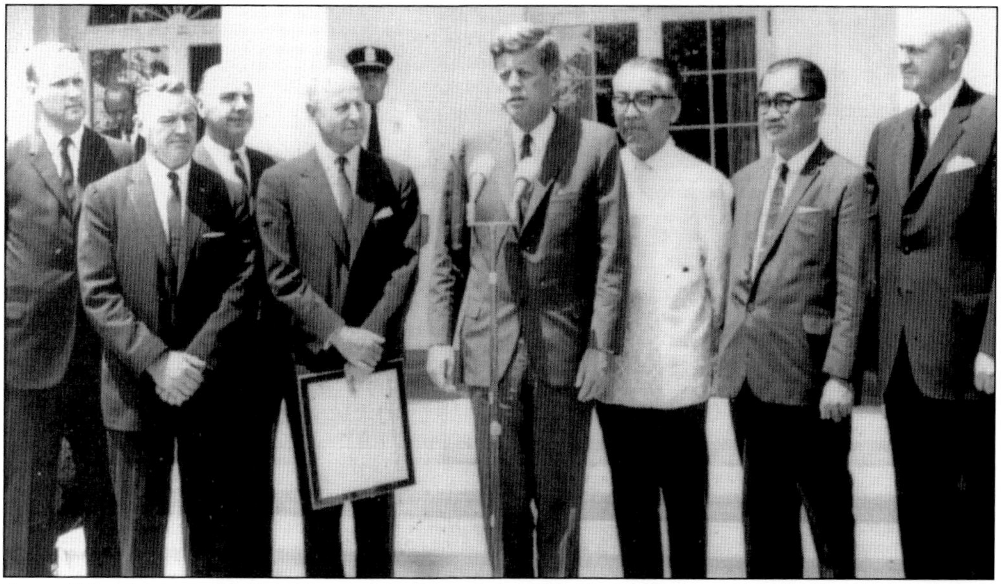

At a Washington, D.C., ceremony, Pres. John. F. Kennedy commends Raytheon for its contributions to the Tools for Freedom program. Raytheon donated 62 tons of tools, equipment, and learning materials, which were sent to the Philippines aboard the *Pioneer Myth*. The donations were consigned to Care (Cooperative for Assistance and Relief) and, ultimately, to a technical school. Raytheon president Charles F. Adams is to the left of President Kennedy, and Philippine ambassador Amelito Mutuc is to the right of Kennedy.

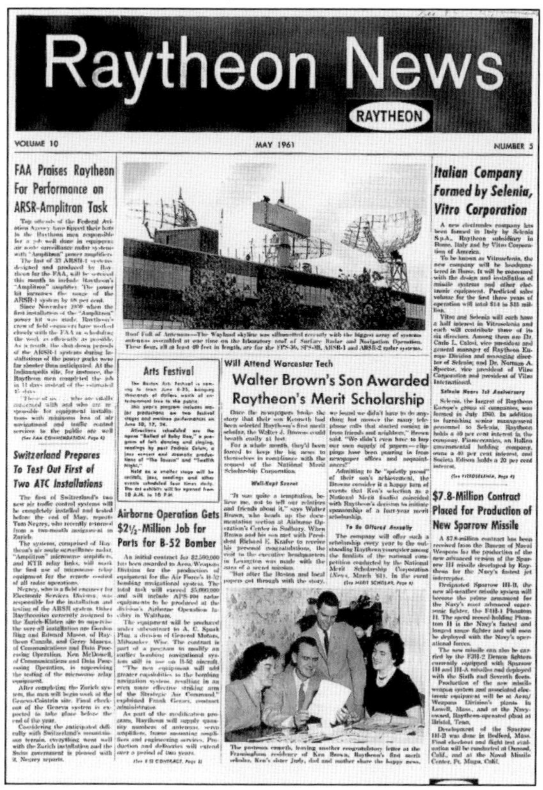

Raytheon News

RAYTHEON

VOLUME 10 MAY 1961 NUMBER 5

FAA Praises Raytheon For Performance on ARSR-Amplitron Task

Arts Festival

Switzerland Prepares To Test Out First of Two ATC Installations

Will Attend Worcester Tech

Walter Brown's Son Awarded Raytheon's Merit Scholarship

Airborne Operation Gets $2½-Million Job for Parts for B-52 Bomber

Italian Company Formed by Selenia, Vitro Corporation

$7.8-Million Contract Placed for Production of New Sparrow Missile

A May 1961 issue of the *Raytheon News* reports the FAA's commendation of Raytheon for completing a power increase modification to 33 air route surveillance radars (ARSRs). The project involved installing a Raytheon-developed Amplitron microwave tube to improve the range of the ARSR by 68 percent. In one case, the upgrade was completed by Raytheon engineers in only 11 days instead of the 45 days that had been allotted.

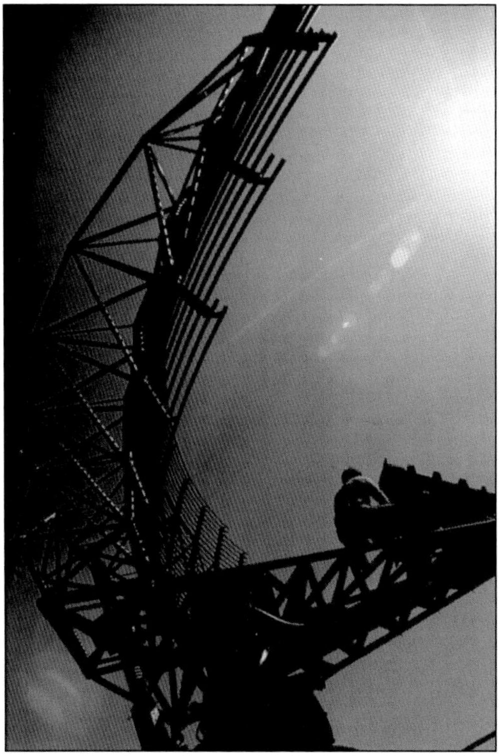

Seen here is the large radar antenna for the U.S. Navy SPS-49 system. SPS-49 is an L-band, long-range, two-dimensional, air-search radar system that provides automatic detection and reporting of targets. It was introduced in the early 1970s.

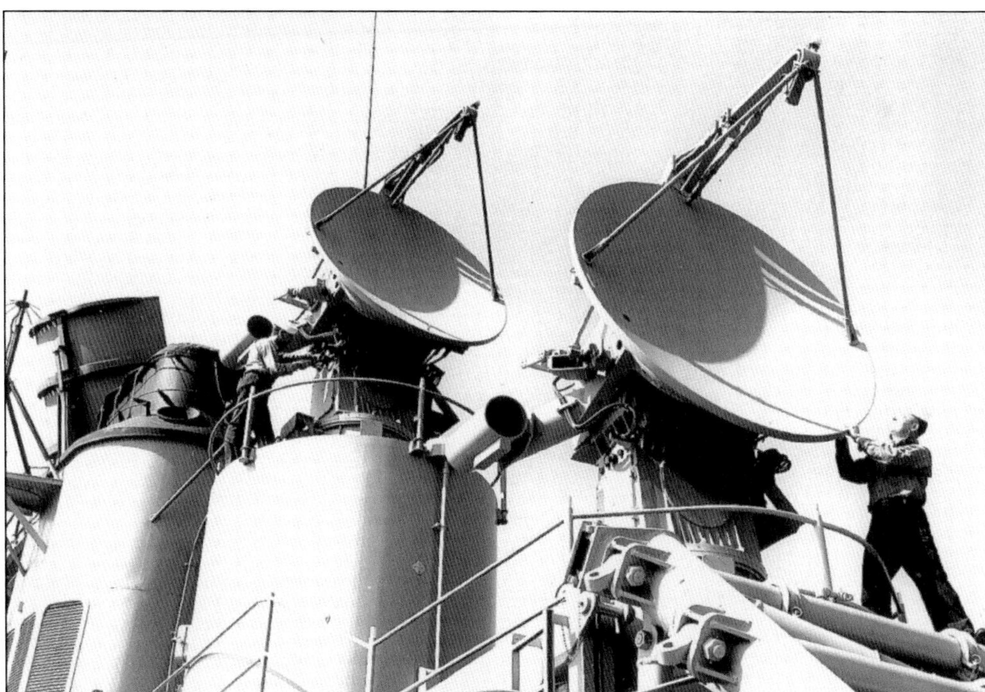

Sailors work on a shipboard antenna for Raytheon's Tartar missile fire-control radar system. The Tartar was an antiaircraft missile that was first fielded by the U.S. Navy in 1962.

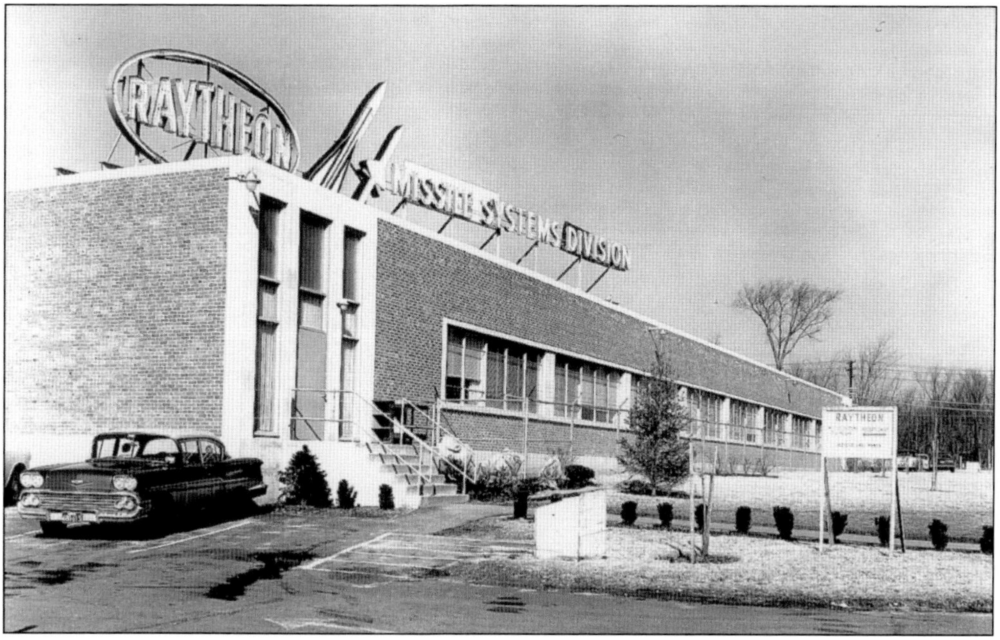

This is one of the buildings used by the Missile Systems Division after 1953, when its operations were moved from Waltham to Bedford and Lowell. The Missile Systems Division headquarters was located in Bedford for many years until a new facility was opened in Tewksbury in 1990.

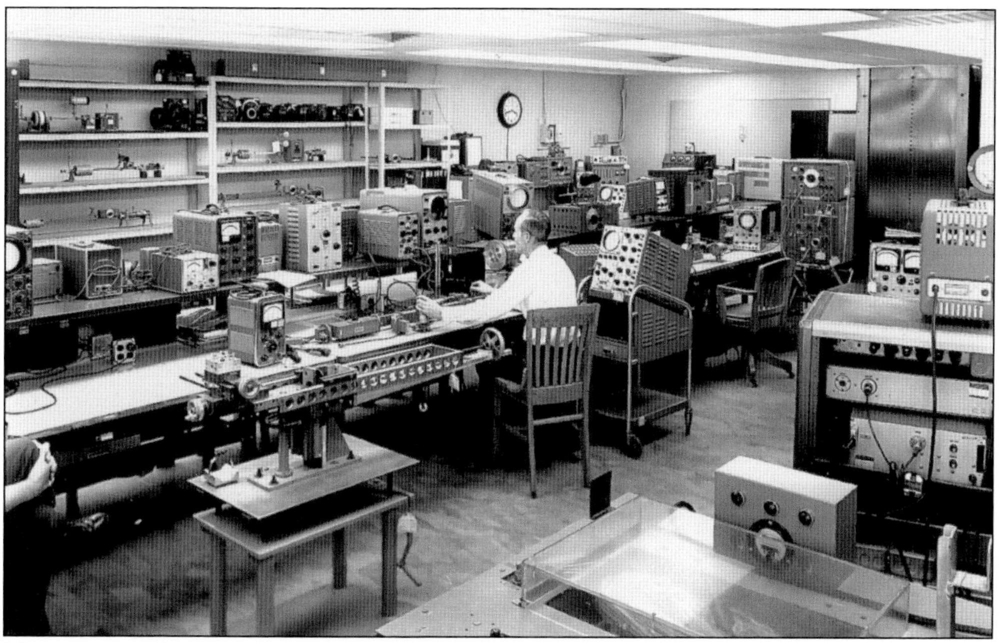

This is a typical 1965 microwave tube pre-testing laboratory. Low-level microwave signals were injected into each tube to assess critical characteristics and to make adjustments prior to final assembly, vacuum pumping, and processing. The microwave tube business remained an important segment of Raytheon's overall operations until the early 1990s and included magnetrons, crossed-field amplifiers (derived from magnetrons), klystrons, and traveling wave tubes.

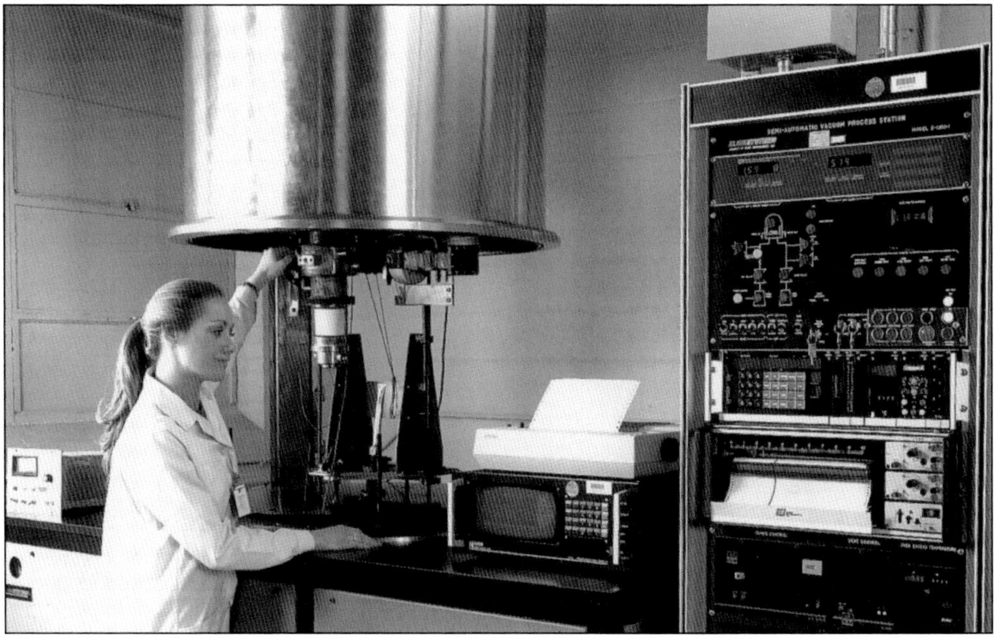

An automatic vacuum bakeout station for crossed-field amplifier tubes had the capability to analyze traces of interior gases that evolved at high temperatures so their sources could be found and eliminated.

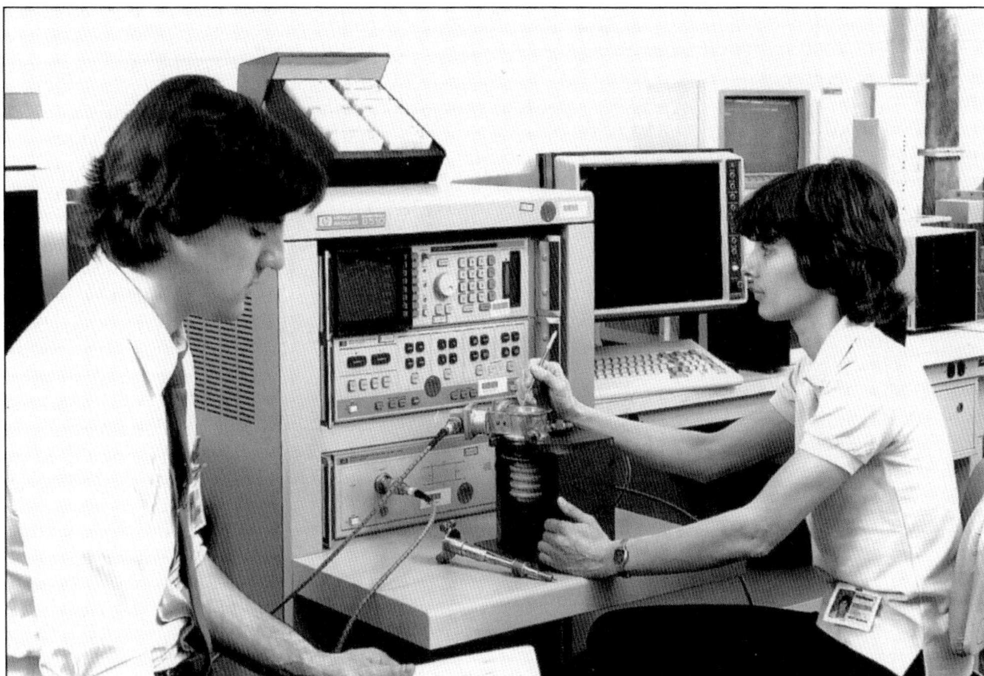

This is a later version of the equipment for non-operational pre-testing (known as a "cold test"). Shown is a unit that could be programmed to automatically run through a series of tests and print out results listing any problem areas. Interior adjustments could then be made to the tube microwave circuits until all specified parameters were met.

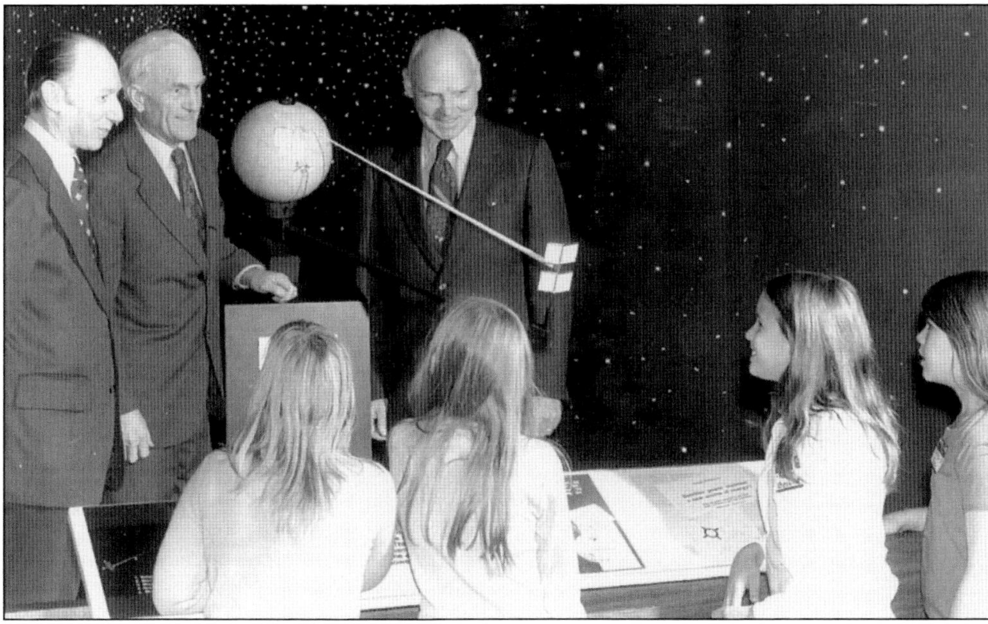

William C. Brown, who joined Raytheon in 1941, was one of its most creative engineers. He was manager of the Magnetron Development Lab during and after World War II, was the inventor of the crossed-field amplifier tube (employed in the Hawk and Patriot missiles, lunar telemetry, and other projects), and generated many other advanced programs. He is seen here at the Boston Museum of Science explaining to a group of children his concept for collecting solar energy in space and beaming it to earth as microwave energy. From left to right are Peter Glaser (from the Arthur D. Little Corporation, a leader of the Solar Power Satellite program), museum director Bradford Washburn, and Brown.

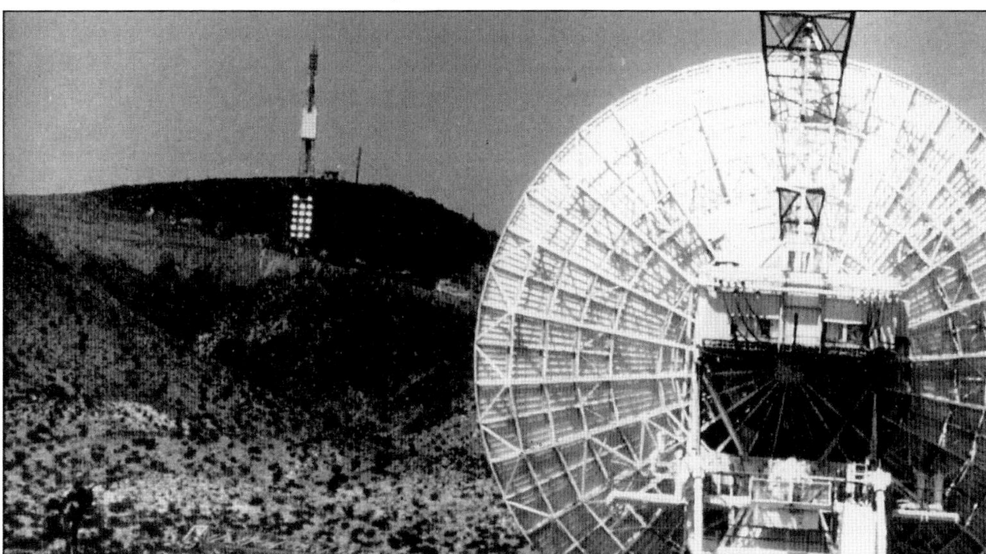

In a demonstration of the feasibility of transmitting microwave power over long distances, this preliminary experiment at a site in Goldstone, California, conducted by Brown in conjunction with Jet Propulsion Laboratory, resulted in beaming power over a distance of one mile at a transmission efficiency of 80 percent.

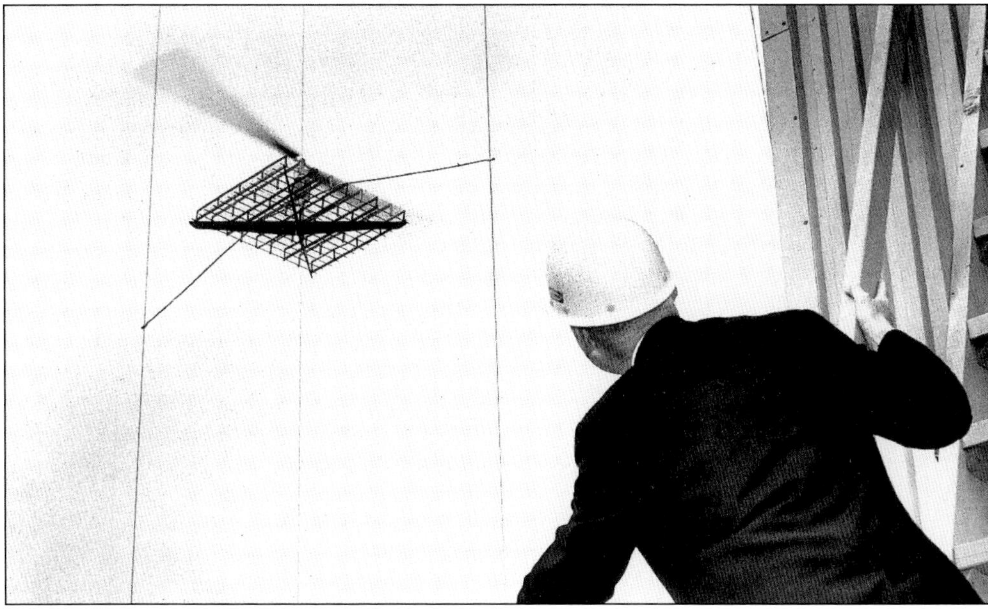

Another of W. C. Brown's programs was the construction of an unmanned, microwave-powered helicopter. A beam of microwave power from the ground was received by a specially designed array or grid of solid-state rectifiers, dubbed a "rectenna," which converted the energy to DC power to run the motor of the helicopter. The technology was evaluated for possible use in surveillance or weather forecasting.

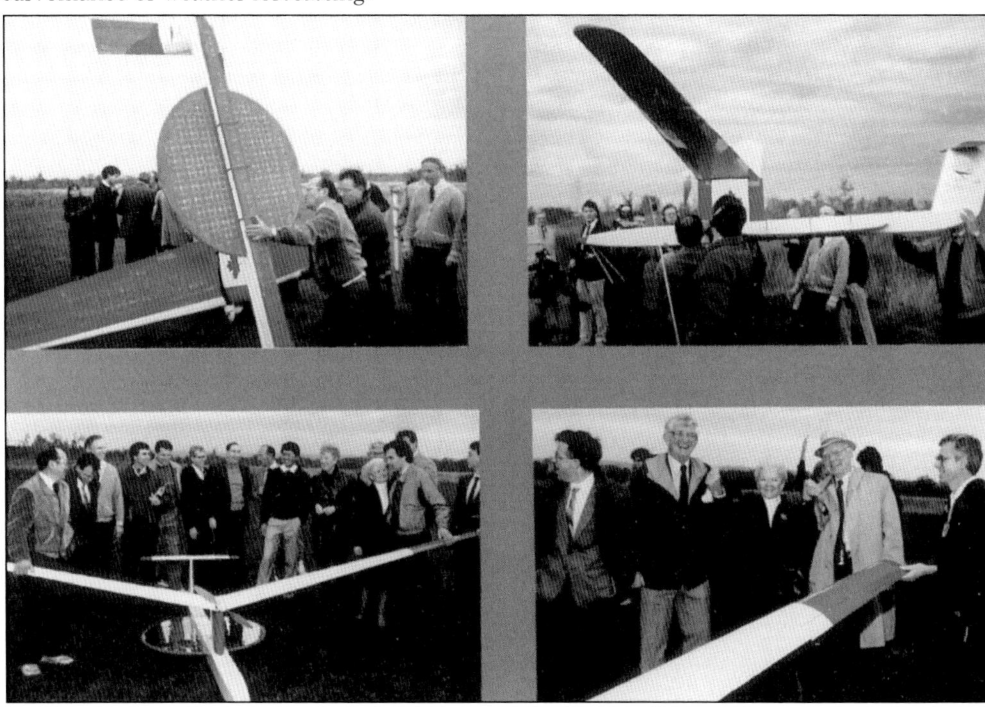

In 1987, a microwave-powered aircraft using Brown's rectenna concept was built and flown in Canada under the auspices of the Canadian Department of Communications. The project was known as the Sharp program.

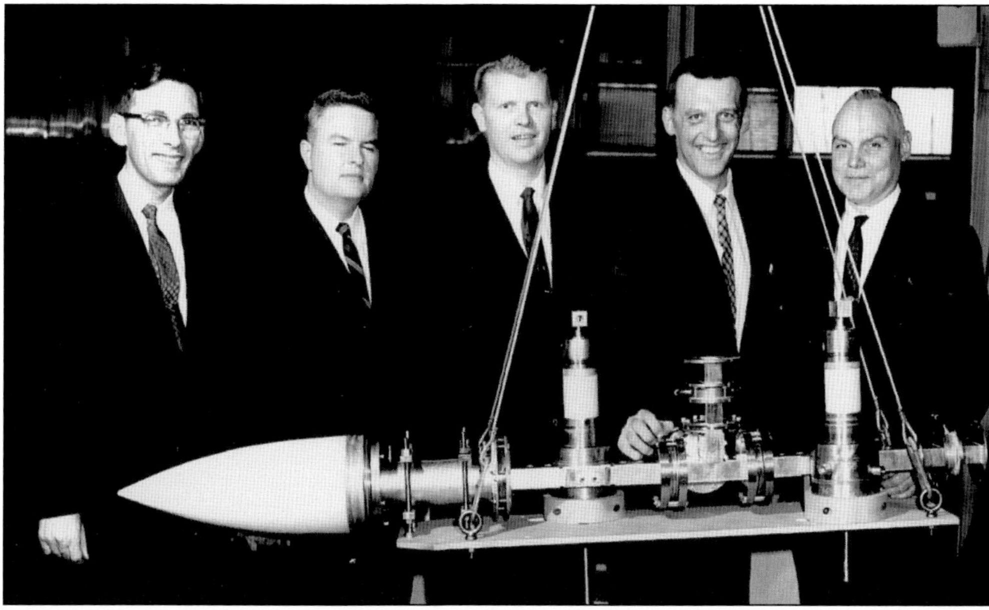

W. C. Brown directed the Raytheon Super Power Laboratory in the 1960s. The group of engineers shown above developed a very high power crossed-field amplifier tube, which achieved a world-record 400 kW of continuous wave (CW) microwave power output at a frequency of 3,000 MHz with an efficiency of 76 percent. Pictured, from left to right, are John Skowron, George Macmaster, John Buckley, Roy Mims, and W. C. Brown.

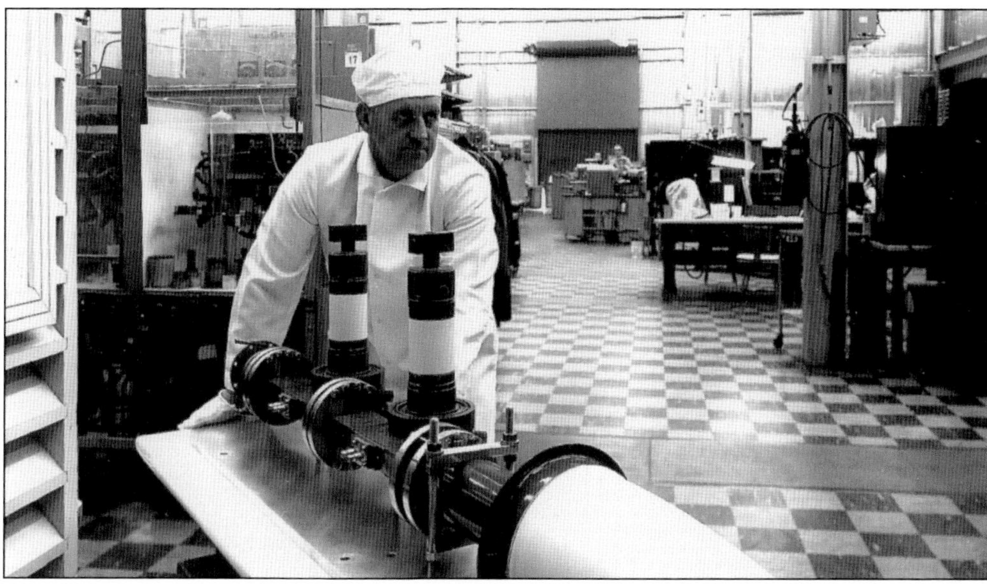

A technician works on the Super Power 400 kW CW crossed-field amplifier. The crossed-field tube classification is derived from the fact that the interior high voltage and magnetic fields are oriented at right angles to each other, resulting in a curved motion of electron flow that then interacts with radio frequency (RF) fields within the tube to amplify microwave power. Crossed-field tubes have the advantage of higher operating efficiency (the ratio of RF power output to the pulsed or DC power input) than other microwave devices; they typically achieve 60 to 75 percent efficiency.

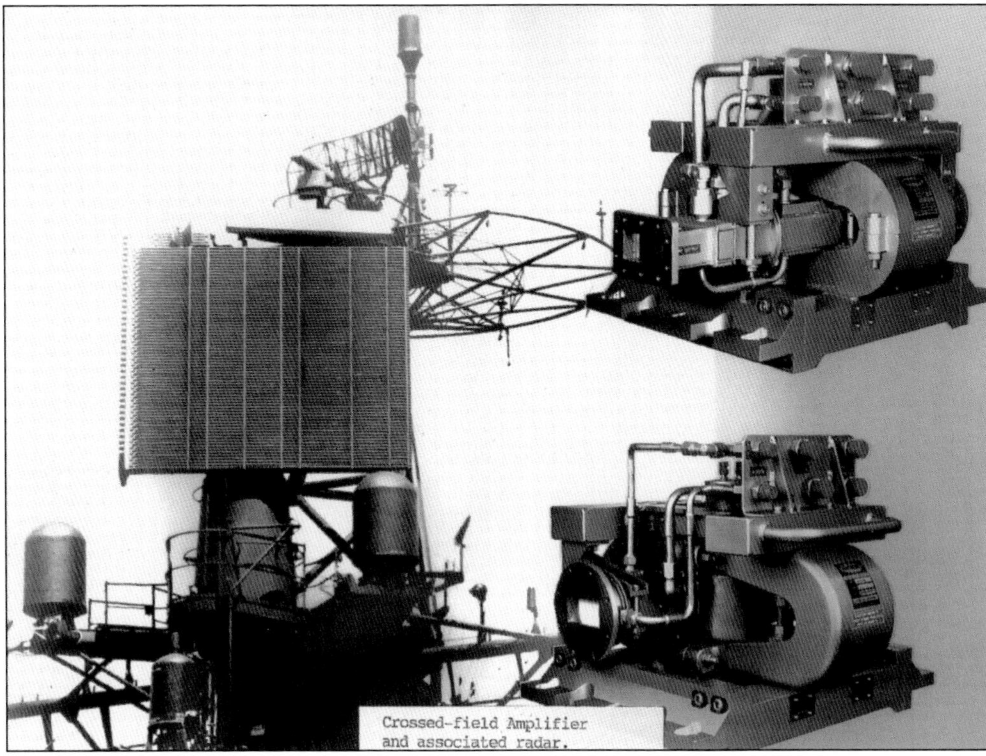

Crossed-field amplifier microwave tubes and their associated radar, an SPS-48, are employed in this military shipboard installation for long-range detection and tracking of aircraft. The SPS-48 used a frequency-scanning antenna that combined mechanical scanning in azimuth and electronic beam steering in elevation.

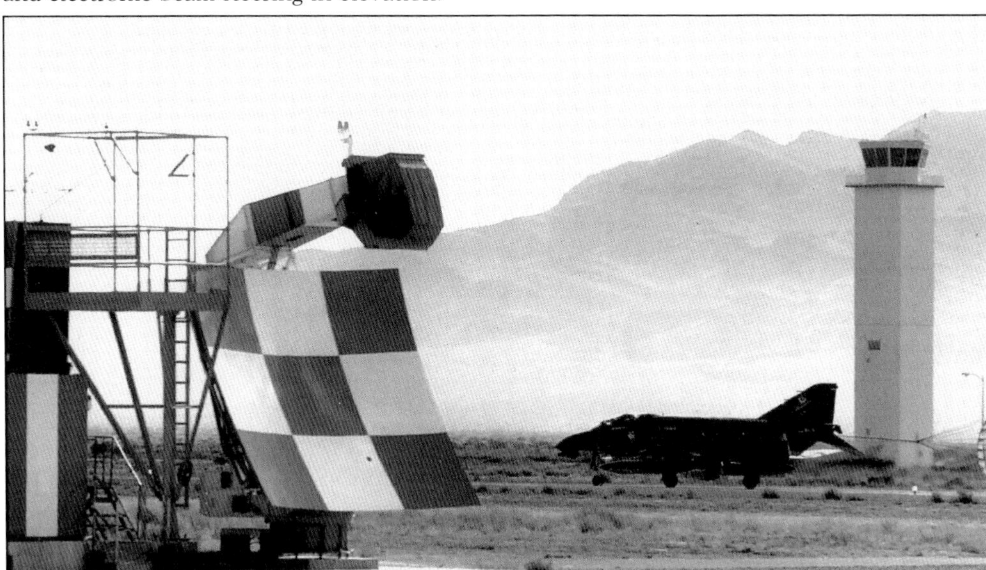

The Raytheon GPN-22 ground control approach radar is tested at Nellis Air Force Base in Nevada. The radar was built to simultaneously track six aircraft on approach to landing. This photograph is from Raytheon's 1979 annual report.

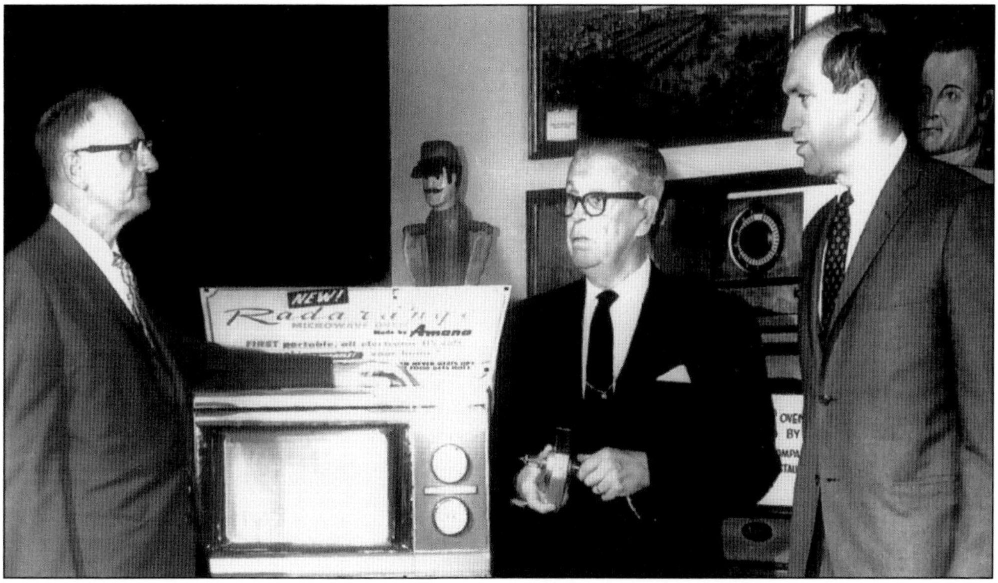

In this mid-1960s photograph, Amana president George Foerstner, Radarange inventor and former Raytheon vice president Percy Spencer, and Raytheon president Tom Phillips pose with a Radarange microwave oven made by Amana. By the time Amana was acquired to help bring his microwave oven to the masses, Spencer had relinquished his responsibilities to others. Spencer died in 1970 at age 76. In recent years, annual worldwide sales of microwave ovens from all manufacturers have exceeded 20 million units.

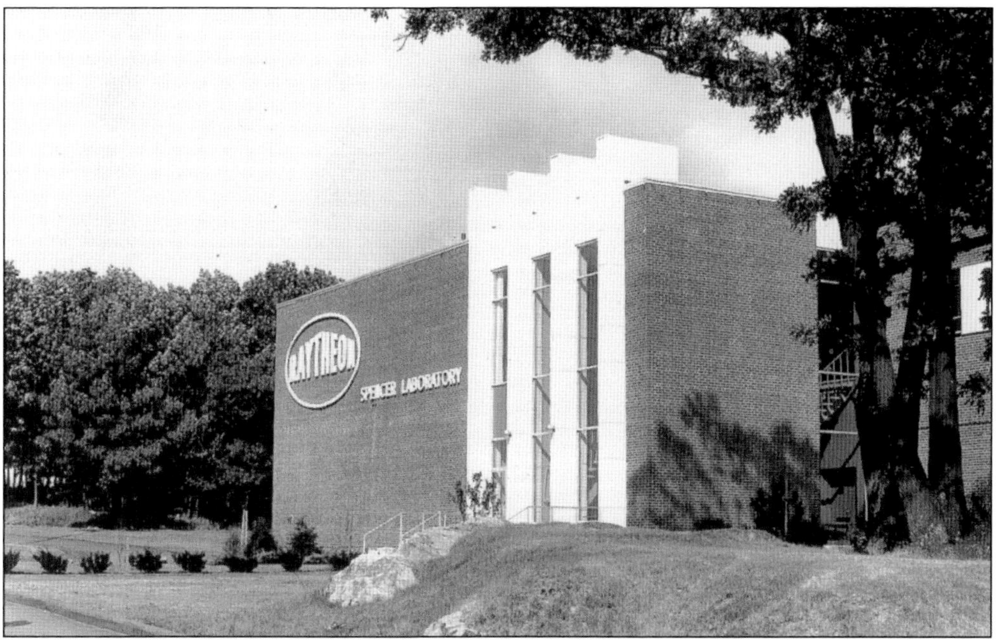

A very attractive laboratory devoted exclusively to the development of microwave tubes was built in Burlington in 1958 and was named Spencer Laboratory in honor of Percy Spencer's lifelong contributions to the success of the company. The facility was active until 1965, when its business was recombined with the Waltham tube plant. The building retains its name but has since been used to house a wide range of corporate activities.

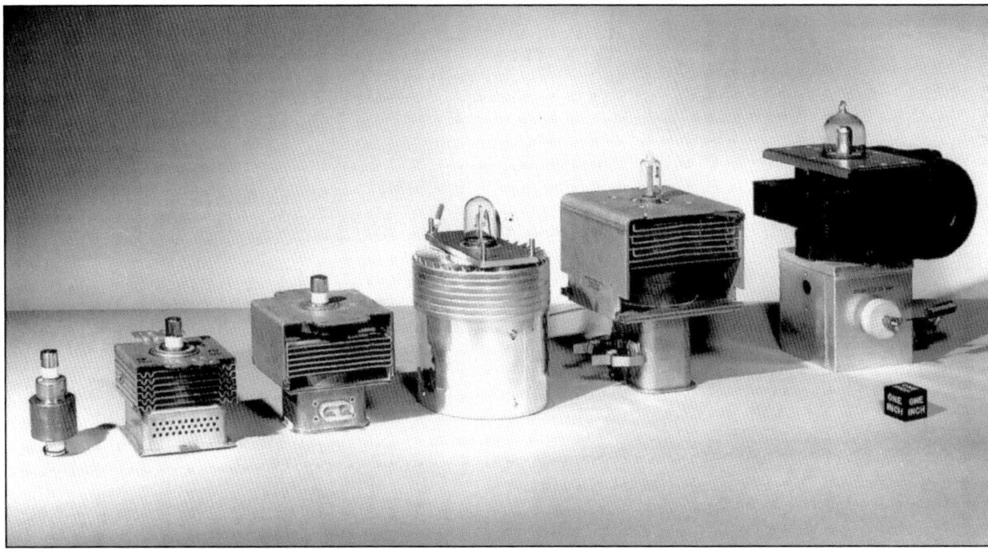

From 1946, when the first Raytheon commercial microwave oven appeared, until the 1980s, when microwave ovens were widely used in homes, the design of the magnetron tubes, which were the heart of the units, underwent many changes. The early tubes (right) were heavy and expensive and were built in much the same manner as the rugged World War II magnetrons that preceded them. Gradually, more efficient magnetic materials were developed, more efficient spurious noise suppression circuits were achieved, and glass elements were replaced with ceramic, leading to reductions in size and cost with improved reliability.

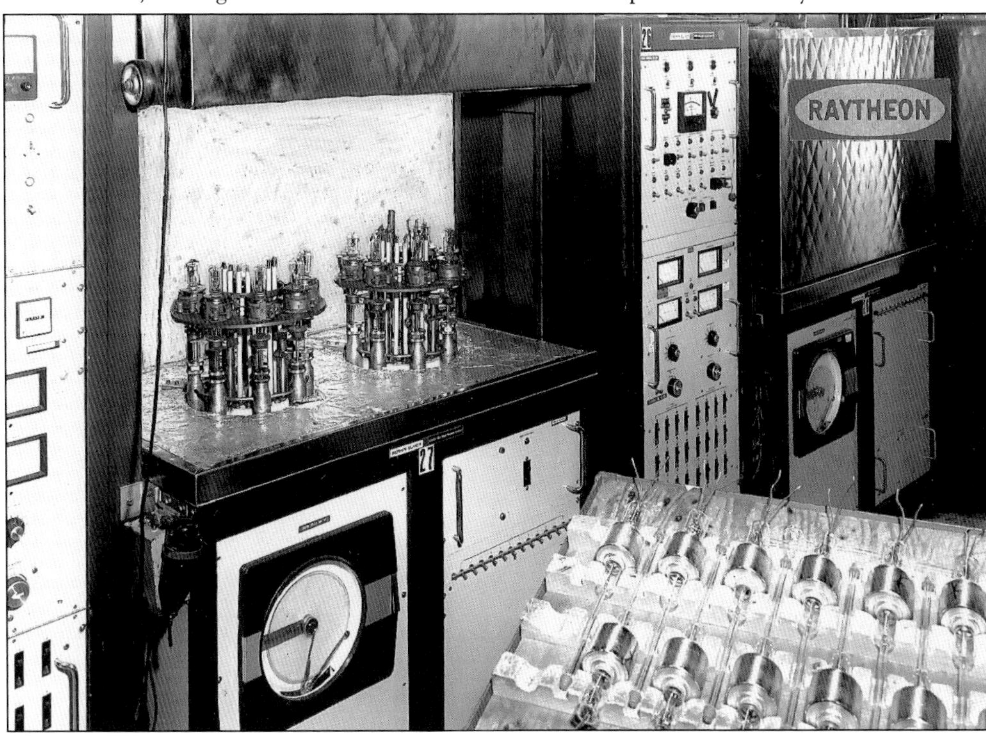

Automatic vacuum-bakeout stations were employed at the Waltham plant for processing the oven magnetrons, helping to achieve high production rates for Amana microwave ovens.

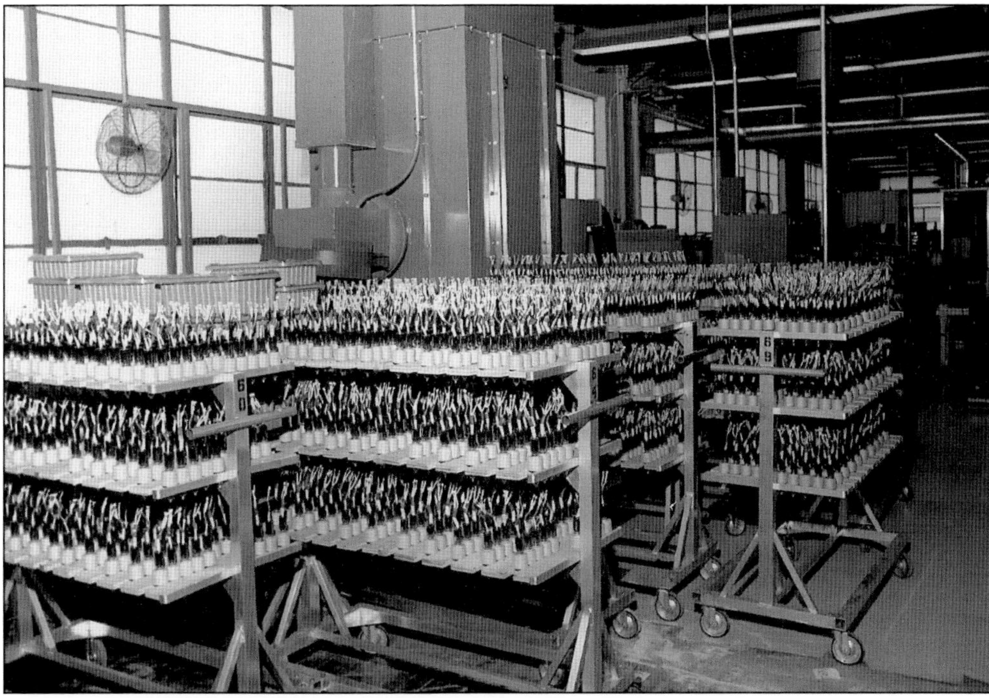

Production of magnetrons for Amana Radarange microwave ovens reached rates of up to 2,000 tubes per day at the Waltham Microwave and Power Tube Division in the 1970s.

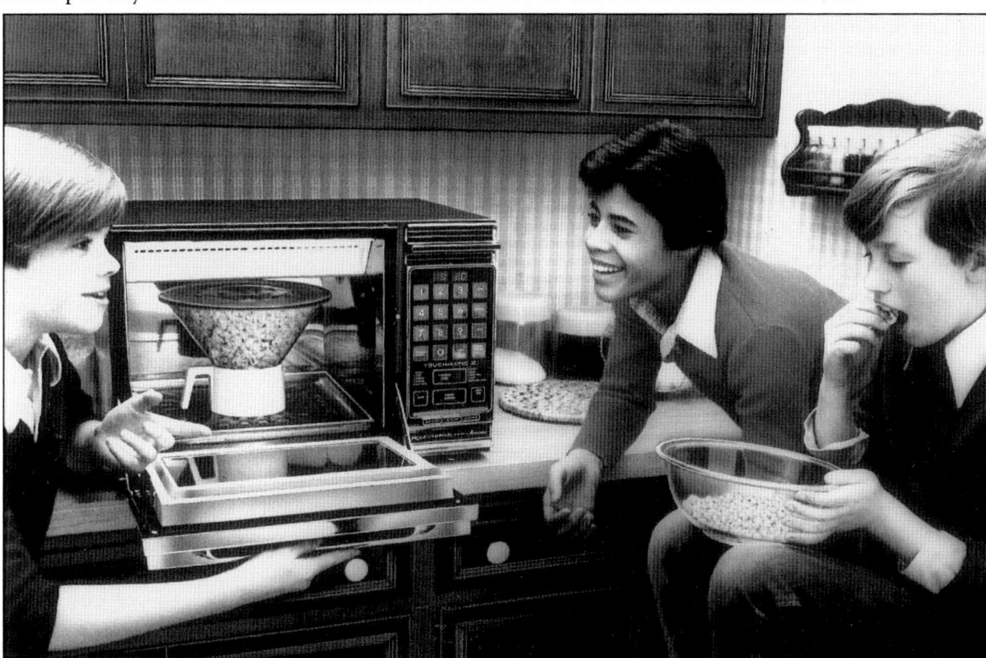

In this publicity photograph, probably from the 1970s, three boys enjoy bowls of popcorn made in their Amana Radarange microwave oven without help from adults. In 1945, popcorn was the first food Percy Spencer deliberately cooked using a magnetron. That event led directly to modern microwave cooking.

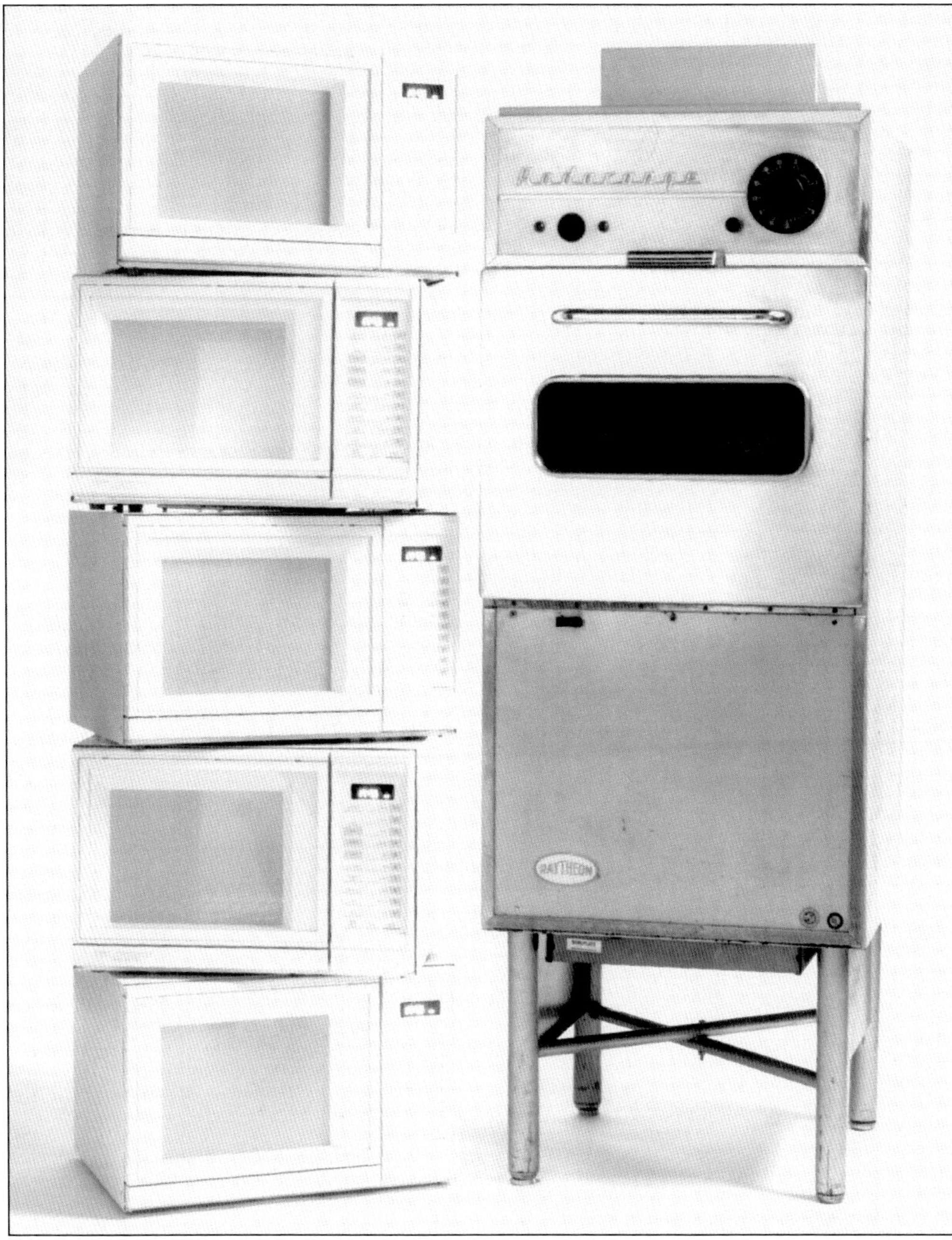

A stack of five modern Amana microwave ovens is about as tall as the one 1946 Raytheon model that belonged to founder Laurence K. Marshall. The modern appliances sell for an insignificantly small price compared to the $100,000 spent on developing Marshall's unit.

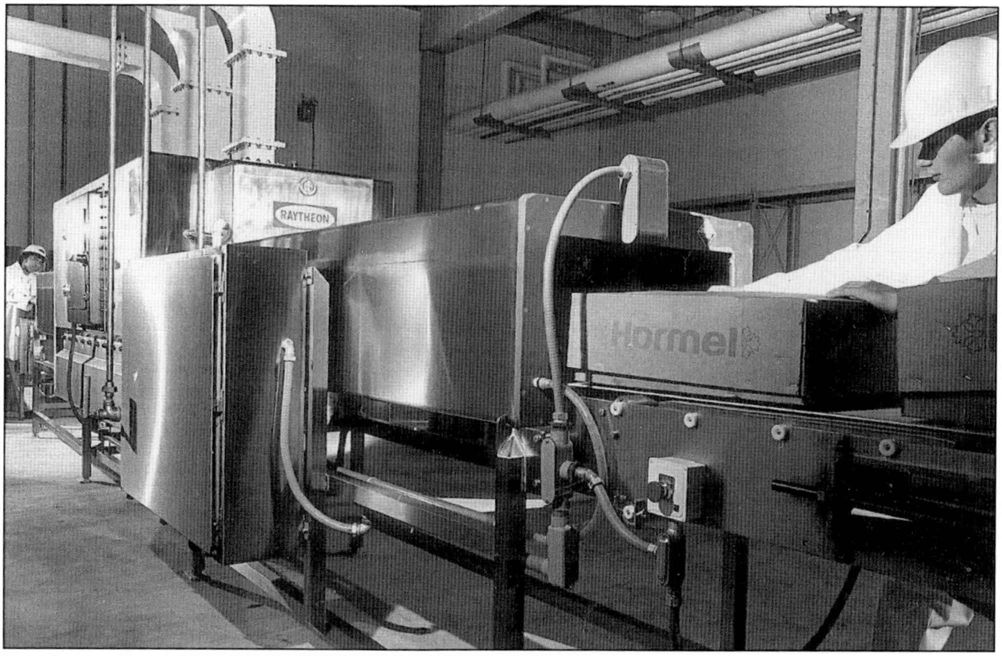

Raytheon also established microwave processing for many large-scale industrial activities. Here, frozen meat is prepared for slicing. This conveyer microwave oven can quick-thaw a 60-pound block of meat from negative 10 degrees to 26 degrees Fahrenheit in four minutes.

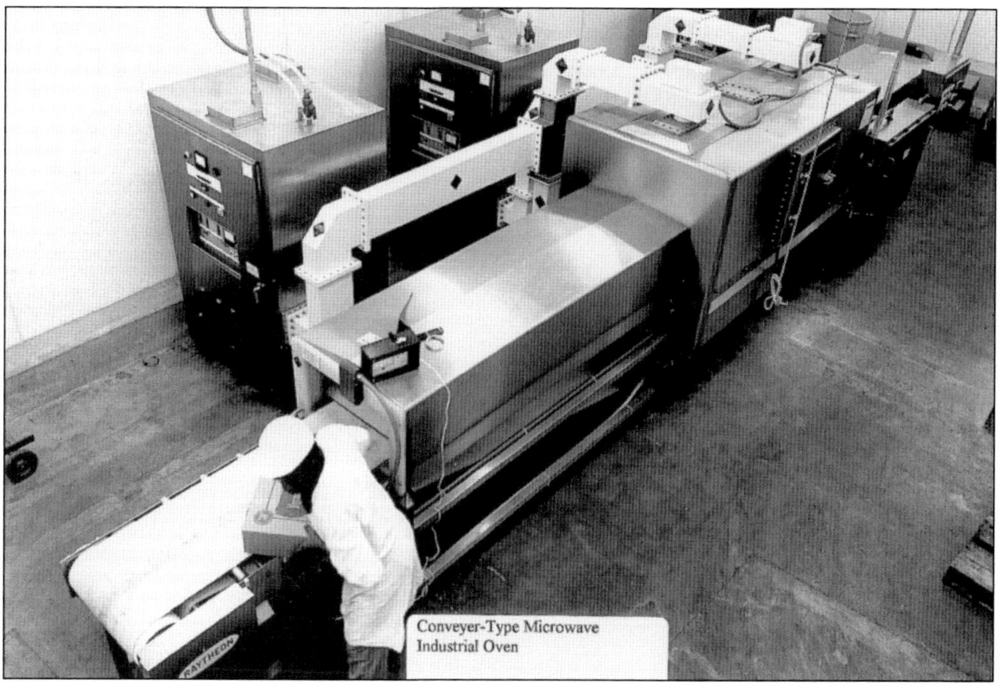

Large single-chamber "batch" microwave ovens and ovens employing conveyer belts were developed. They have been used for such varied applications as processing rubber tires, frying potato chips, and softening frozen meat. The appliances were purchased by customers in the U.S. and in several foreign countries, including China.

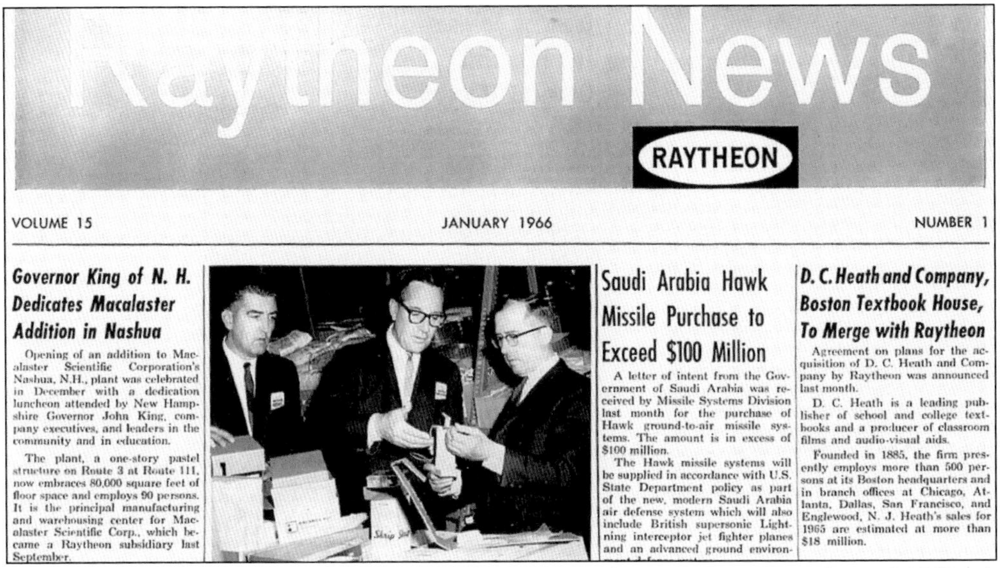

Raytheon News

RAYTHEON

VOLUME 15 JANUARY 1966 NUMBER 1

Governor King of N. H. Dedicates Macalaster Addition in Nashua

Opening of an addition to Macalaster Scientific Corporation's Nashua, N.H., plant was celebrated in December with a dedication luncheon attended by New Hampshire Governor John King, company executives, and leaders in the community and in education.

The plant, a one-story pastel structure on Route 3 at Route 111, now embraces 80,000 square feet of floor space and employs 90 persons. It is the principal manufacturing and warehousing center for Macalaster Scientific Corp., which became a Raytheon subsidiary last September.

Saudi Arabia Hawk Missile Purchase to Exceed $100 Million

A letter of intent from the Government of Saudi Arabia was received by Missile Systems Division last month for the purchase of Hawk ground-to-air missile systems. The amount is in excess of $100 million.

The Hawk missile systems will be supplied in accordance with U.S. State Department policy as part of the new, modern Saudi Arabia air defense system which will also include British supersonic Lightning interceptor jet fighter planes and an advanced ground environ-

D. C. Heath and Company, Boston Textbook House, To Merge with Raytheon

Agreement on plans for the acquisition of D. C. Heath and Company by Raytheon was announced last month.

D. C. Heath is a leading publisher of school and college textbooks and a producer of classroom films and audio-visual aids.

Founded in 1885, the firm presently employs more than 500 persons at its Boston headquarters and in branch offices at Chicago, Atlanta, Dallas, San Francisco, and Englewood, N. J. Heath's sales for 1965 are estimated at more than $18 million.

The Hawk missile program has been a major factor in Raytheon's success since the mid-1950s. A *Raytheon News* item from January 1966 announced a $100 million order for the system from Saudi Arabia. Significantly, the same issue noted the merger of the D. C. Heath publishing company with Raytheon. Under the leadership of Tom Phillips, Raytheon attempted to balance its successes in the highly cyclical defense business with complementary enterprises such as D. C. Heath.

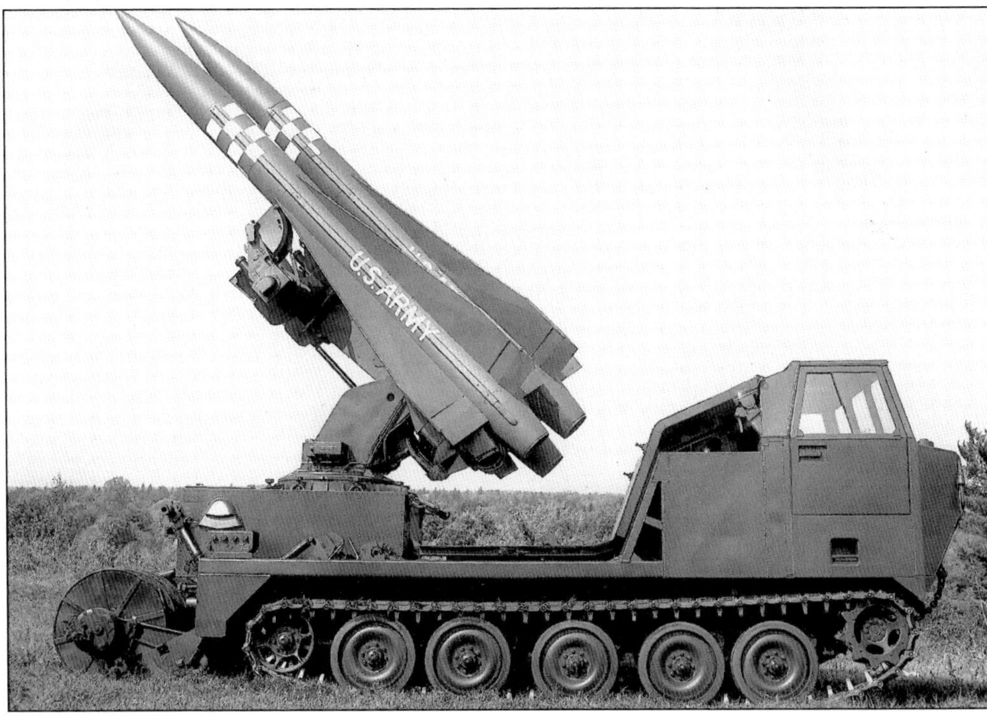

The Hawk system was Raytheon's first complete prime missile contract. Following closely on the success of the earlier Lark and Sparrow missile work using FM-CW radar guidance, Hawk development commenced in 1952. Seen here are mobile launchers that make the system especially versatile in the field.

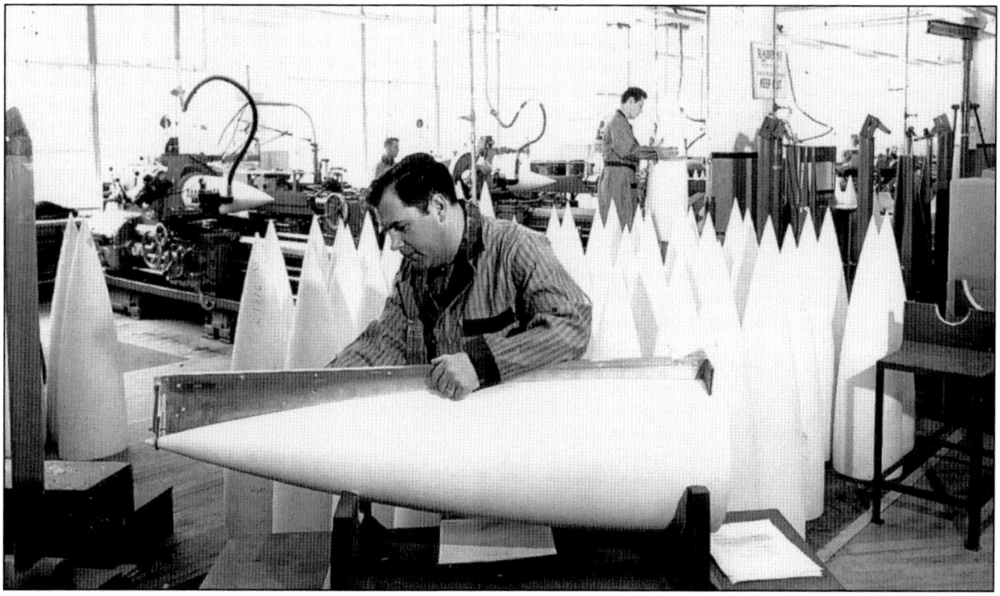

The Hawk's excellent capability for tracking and destroying low-flying aircraft has resulted in its extensive deployment worldwide for antiaircraft defense. While other branches of the company were pursuing commercial enterprises, Raytheon's defense and missile operations have always provided a significant base of military business. Here we see a worker checking the surface contour on nose cones for Hawk missiles.

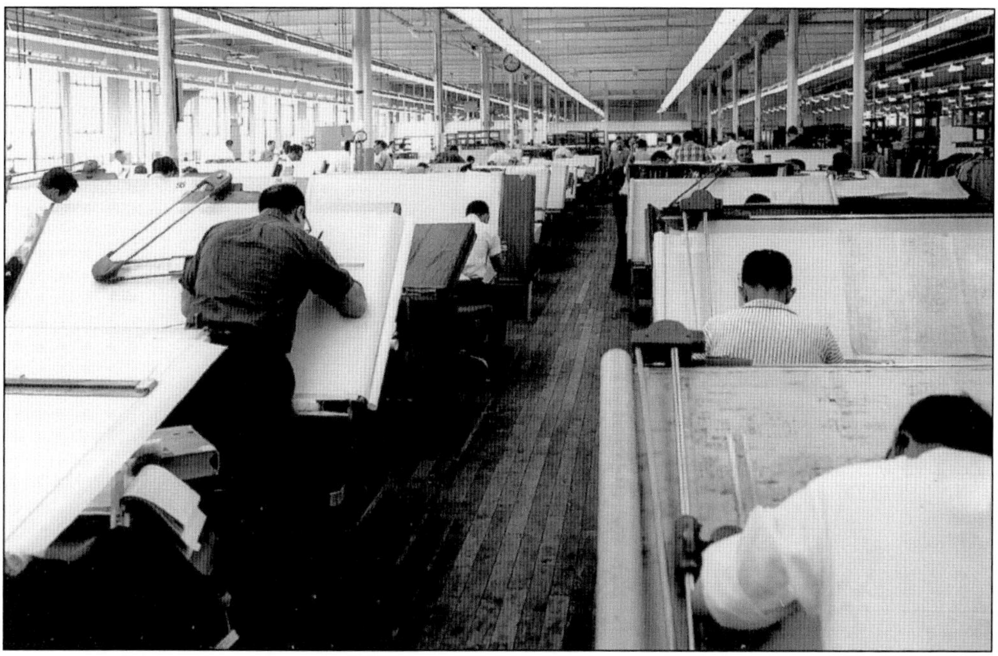

In the early decades of development of the Hawk system, computer-aided drafting had not yet appeared, so all of the drawings had to be done in the traditional hand method, line by line. The prime contract was awarded in 1954, and a production buildup occurred over the years 1958–1962. Hawk has continued for many years since, with sales not only to the U.S. but also to various foreign countries.

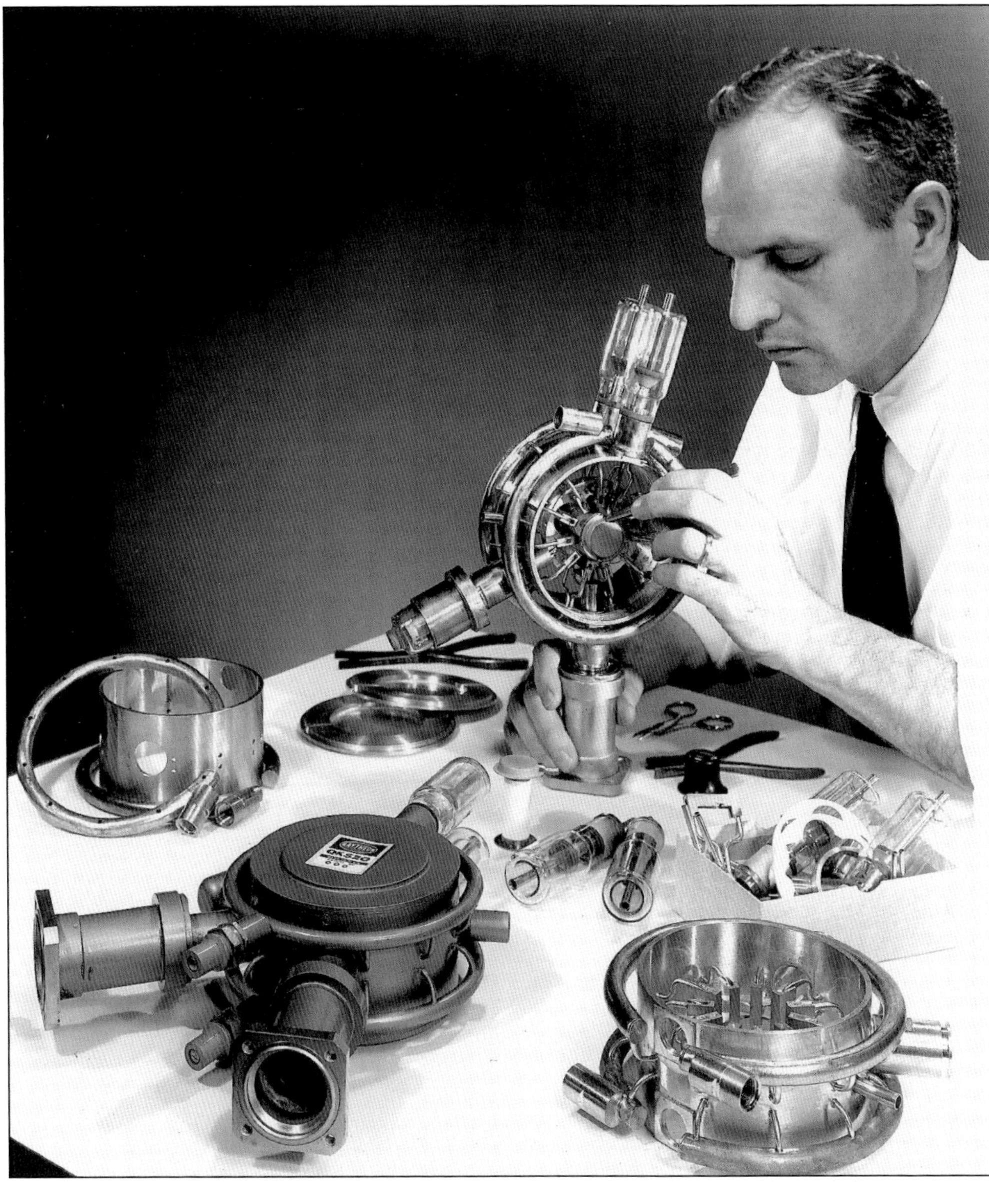

The main microwave power source for generating output signals from the Hawk Acquisition Radar system was this Stabilotron tube, another invention of W. C. Brown. The device was chosen for its high efficiency, good frequency stability, and excellent RF output spectrum quality. This engineer is working on the interior microwave circuit for the Stabilotron tube. The electronics for the Hawk have been wholly reengineered a number of times to take advantage of new technologies, such as transistors and, later, microcircuits.

The Saudi Arabian minister of defense and his party visited Raytheon in 1966 in connection with the $100 million purchase of Hawk defense systems for his country. They viewed a Hawk battery at the Bedford facility, then went to the Lexington corporate offices for further briefings and to meet company officials and Gov. John Volpe.

Prince Sultan of Saudi Arabia Visitor at Raytheon

Prince Sultan, Saudi Arabia's minister of Defense and Aviation, and his party visited Raytheon last month for a one-day conference on the Saudi Arabian $100 million order for Hawk missile systems.

The Saudi Arabian party, accompanied by Col. William J. Hogan, Raytheon's regional manager of International Activities, Washington office, was flown into Hanscom Field, Bedford, Feb. 23. Board Chairman C. F. Adams and Senior Vice President D. B. Holmes met the visitors at the field and rode with them to Lexington after the group viewed a Hawk battery set up for their inspection at Bedford.

President T. L. Phillips greeted the guests at Lexington where briefings were given to Prince Sultan on Raytheon's background, experience, capabilities and equipment lines including those in the education field.

Guests at the luncheon held for Prince Sultan in the executive dining room at Lexington included Massachusetts Governor John A. Volpe, Saudi Arabian Ambassador to the U.S. Ibrahim Al-Sowayel, Brig. Gen. Ibrahim Al-Malik and Mohammed Khalas, official interpreter.

Attending from Raytheon besides Chairman Adams, President Phillips, Senior Vice President Holmes and Colonel Hogan were M. W. Fossier, vice president and assistant general manager — technical, Missile Systems Division; R. G. Hennemuth, vice president — Industrial Relations, and J. A. Grehan, manager of overseas Hawk programs, Missile Systems Division.

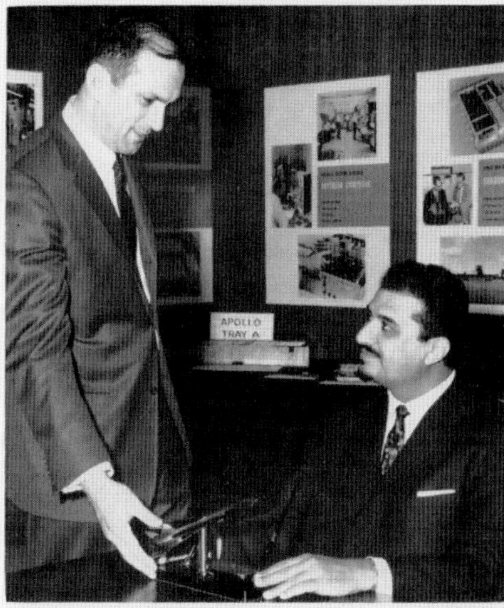

MINISTER OF DEFENSE AND AVIATION for Saudi Arabia, Prince Sultan, is presented with a Hawk missile desk set by President T. L. Phillips in board room at Lexington executive offices.

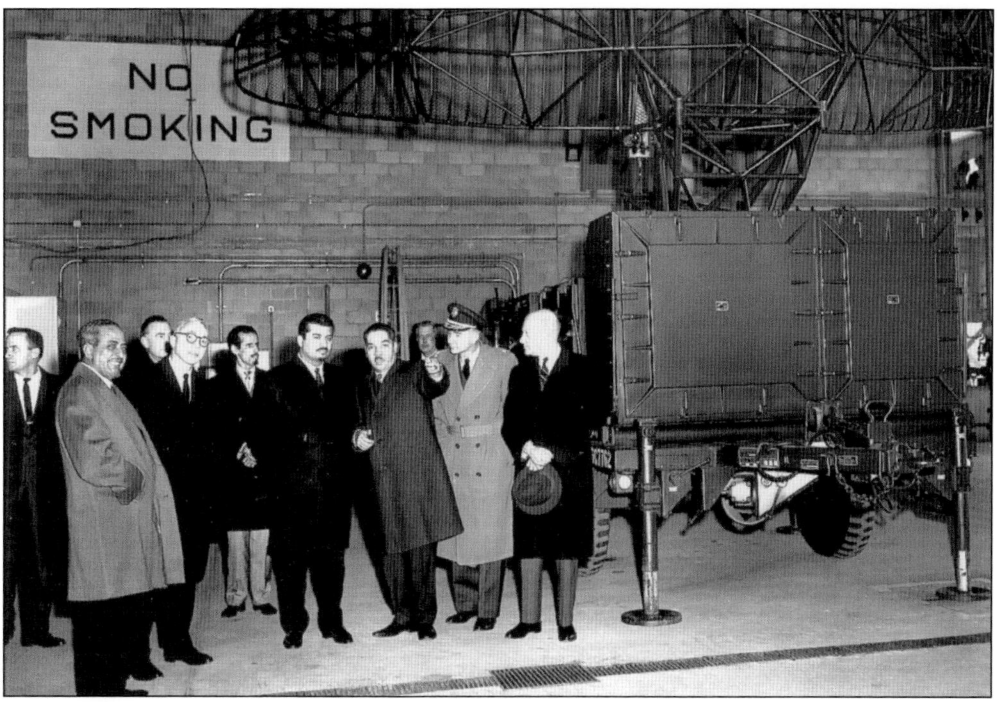

Prince Sultan of Saudi Arabia (center), Raytheon chairman Charles Francis Adams (far right), and senior vice president D. Brainerd Holmes (second from left) view a Hawk battery at the Bedford plant in February 1966.

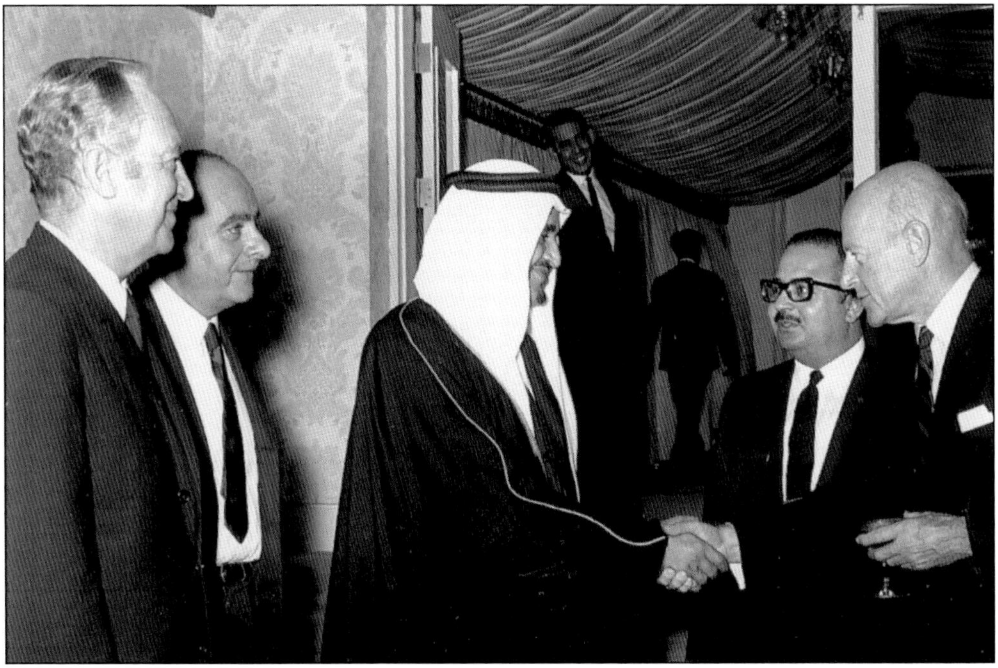

King Faisal of Saudi Arabia also visited Raytheon in June 1966 for briefings on the Hawk missile defense systems that his country was purchasing. To the right is Charles F. Adams.

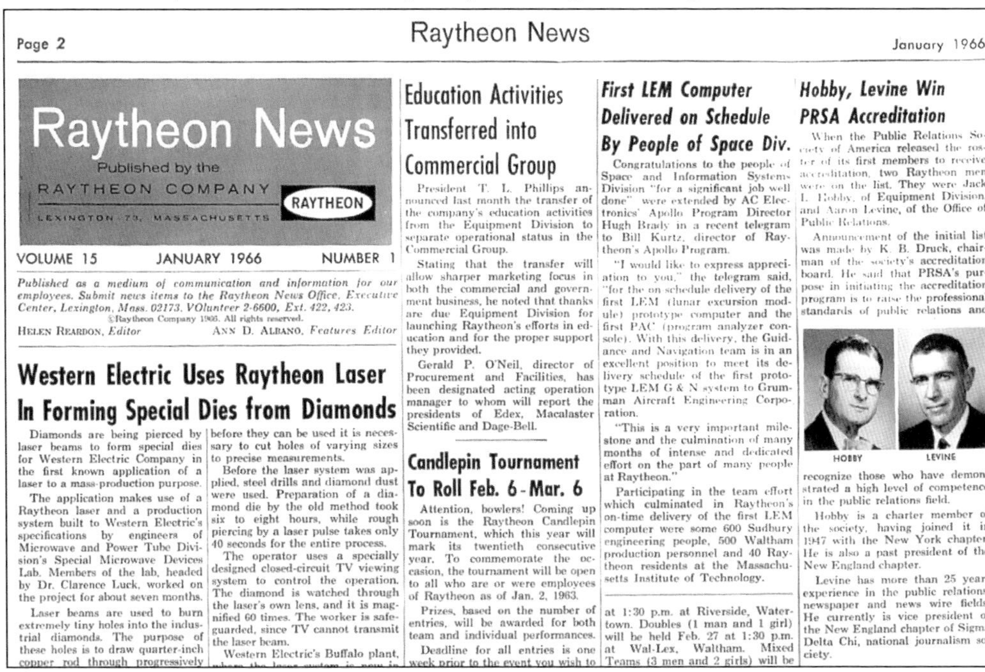

Page 2 Raytheon News January 1966

Raytheon News

Published by the RAYTHEON COMPANY

LEXINGTON 73, MASSACHUSETTS

RAYTHEON

VOLUME 15 JANUARY 1966 NUMBER 1

Published as a medium of communication and information for our employees. Submit news items to the Raytheon News Office, Executive Center, Lexington, Mass. 02173. VOlunteer 2-6600, Ext. 422, 423.

©Raytheon Company 1966. All rights reserved.

HELEN REARDON, *Editor* ANN D. ALBANO, *Features Editor*

Western Electric Uses Raytheon Laser In Forming Special Dies from Diamonds

Diamonds are being pierced by laser beams to form special dies for Western Electric Company in the first known application of a laser to a mass-production purpose.

The application makes use of a Raytheon laser and a production system built to Western Electric's specifications by engineers of Microwave and Power Tube Division's Special Microwave Devices Lab. Members of the lab, headed by Dr. Clarence Luck, worked on the project for about seven months.

Laser beams are used to burn extremely tiny holes into the industrial diamonds. The purpose of these holes is to draw quarter-inch copper rod through progressively before they can be used it is necessary to cut holes of varying sizes to precise measurements.

Before the laser system was applied, steel drills and diamond dust were used. Preparation of a diamond die by the old method took six to eight hours, while rough piercing by a laser pulse takes only 40 seconds for the entire process.

The operator uses a specially designed closed-circuit TV viewing system to control the operation. The diamond is watched through the laser's own lens, and it is magnified 60 times. The worker is safeguarded, since TV cannot transmit the laser beam.

Western Electric's Buffalo plant,

Education Activities Transferred into Commercial Group

President T. L. Phillips announced last month the transfer of the company's education activities from the Equipment Division to separate operational status in the Commercial Group.

Stating that the transfer will allow sharper marketing focus in both the commercial and government business, he noted that thanks are due Equipment Division for launching Raytheon's efforts in education and for the proper support they provided.

Gerald P. O'Neil, director of Procurement and Facilities, has been designated acting operation manager to whom will report the presidents of Edex, Macalaster Scientific and Dage-Bell.

Candlepin Tournament To Roll Feb. 6 - Mar. 6

Attention, bowlers! Coming up soon is the Raytheon Candlepin Tournament, which this year will mark its twentieth consecutive year. To commemorate the occasion, the tournament will be open to all who are or were employees of Raytheon as of Jan. 2, 1963.

Prizes, based on the number of entries, will be awarded for both team and individual performances.

Deadline for all entries is one week prior to the event you wish to

at 1:30 p.m. at Riverside, Watertown. Doubles (1 man and 1 girl) will be held Feb. 27 at 1:30 p.m. at Wal-Lex, Waltham. Mixed Teams (3 men and 2 girls) will be

First LEM Computer Delivered on Schedule By People of Space Div.

Congratulations to the people of Space and Information Systems Division "for a significant job well done" were extended by AC Electronics' Apollo Program Director Hugh Brady in a recent telegram to Bill Kurtz, director of Raytheon's Apollo Program.

"I would like to express appreciation to you," the telegram said, "for the on-schedule delivery of the first LEM (lunar excursion module) prototype computer and the first PAC (program analyzer console). With this delivery, the Guidance and Navigation team is in an excellent position to meet its delivery schedule of the first prototype LEM G & N system to Grumman Aircraft Engineering Corporation.

"This is a very important milestone and the culmination of many months of intense and dedicated effort on the part of many people at Raytheon."

Participating in the team effort which culminated in Raytheon's on-time delivery of the first LEM computer were some 600 Sudbury engineering people, 500 Waltham production personnel and 40 Raytheon residents at the Massachusetts Institute of Technology.

Hobby, Levine Win PRSA Accreditation

When the Public Relations Society of America released the roster of its first members to receive accreditation, two Raytheon men were on the list. They were Jack L. Hobby, of Equipment Division, and Aaron Levine, of the Office of Public Relations.

Announcement of the initial list was made by K. B. Druck, chairman of the society's accreditation board. He said that PRSA's purpose in initiating the accreditation program is to raise the professional standards of public relations and

HOBBY LEVINE

recognize those who have demonstrated a high level of competence in the public relations field.

Hobby is a charter member of the society, having joined it in 1947 with the New York chapter. He is also a past president of the New England chapter.

Levine has more than 25 years experience in the public relations, newspaper and news wire fields. He currently is vice president of the New England chapter of Sigma Delta Chi, national journalism society.

The January 1966 issue of the *Raytheon News* reported that Raytheon's Space and Information Systems Division had delivered the first lunar excursion module computer on schedule for the Apollo program. Involved in the effort were approximately 600 engineering personnel from the Sudbury plant, 500 production workers from the Waltham plant, and 50 Raytheon resident scientists at MIT's Instrumentation Lab.

Raytheon played an important role in one of mankind's greatest achievements: the successful Apollo lunar landing missions of the late 1960s. The guidance computers that directed the Apollo vehicles on these voyages were designed by the MIT Instrumentation Lab (now the C. S. Draper Lab) and built by Raytheon. Many other components, such as the control display keyboard and the crossed-field amplifier tube (which transmitted all telemetry and television pictures from the moon) were developed and produced by Raytheon for these historic missions.

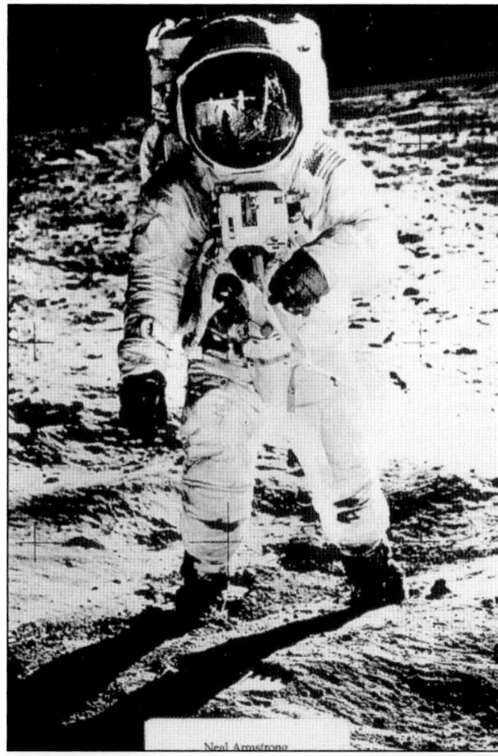

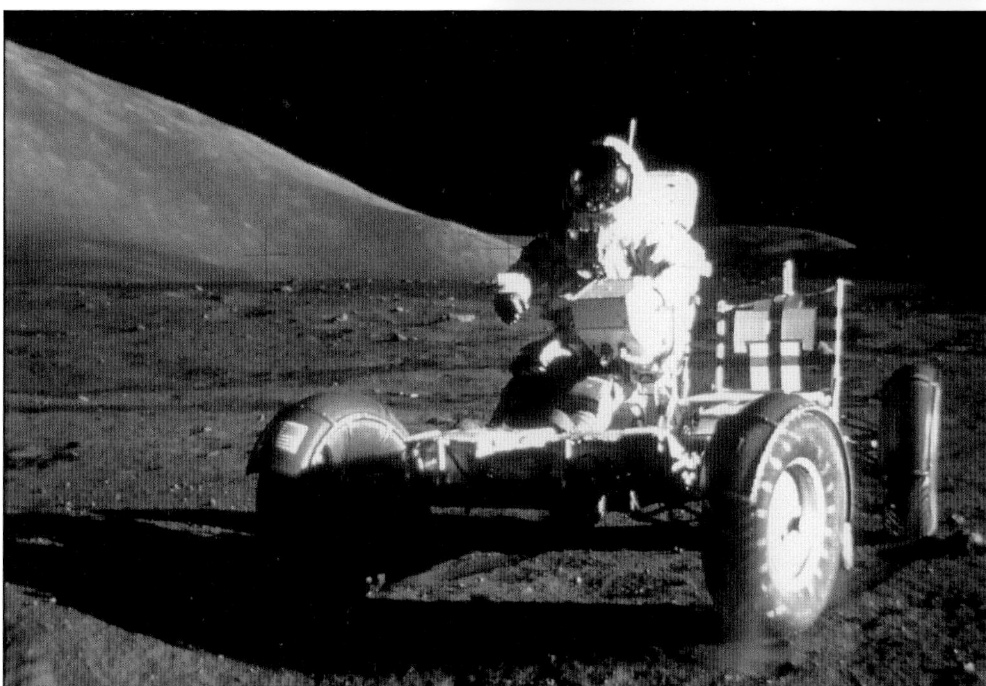

This remarkable photograph shows the lunar rover exploring the surface of the moon. The fact that people on earth were able to share in the experience of exploring the moon almost in real time was due to the efficient and powerful television and telemetry components supplied by Raytheon.

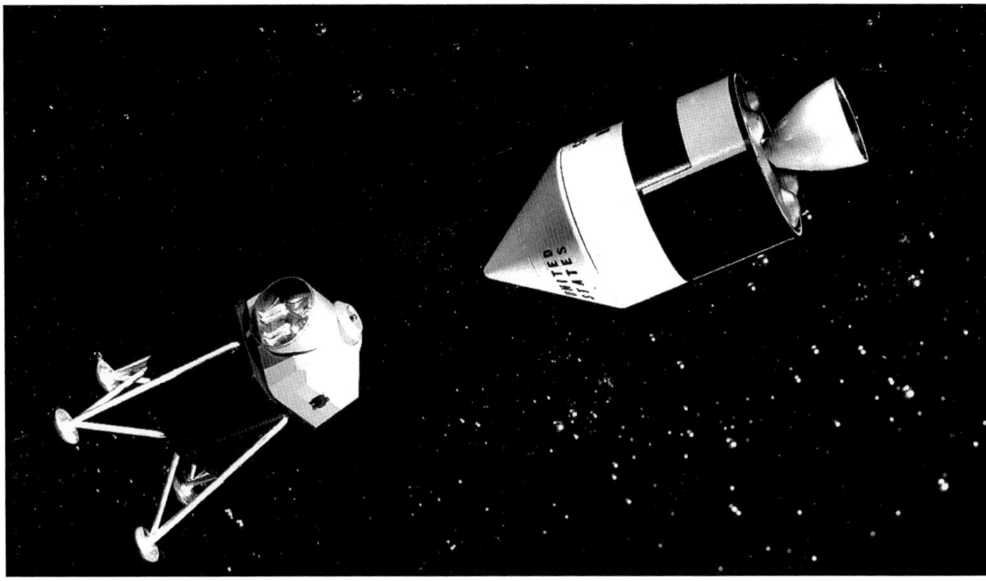

This is an artist's conception of the lunar excursion module (LEM), designed to land astronauts on the moon's surface, as it prepares to dock with the command module (right). The command module carried the astronauts from earth orbit to the moon, waited in orbit around the moon until the return of the LEM, and then returned the astronauts to earth. Longtime Raytheon executive D. Brainerd Holmes served as a director of manned space flight at NASA in the early 1960s and helped establish the Apollo program.

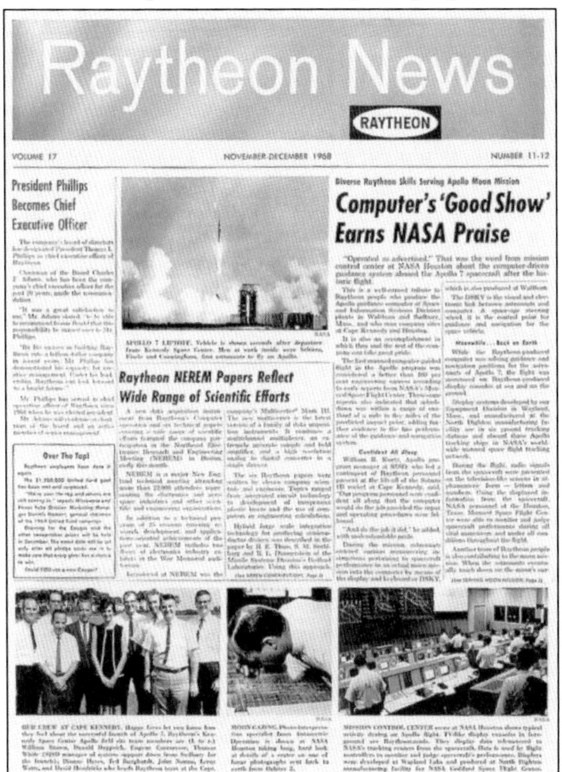

Raytheon News

RAYTHEON

VOLUME 17 NOVEMBER-DECEMBER 1968 NUMBER 11-12

President Phillips Becomes Chief Executive Officer

Diverse Raytheon Skills Serving Apollo Moon Mission

Computer's 'Good Show' Earns NASA Praise

"Operated as advertised." That was the word from mission control center at NASA Houston about the computer-driven guidance system aboard the Apollo 7 spacecraft after the historic flight.

Confident All Along

Raytheon NEREM Papers Reflect Wide Range of Scientific Efforts

Over The Top!

In 1968, the first manned computer-guided flight was conducted by the Apollo 7 spacecraft in a 10-day earth-orbital mission intended to test all systems that would be needed for a trip to the moon. It was guided by a Raytheon-built computer to within one and a half miles of the intended splashdown point near Bermuda. Confidence built during this mission, allowing the next mission, Apollo 8, to make an orbital trip to the moon.

This 1965 image shows the display and keyboard (DSKY) manufactured by Raytheon. It was aboard all Apollo spacecraft, providing astronauts with visual and electronic links to the guidance computer and spacecraft systems.

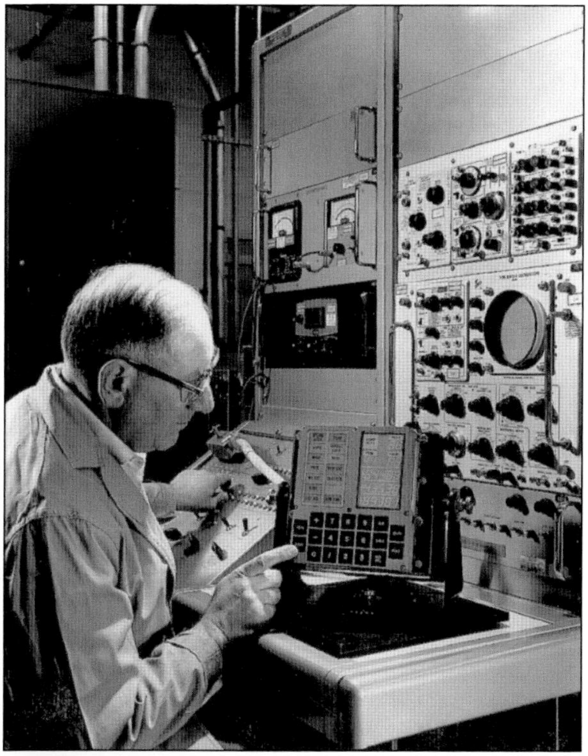

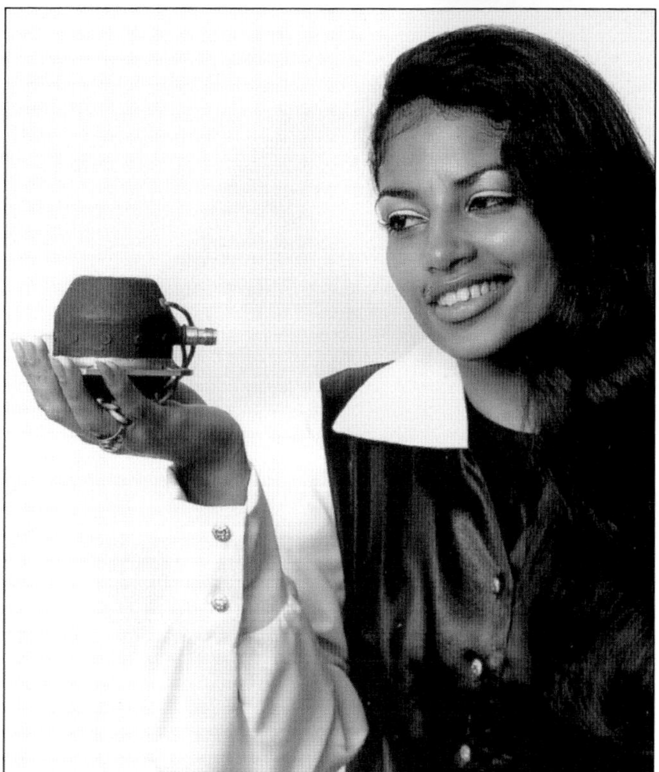

All telemetry and television pictures from the LEM on the moon's surface were transmitted by one of these 20-watt crossed-field amplifier tubes, which were developed by Wesley Teich of Raytheon's Microwave and Power Tube Division. They were based on the principle invented by W. C. Brown in the 1950s.

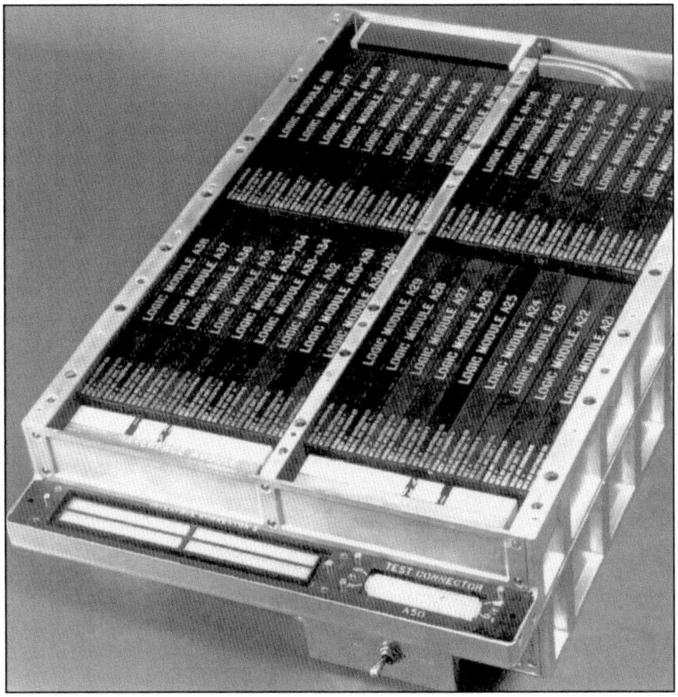

The Apollo guidance computer was designed by an MIT team (led by Charles Stark Draper) and was built by Raytheon. This was the first computer ever built entirely with integrated circuits, and it had unprecedented computing power for its size and weight. By the standards of today, it was puny and had scarcely any memory; but with more than 4,000 chips in each machine, it was an engineering marvel. One source suggests that the 75 units built as part of the program probably consumed a significant fraction of all the chips being produced at the time.

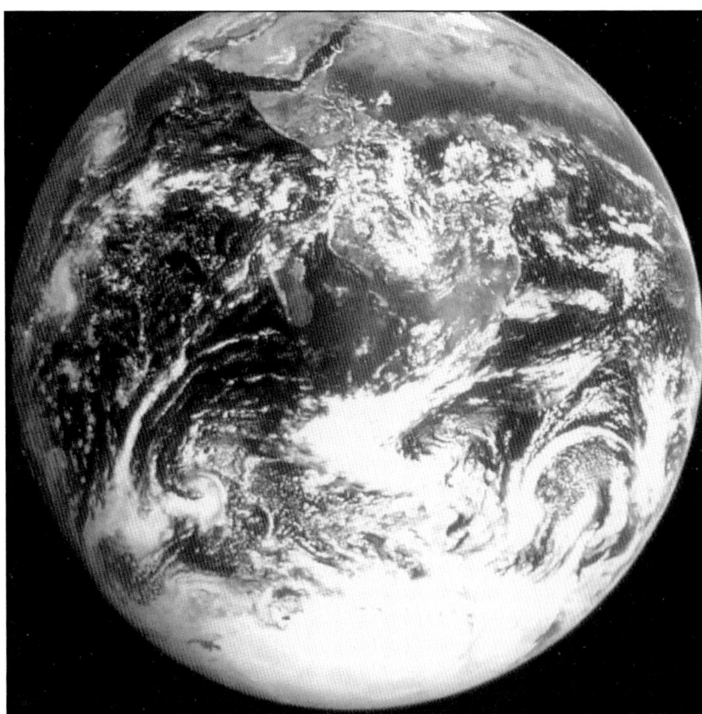

This photograph of earth seen from outer space was taken during one of the Apollo moon trips. During this period, Raytheon also produced a circular slide rule (now something of a collectable) called the Apollo 11 Mission Analyzer. It illustrated the series of events in the first lunar lander mission from liftoff to splashdown.

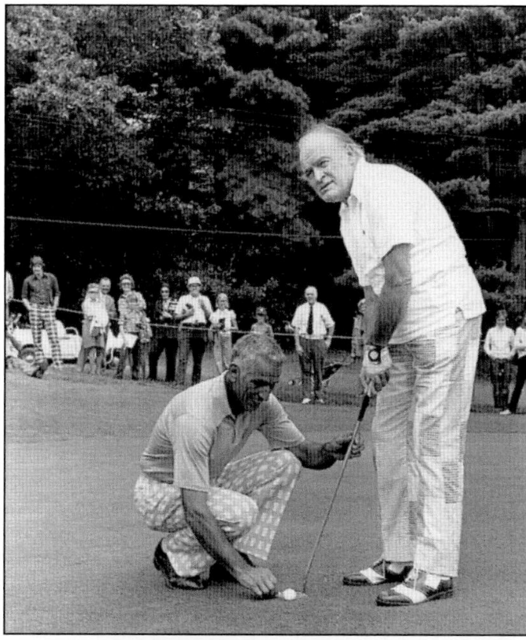

Throughout its history, Raytheon has paid attention to the special needs and capabilities of its people. Raytheon employee Joe Lazaro, seven times the blind golfing champion of the United States and also a president of the U.S. Blind Golfers Association, was one of those people. Entertainer Bob Hope visited the blind golfing tournaments on several occasions. In this photograph, Hope is getting help lining up a shot from Lazaro.

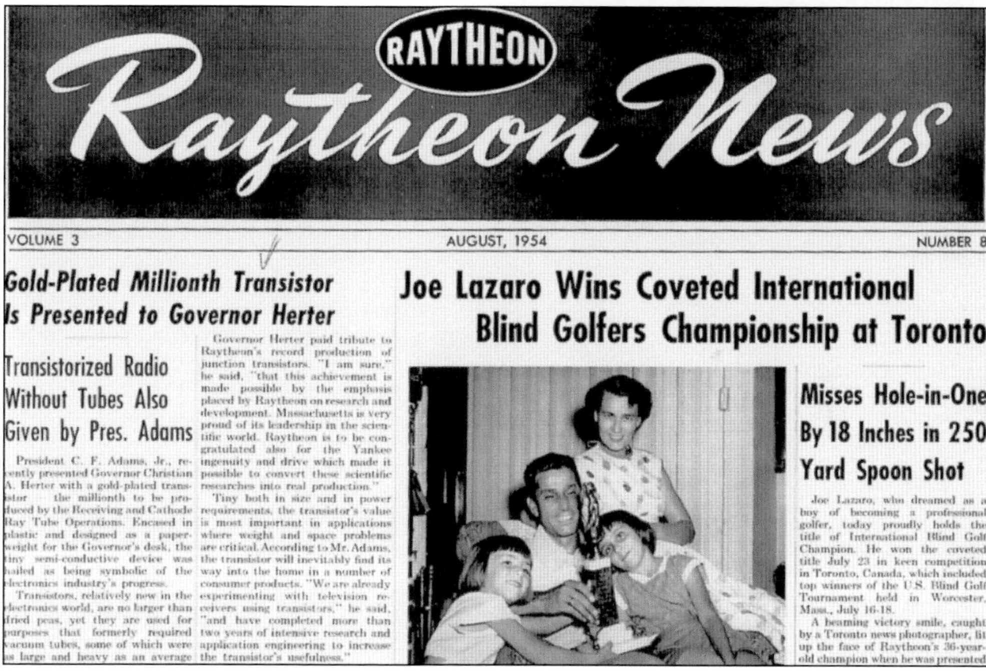

RAYTHEON

Raytheon News

VOLUME 3 — AUGUST, 1954 — NUMBER 8

Gold-Plated Millionth Transistor Is Presented to Governor Herter

Transistorized Radio Without Tubes Also Given by Pres. Adams

President C. F. Adams, Jr., recently presented Governor Christian A. Herter with a gold-plated transistor the millionth to be produced by the Receiving and Cathode Ray Tube Operations. Encased in plastic and designed as a paperweight for the Governor's desk, the tiny semi-conductive device was hailed as being symbolic of the electronics industry's progress.

Transistors, relatively new in the electronics world, are no larger than dried peas, yet they are used for purposes that formerly required vacuum tubes, some of which were as large and heavy as an average

Governor Herter paid tribute to Raytheon's record production of junction transistors. "I am sure," he said, "that this achievement is made possible by the emphasis placed by Raytheon on research and development. Massachusetts is very proud of its leadership in the scientific world. Raytheon is to be congratulated also for the Yankee ingenuity and drive which made it possible to convert these scientific researches into real production."

Tiny both in size and in power requirements, the transistor's value is most important in applications where weight and space problems are critical. According to Mr. Adams, the transistor will inevitably find its way into the home in a number of consumer products. "We are already experimenting with television receivers using transistors," he said, "and have completed more than two years of intensive research and application engineering to increase the transistor's usefulness."

Joe Lazaro Wins Coveted International Blind Golfers Championship at Toronto

Misses Hole-in-One By 18 Inches in 250 Yard Spoon Shot

Joe Lazaro, who dreamed as a boy of becoming a professional golfer, today proudly holds the title of International Blind Golf Champion. He won the coveted title July 23 in keen competition in Toronto, Canada, which included top winners of the U.S. Blind Golf Tournament held in Worcester, Mass., July 16-18.

A beaming victory smile, caught by a Toronto news photographer, lit up the face of Raytheon's 36-year-old champion when he was presented

Blinded by a land mine explosion in World War II, Lazaro returned from the war and took a position in Raytheon's Microwave and Power Tube salvage department. He even found time to write a book, *The Right Touch*, on his golfing techniques. Blind golfers got their start in the 1920s. During World War II, they proposed to the Veterans Administration that the sport would be a positive activity for servicemen who had lost their sight. The VA agreed and continues to support this work today. Lazaro usually scored in the upper 90s to low 100s and modestly gave much of the credit to his caddy and coach, John Callahan. The Lazaro Trophy is named in his honor.

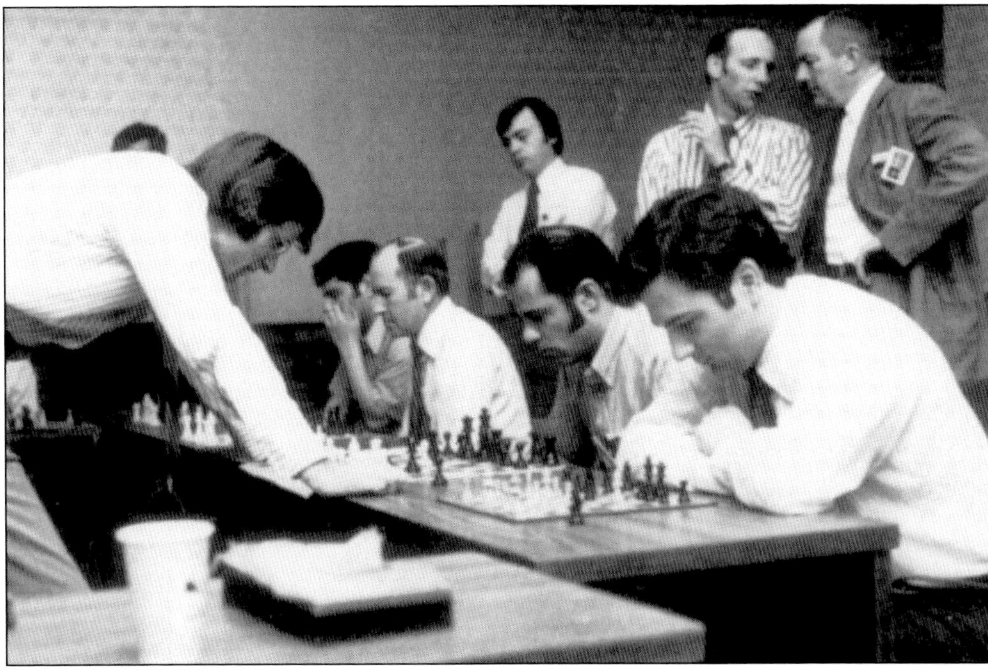

As reported in the *Raytheon Missile Messenger* newsletter of January–February 1975, Mike Hart of the Systems Design Lab faced 12 opponents simultaneously in a lunchtime chess match. Hart was rated as one of the top chess players in Massachusetts. An engineer from Worcester Polytechnic Institute, he joined Raytheon in 1969.

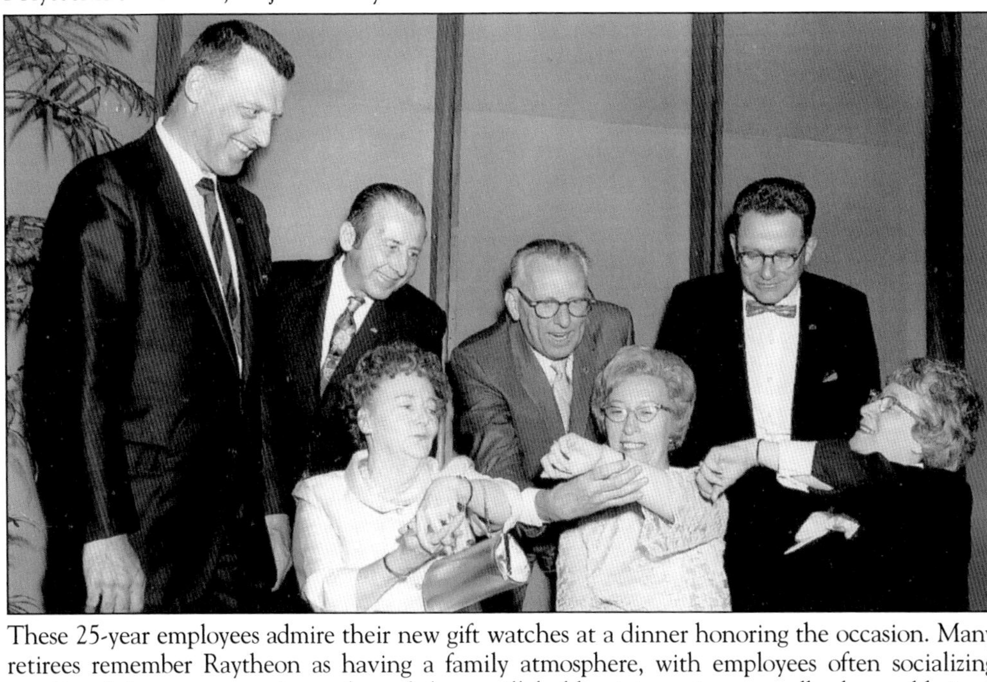

These 25-year employees admire their new gift watches at a dinner honoring the occasion. Many retirees remember Raytheon as having a family atmosphere, with employees often socializing outside of the company. A number of them still hold mini-reunions to talk about old times and catch up on their latest activities. The Association of Raytheon Company Retirees can be contacted at 336 Baker Avenue, Concord, Massachusetts, 01742 or at www.raytheonretirees.org.

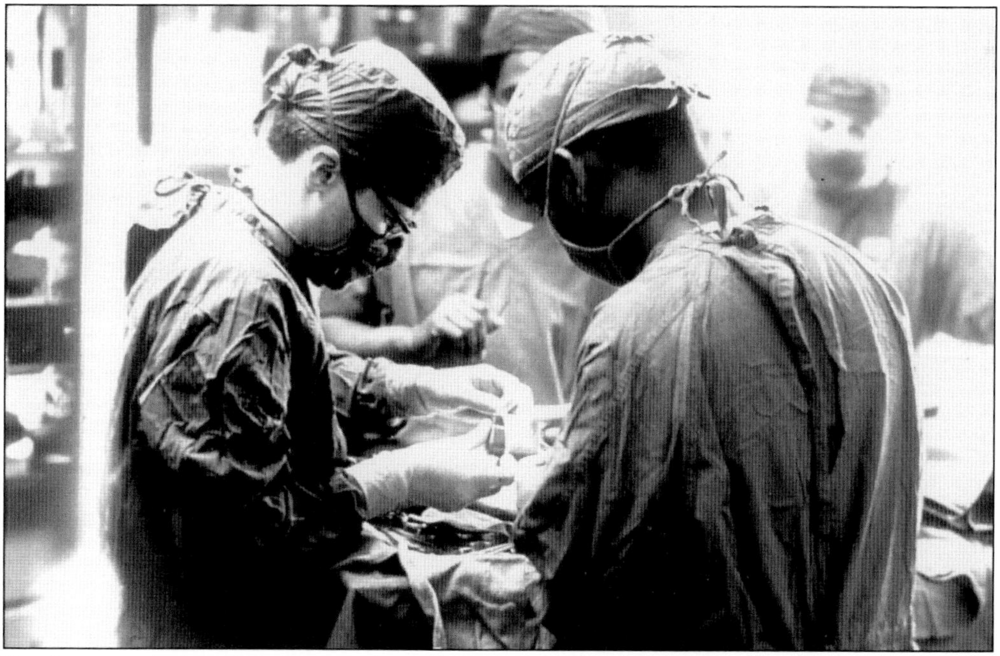

Raytheon worked with American Optical Company, Arconunlear and Medtronic to produce cardiac pacemakers, providing the transistors and circuit modules for implantation in a large number of patients to correct serious heart irregularities.

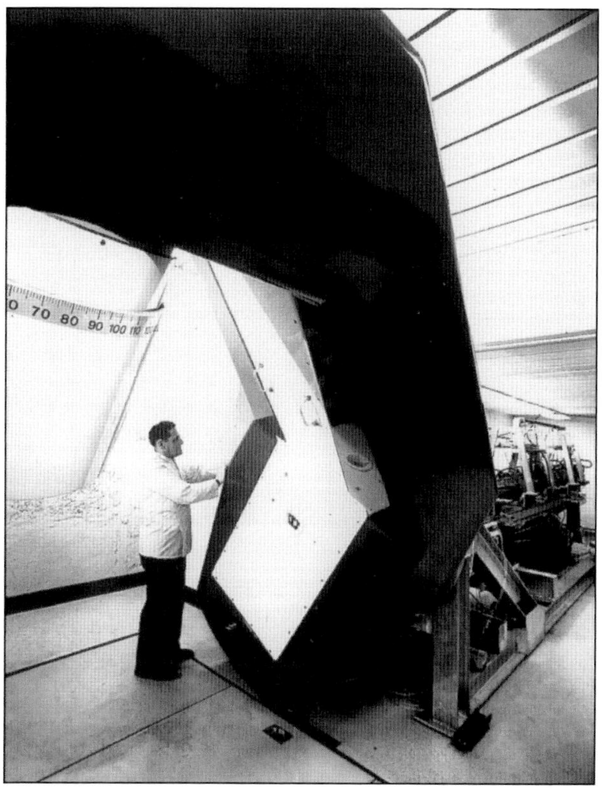

This is a view of the linear accelerator built for radiotherapy of cancer at the University of Texas's M. D. Anderson Hospital and Tumor Institute. It produced an accelerated electron beam with energies up to 12 million electron volts and generated x-rays having energies of 25 million volts.

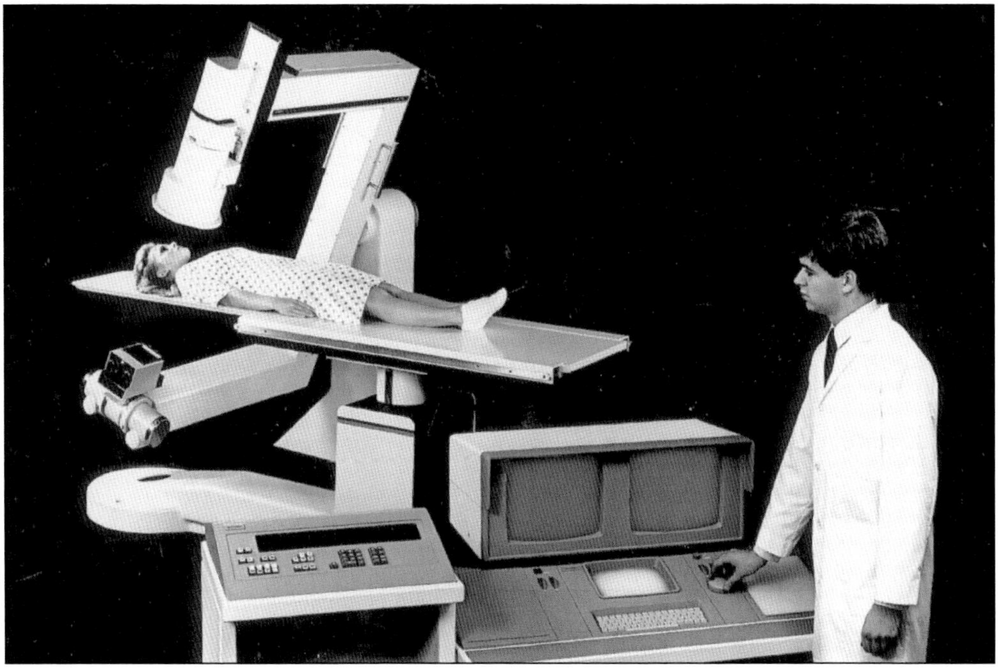

This is an example of the medical x-ray equipment produced by Raytheon's Machlett Laboratories in Stamford, Connecticut, during the 1970s.

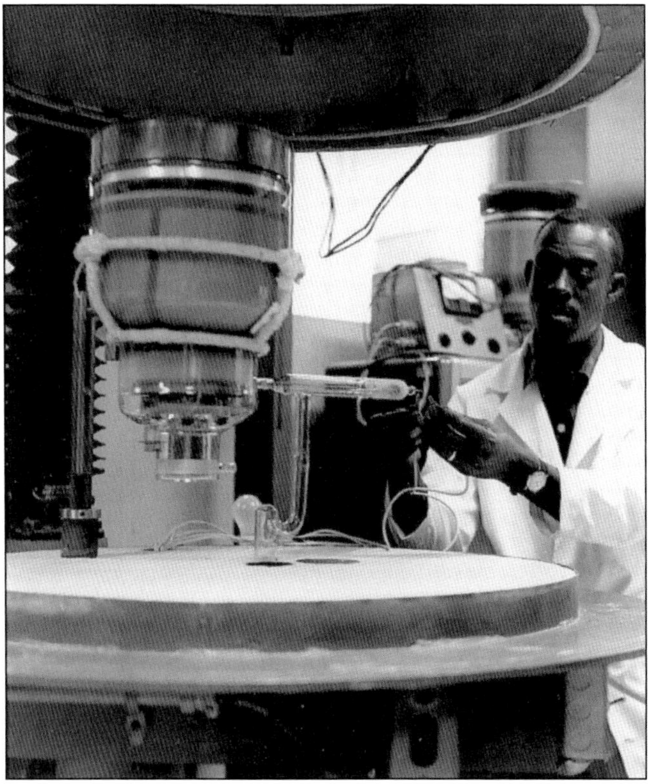

A technician at Machlett Labs works on the processing of a large glass industrial tube. Machlett has specialized in high-powered thyratrons, x-ray tubes, and transmitting tubes, as well as complete medical equipment.

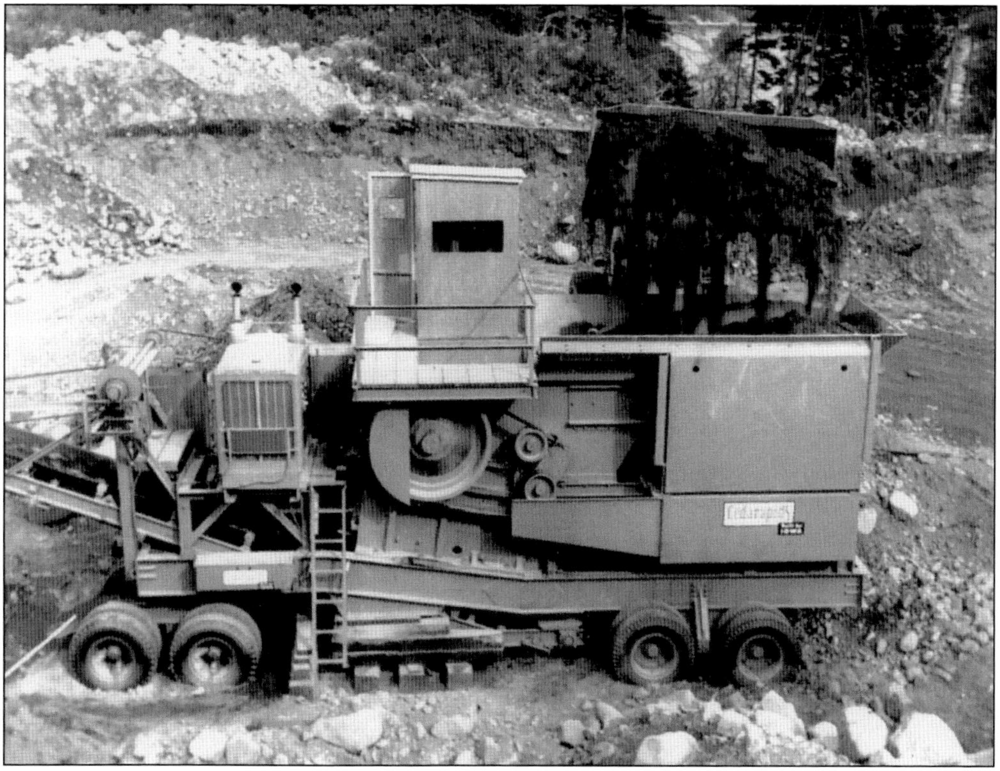

One of Raytheon's acquisitions was the Iowa Manufacturing Company, which specialized in large equipment for construction, rock crushing, and road paving. After its acquisition, the company was renamed Cedar Rapids. In this photograph, Cedar Rapids equipment is shown at a site in Ecuador.

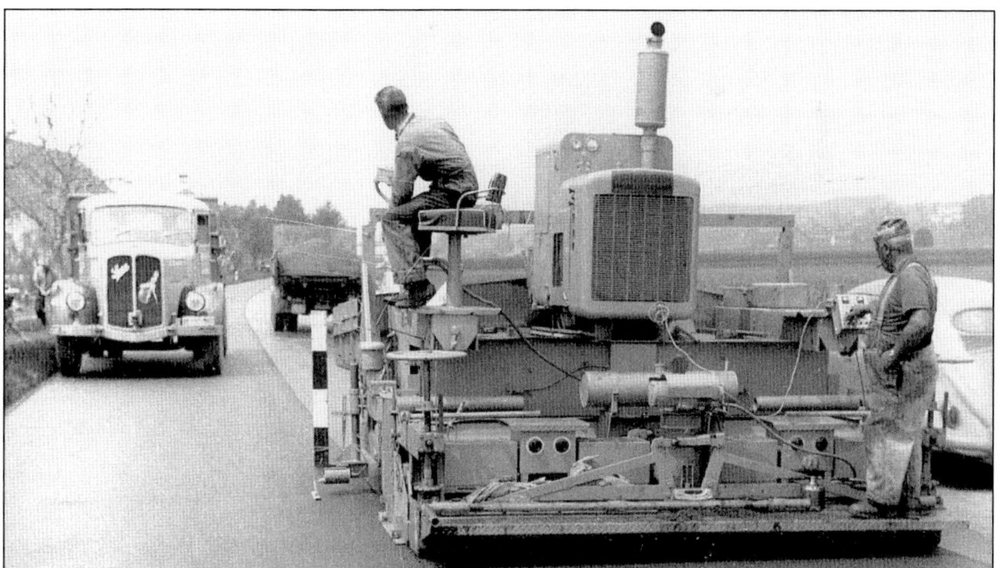

Here, a Cedar Rapids BSF-2 road-paving machine is hard at work in Switzerland on a warm summer day.

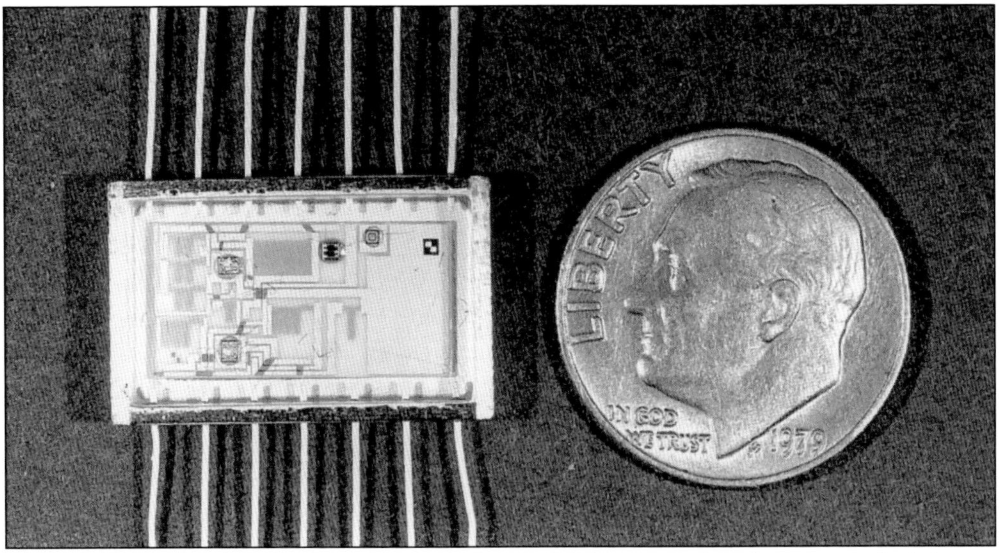

The Semiconductor Operation in Mountain View, California, produced a variety of solid-state devices and integrated circuits. The microscopic size of these circuits is illustrated by their comparison with a 1979 U.S. dime. Although Raytheon did not regain the dominant position it held in the solid-state world of the 1950s, the company continued to play an important role in the evolution of this technology through each successive generation.

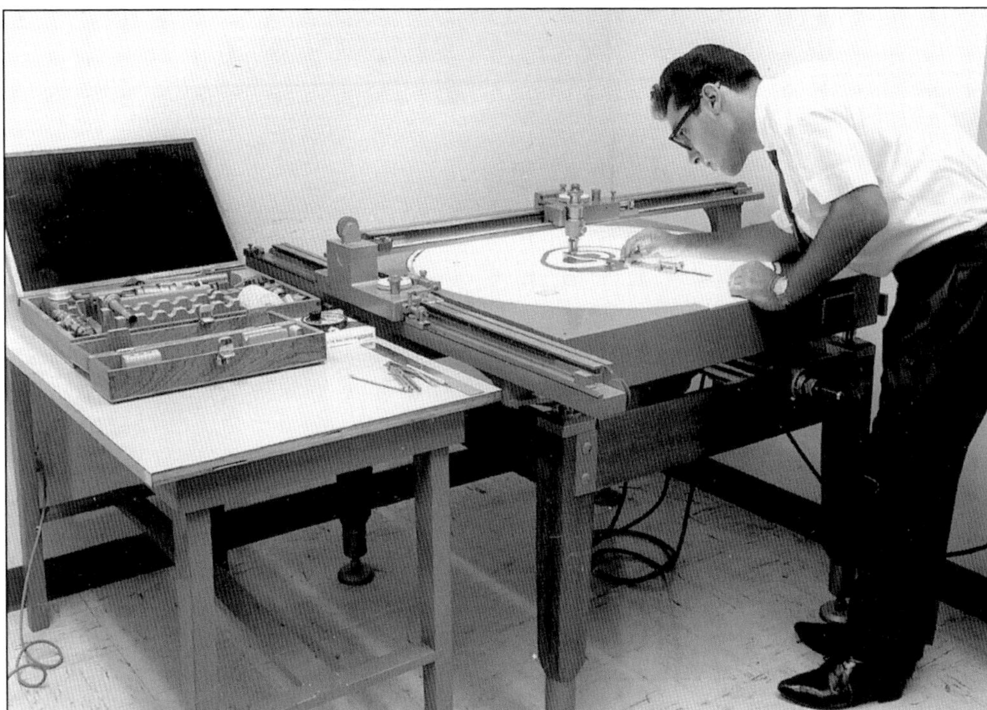

The design and layout of microcircuits is performed on an enlarged scale by this engineer, then photographically reduced to microscopic size for fabrication. Without this technology, the miniaturization of computers, radios, televisions, hearing aids, and other electronic equipment would not have been possible.

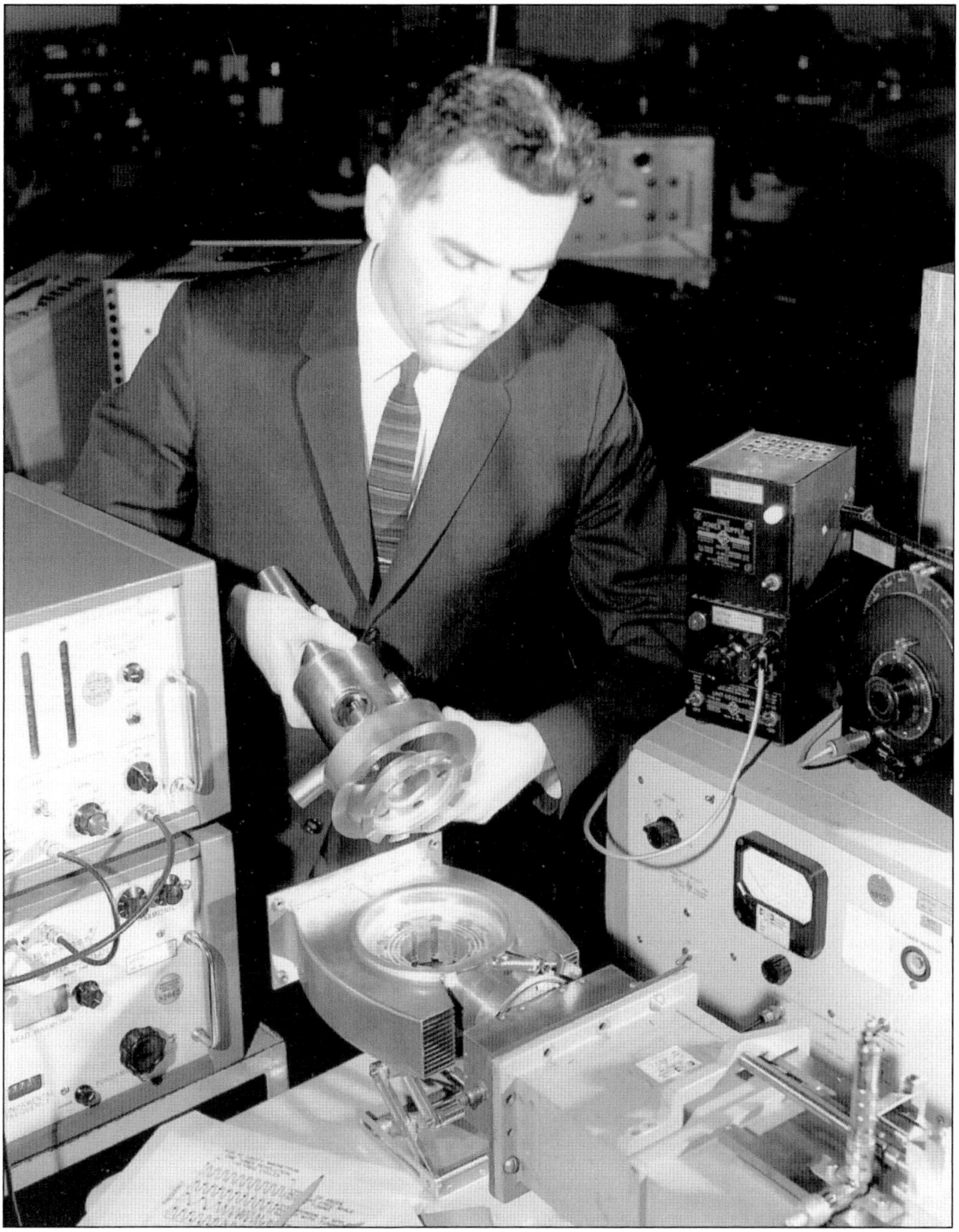

Coauthor Bob Edwards is shown in this 1964 photograph with one of his rotary-tuned magnetrons. The concept of rapid frequency jumping using high-power, inexpensive magnetrons to avoid radar jamming was used in Europe and Japan, but it never became popular in the United States. The advent of traveling wave tube amplifiers with a wider frequency bandwidth and a high gain of 30 dB superseded this method, offering electronic control of frequency output from a low-power source.

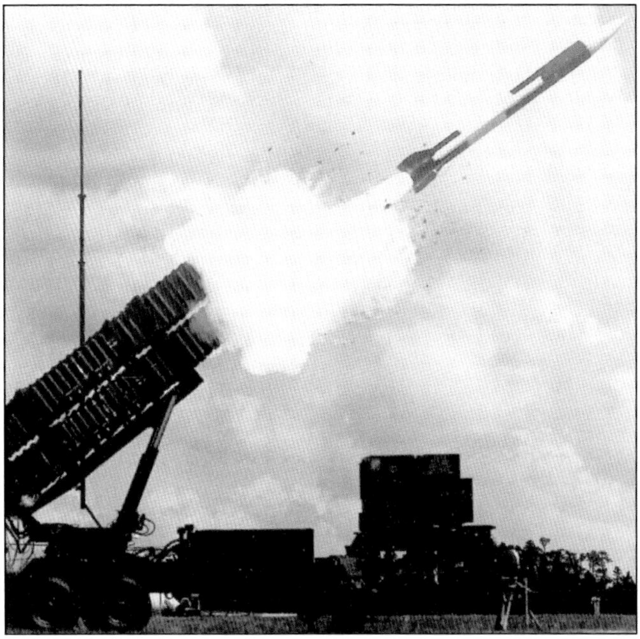

In this photograph, a SAM-D missile is fired from its canister enclosure to intercept attacking aircraft. By the time it went into production, the Sam-D was renamed the Patriot missile. It was later hastily adapted for action against Soviet-designed Scud missiles in the Gulf War. Many countries are buying the latest versions of Patriot systems for their air defense.

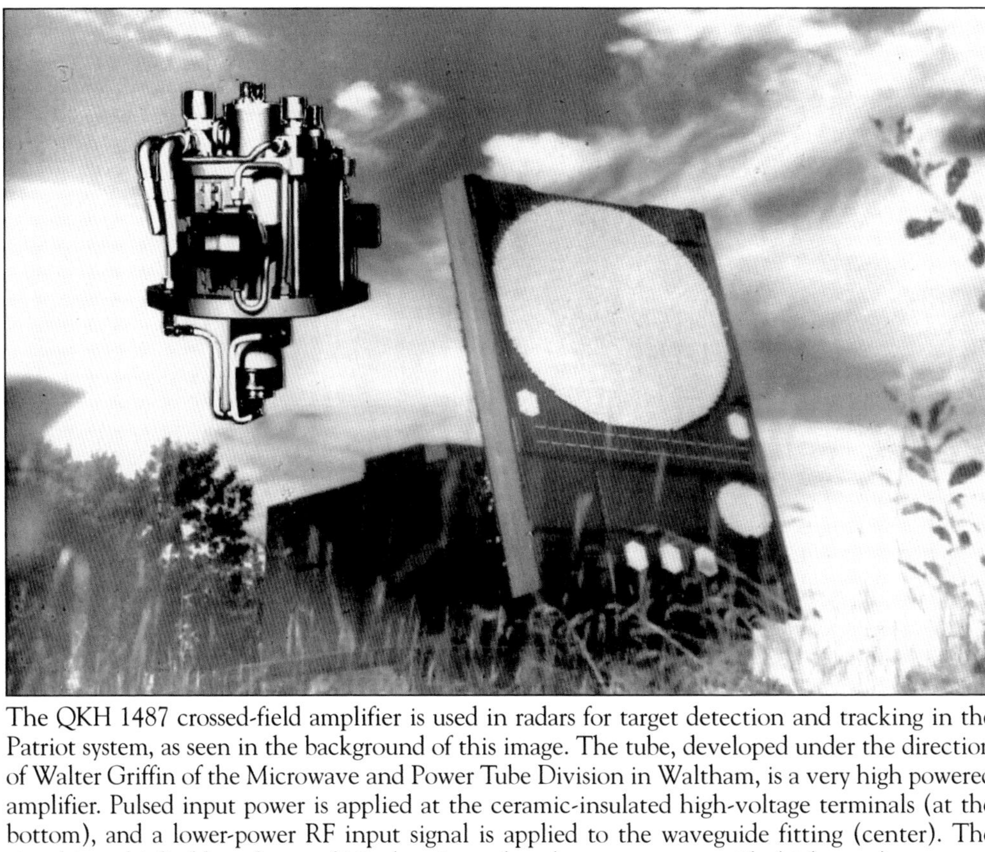

The QKH 1487 crossed-field amplifier is used in radars for target detection and tracking in the Patriot system, as seen in the background of this image. The tube, developed under the direction of Walter Griffin of the Microwave and Power Tube Division in Waltham, is a very high powered amplifier. Pulsed input power is applied at the ceramic-insulated high-voltage terminals (at the bottom), and a lower-power RF input signal is applied to the waveguide fitting (center). The signal is multiplied by a factor of 10 when it reaches the output waveguide (right rear).

A typical traveling wave tube, such as the type used in satellites and aircraft radars, has a row of doughnut-shaped magnets surrounding the internal electron beam to maintain it in sharp focus. These high-energy Samarium Cobalt magnets were produced by the Microwave and Power Tube Division's Magnet Laboratory. They are several times more powerful than more conventional alnico permanent magnets, resulting in a significant savings in weight and an improved performance.

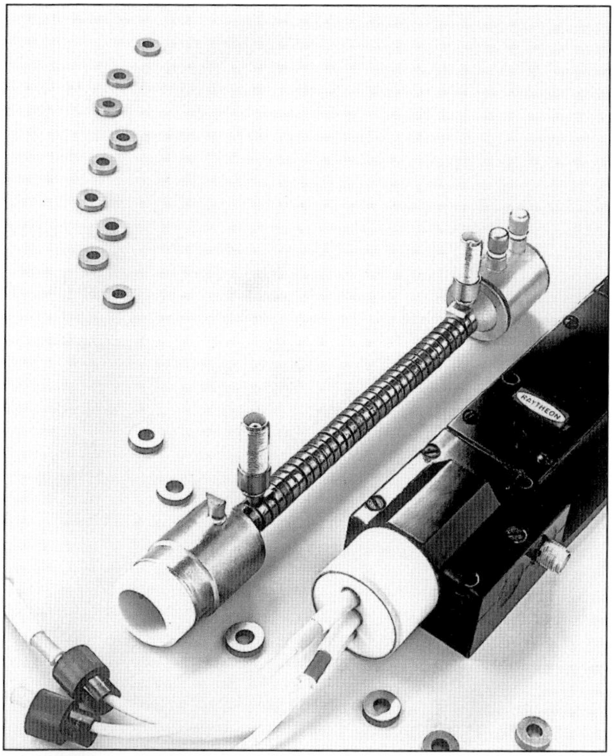

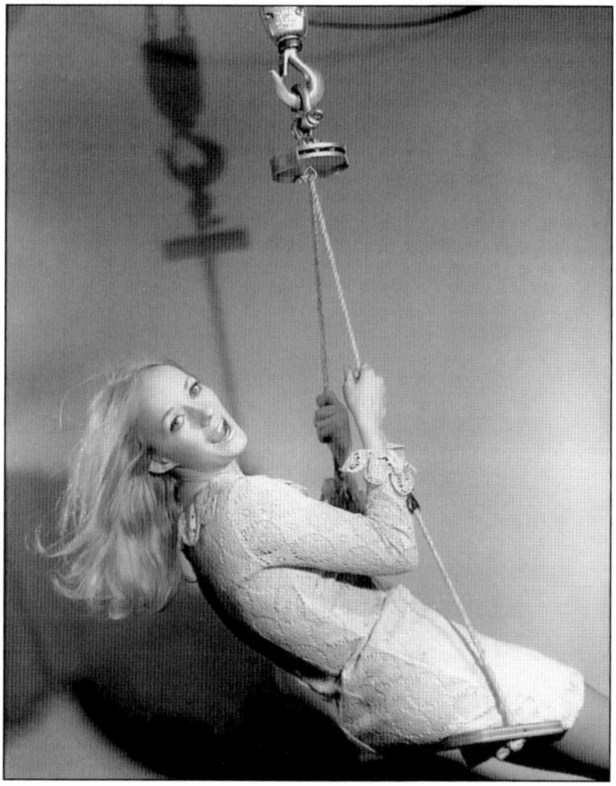

This model was suspended on a swing held up by a ring of high-energy Samarium Cobalt magnets to demonstrate their amazing strength. They are the same type of magnets used in traveling wave tubes.

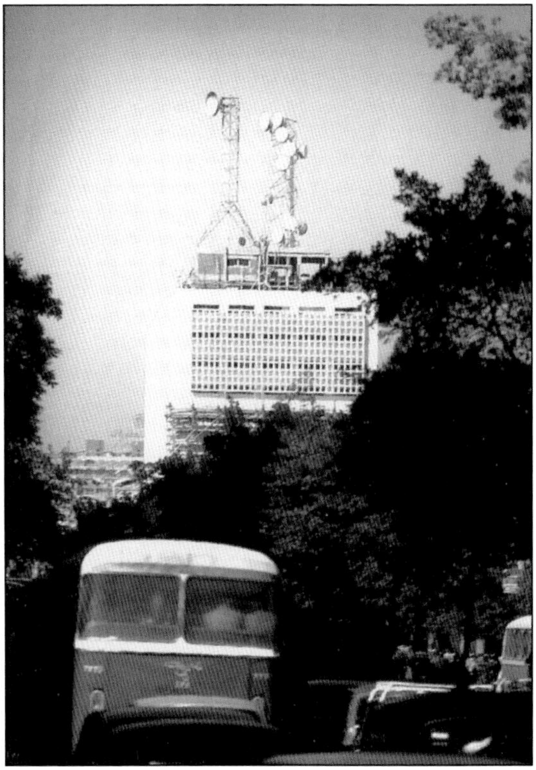

The replacement of Cairo's out-of-date underground telephone wires by a series of microwave repeater towers was chronicled in *Raytheon* magazine in 1981. Prior to the introduction of Raytheon's microwave technology, the old, poorly insulated underground wires would flood during the area's infrequent rain storms, shutting down large segments of Cairo's phone system and forcing businesses to rely on runners to carry important messages.

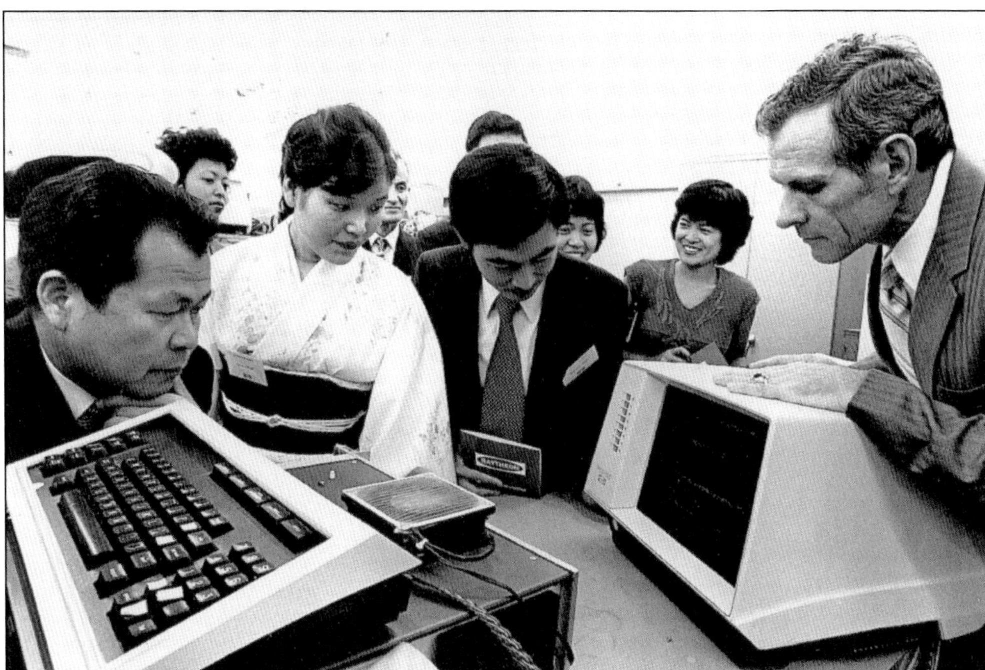

Frank Taylor of Raytheon Data Systems in Norwood demonstrates the capability of a programmable terminal to print out Japanese characters. His audience was part of a 36-person Japanese delegation on a cultural exchange with Boston University in 1975.

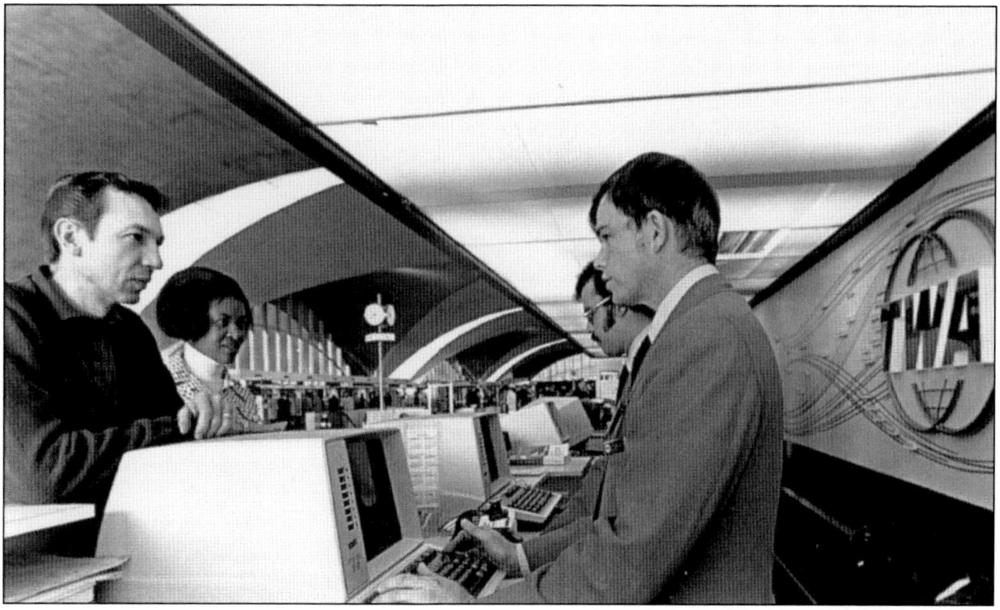

Raytheon has been involved in computing in a number of ways over the years, starting with the Raydac, a digital computer built for the navy's Bureau of Aeronautics in the early 1950s. Here, a group of Raytheon airline reservation computers is in use at a TWA airline ticket counter in 1974. These devices accelerated the passenger-handling process significantly, and they soon became widely used by all the major airlines.

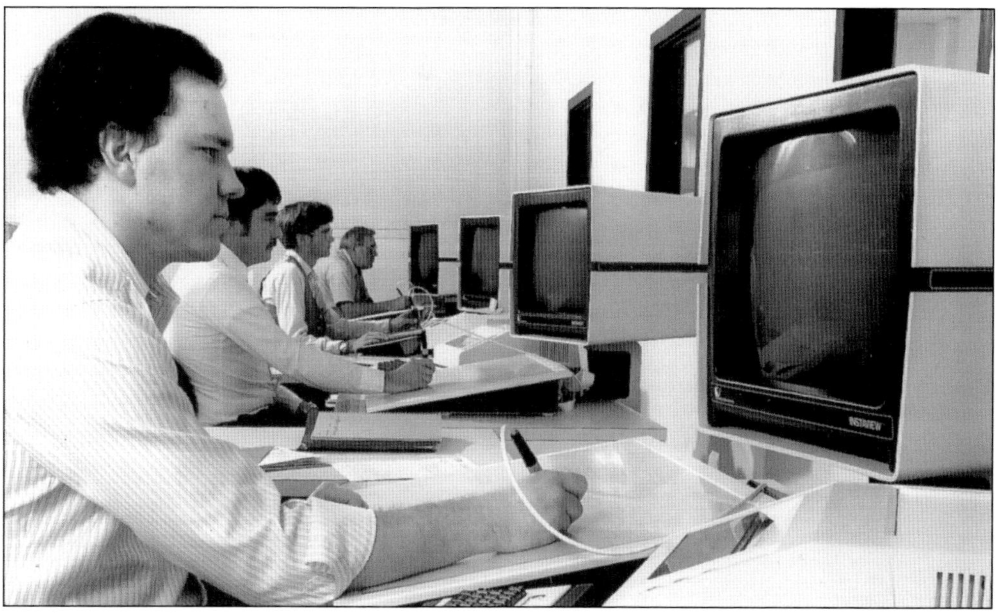

Raytheon was also a consumer of computing power. By 1981, computer-aided drafting (CAD) had begun to replace manual methods, as evidenced in these views of the Microwave and Power Tube Division. CAD allowed the assessment of spacing between parts, preventing interferences. It also let the designer rotate parts and assemblies to view them from other angles and permitted assemblies to be "built" before parts were even manufactured. Electronic storage of images eliminated bulky, hard-to-catalog paper drawings.

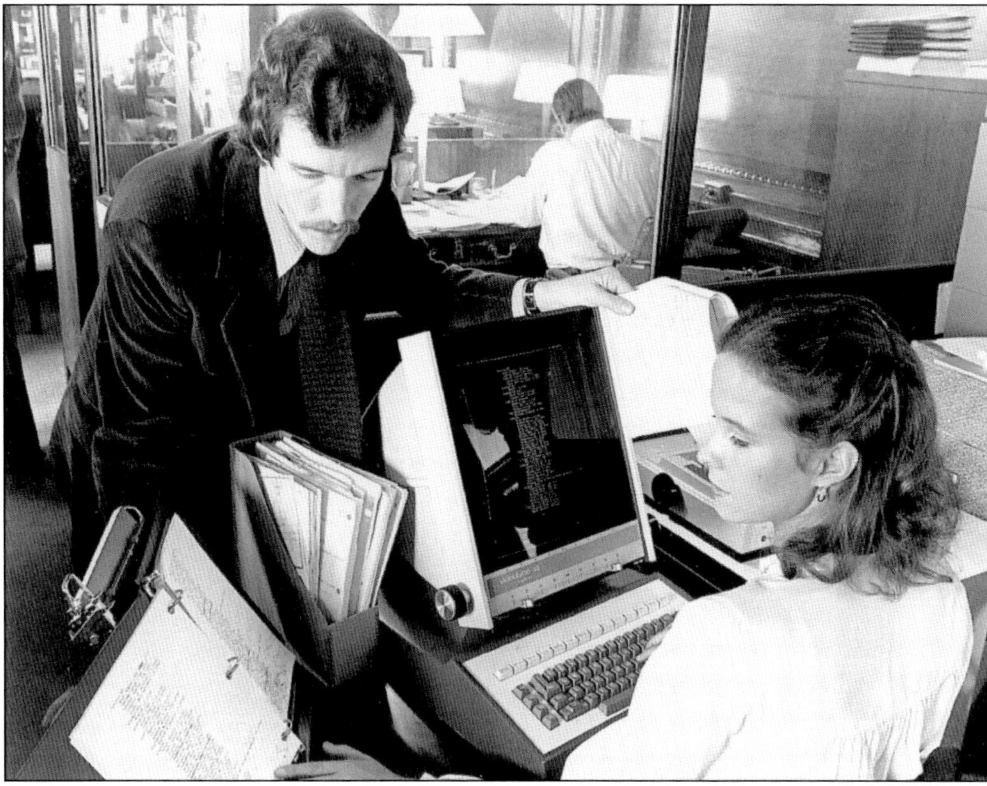

Raytheon also staked a claim to the burgeoning market for word processors, which first appeared as early as the mid-1960s in the form of typewriters with electronic memory. By the early 1970s, Raytheon pioneered the Lexitron, which featured a video screen, electronic storage, and a printer. Here, a Lexitron word processor is used in 1978 at the Library of Congress.

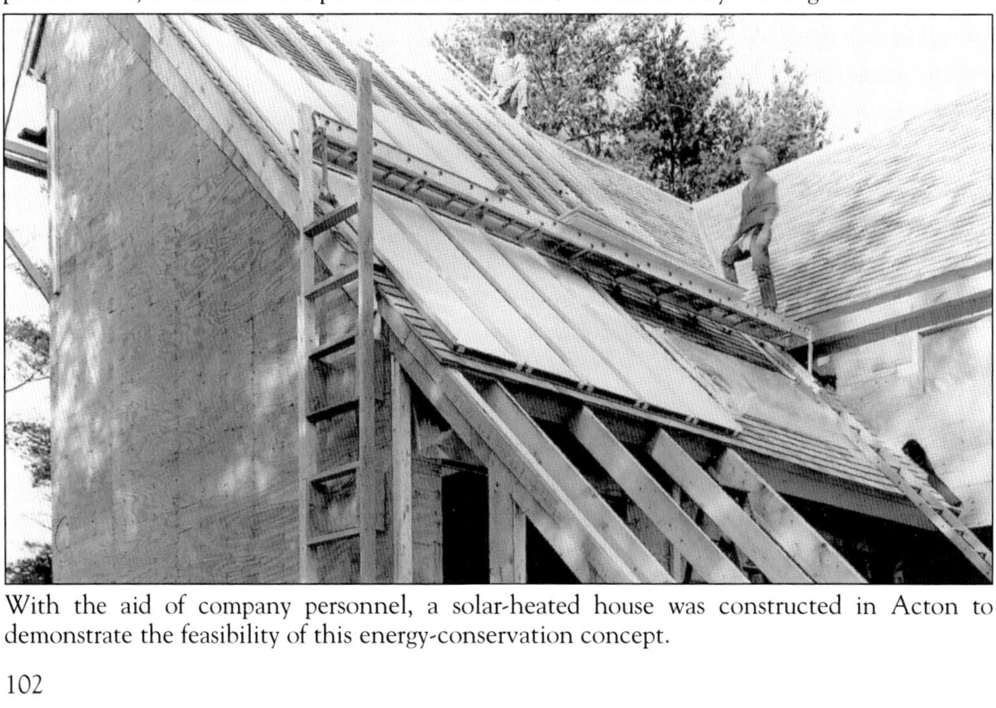

With the aid of company personnel, a solar-heated house was constructed in Acton to demonstrate the feasibility of this energy-conservation concept.

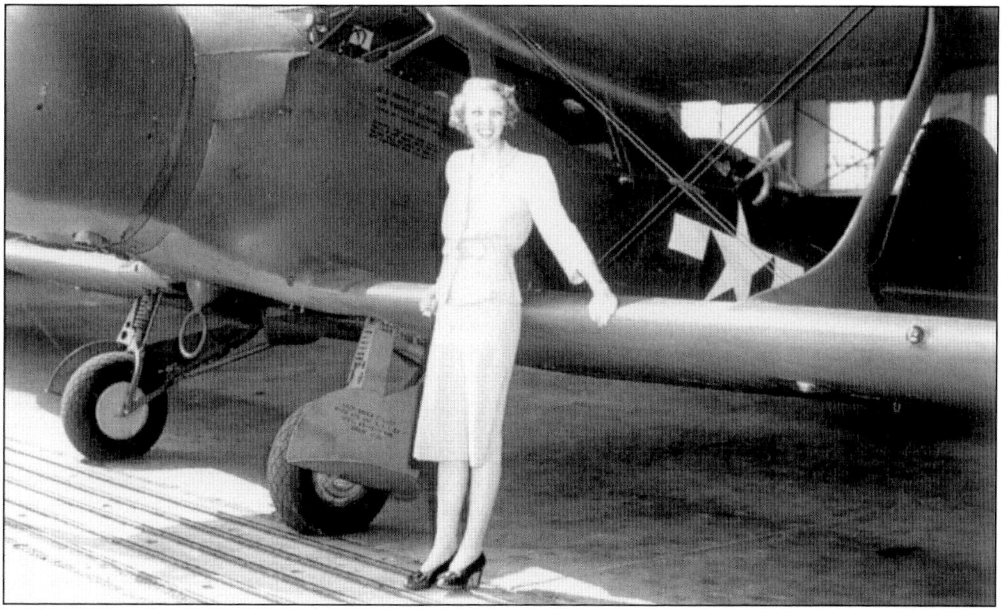

Walter Beech and his wife, Olive Ann Beech, headed Beech Aircraft, which joined Raytheon in 1980. Olive Beech is shown here with the famous Beech Staggerwing biplane, a unique design in which the lower wing was located forward of the upper wing. The plane, produced from 1932 until 1947, set many speed records in the 1930s. Olive showed an unusual financial aptitude at an early age, and she was assigned the responsibility of writing checks and paying the household bills at age 11. She directed the company after her husband's death in 1950. Beech Aircraft grew from 10 employees to 10,000 between 1932 and 1982.

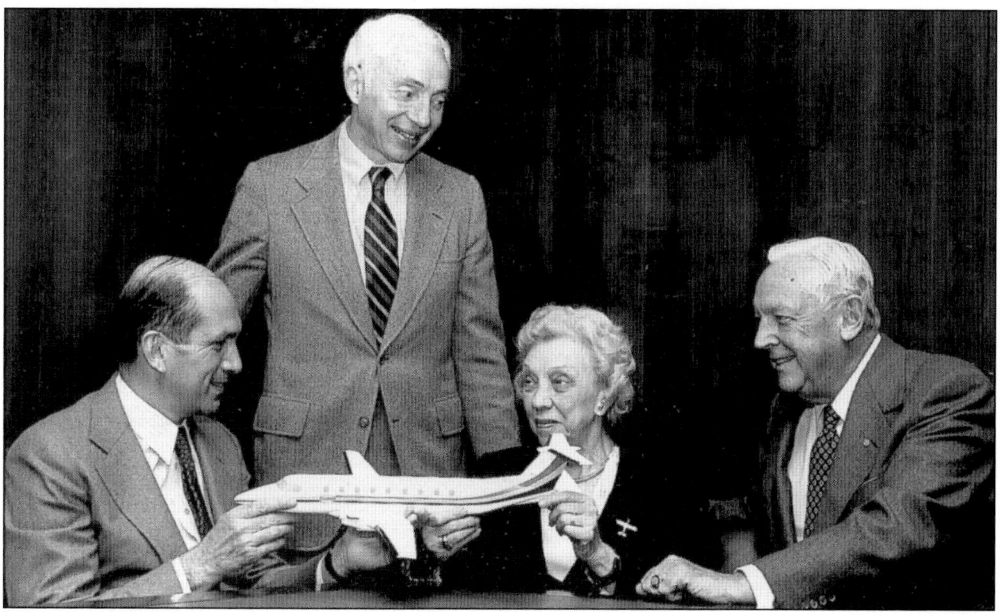

Olive Beech, a cofounder and cochairman of Beech Aircraft Company, is shown in 1980 on the occasion of her election to Raytheon's board of directors. At the left is Raytheon's board chairman, Tom Phillips; standing is Raytheon president D. Brainerd Holmes; and at the right is Beech chairman Frank Hendrick.

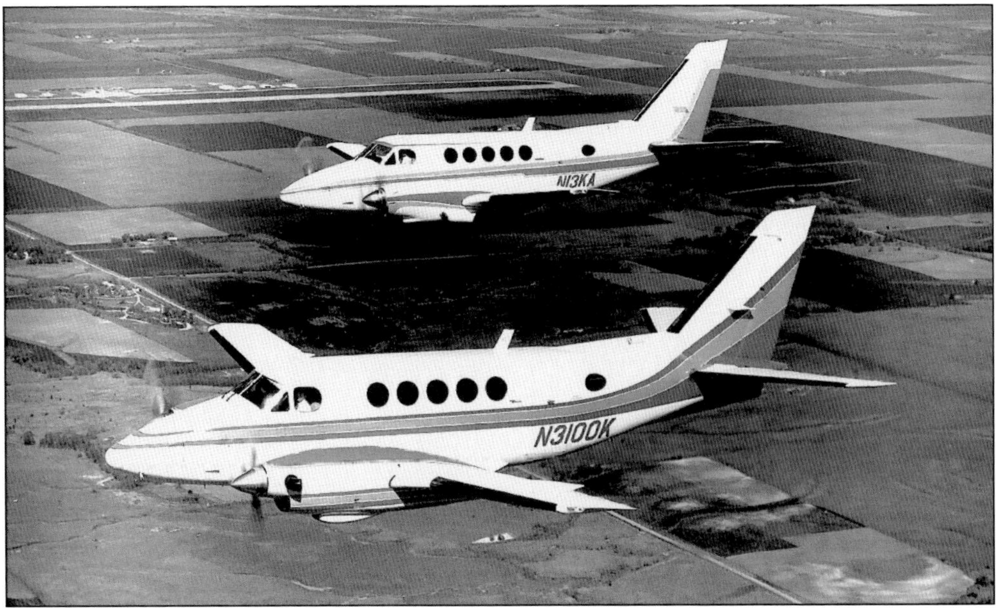

Beech Aircraft has been a dominant producer of small commercial planes that are well suited for individuals, businesses, passenger flights, and freight operations and are appropriate for small and midsized airports.

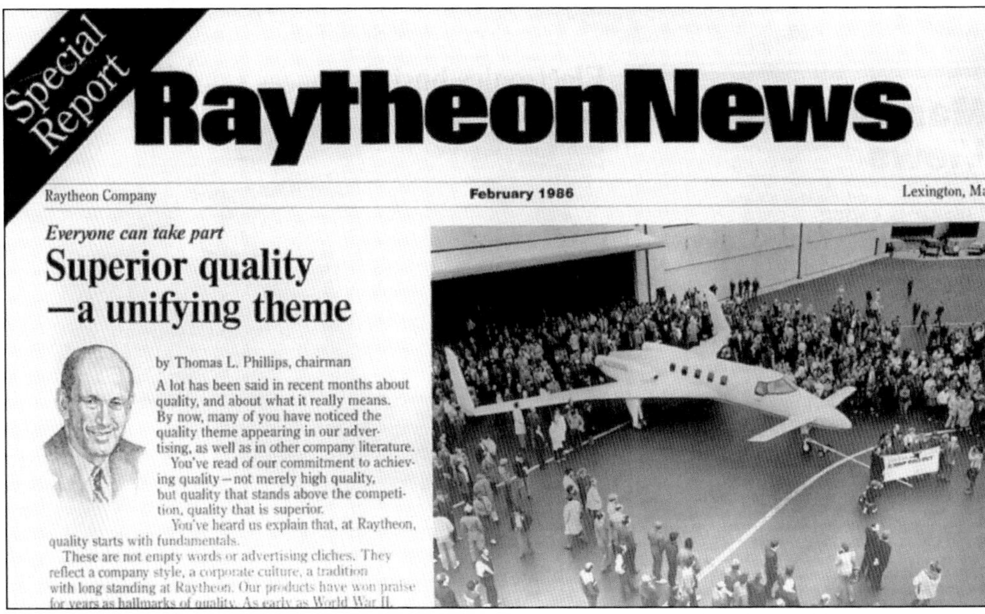

Special Report

RaytheonNews

Raytheon Company | February 1986 | Lexington, Ma

Everyone can take part

Superior quality —a unifying theme

by Thomas L. Phillips, chairman

A lot has been said in recent months about quality, and about what it really means. By now, many of you have noticed the quality theme appearing in our advertising, as well as in other company literature.

You've read of our commitment to achieving quality—not merely high quality, but quality that stands above the competition, quality that is superior.

You've heard us explain that, at Raytheon, quality starts with fundamentals.

These are not empty words or advertising cliches. They reflect a company style, a corporate culture, a tradition with long standing at Raytheon. Our products have won praise for years as hallmarks of quality. As early as World War II,

The February 1986 *Raytheon News* reported the much anticipated rollout of Beech Aircraft's "Starship 1," a revolutionary design created with help from Burt Rutan. The plane, which could carry up to 11 people, was constructed of high-strength synthetic fiber materials, and with its pusher engines, it could cruise at 41,000 feet at speeds of 400 miles per hour. Its development was begun in 1983. Because of its radical new design and its novel construction, the plane required major changes in order to obtain FAA certification; these changes impacted its economics and performance. Ultimately, only a limited number of the planes were completed, but the influential design was an important aviation milestone.

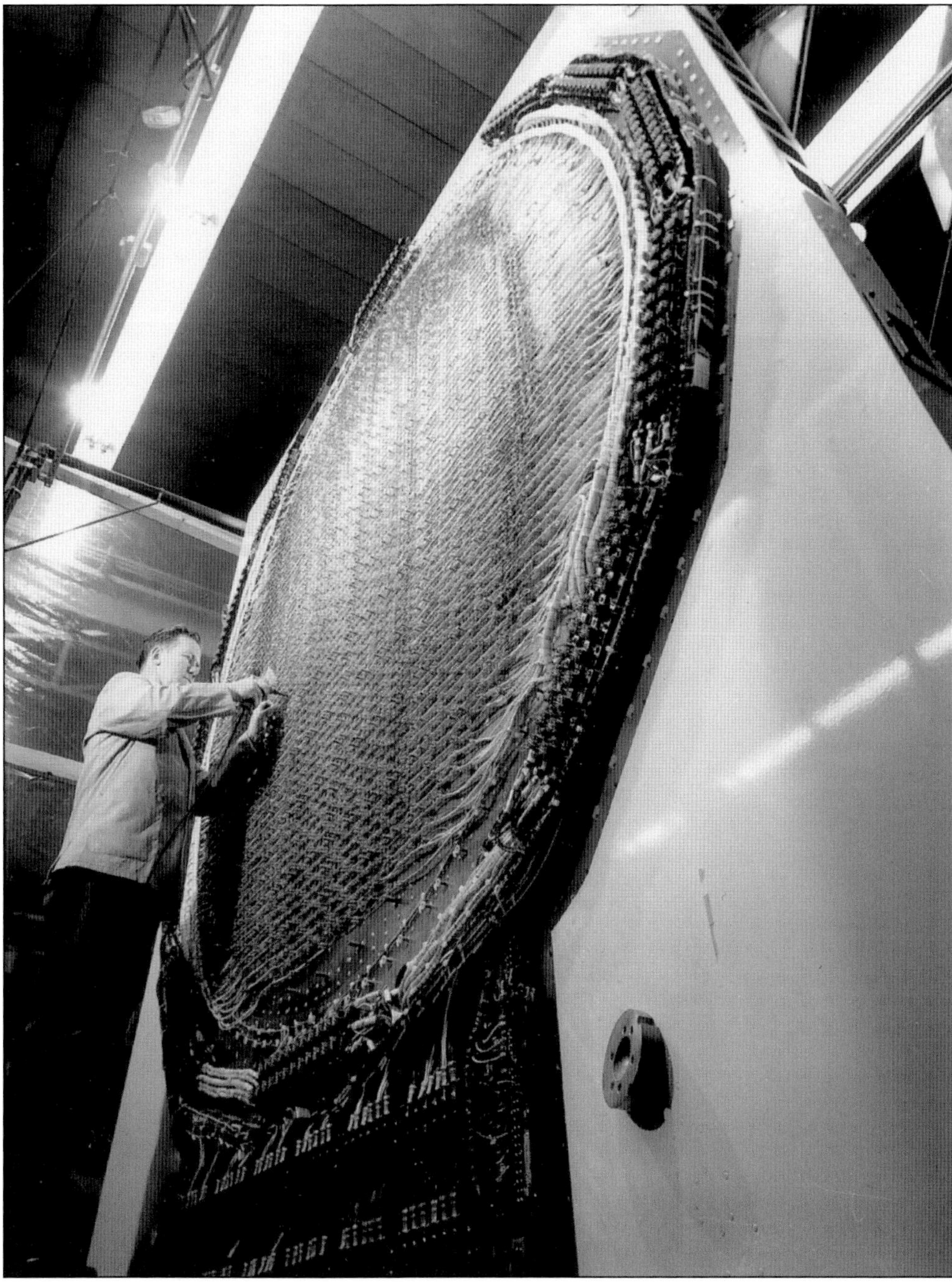

In this image, a technician works on the wire-wrap connections at the rear of the phased array antenna for the SAM-D missile system (which later became the Patriot). One of these antennas has a face with a 10-foot diameter. Unlike early mechanically scanned antennas, phased arrays can move the radar beam electronically for target tracking. The SAM-D program was managed by the U.S. Army Missile Command at Redstone Arsenal in Huntsville, Alabama.

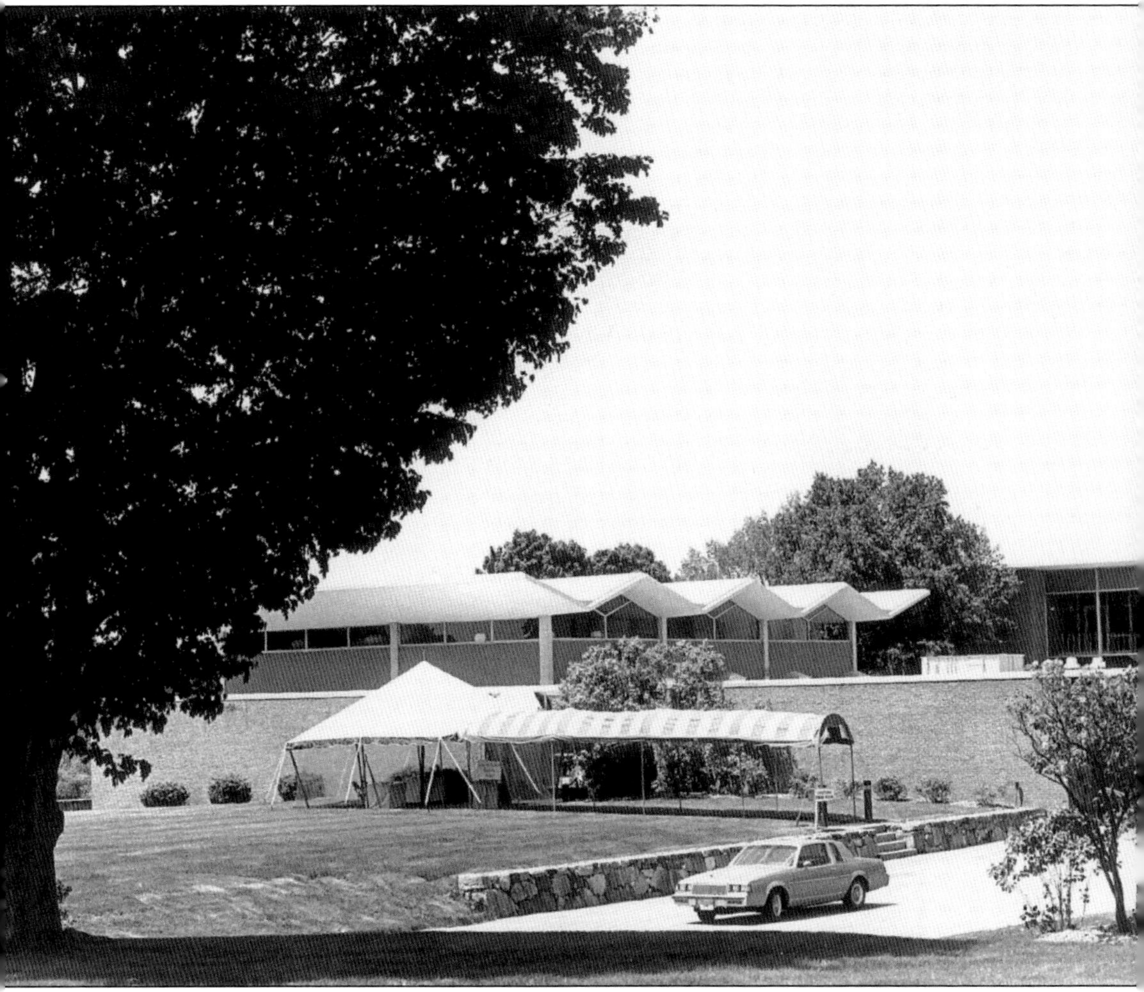

A new headquarters was opened in Lexington in 1961 on a large site overlooking Route 128, the "technology highway." A separate building nearby housed the Raytheon Research Division, and another later housed the D. C. Heath Publishing Company, acquired in 1966.

Five

WINNING THE COLD WAR

The cold war, which began shortly after World War II, sprang from the stark differences between the western Allies and the totalitarian government of the Soviet Union. It comprised a long period of fierce political and economic competition overshadowed by an arms race that always seemed in real danger of turning into a general conflagration.

In these decades of insecurity that witnessed the sudden emergence of the Soviet Union as a nuclear power, Americans often perceived themselves to be vulnerable—and they often were. While some aspects of the cold war, such as the fabled "missile gap" of the late 1950s, proved to be illusory, there was nothing illusory about the steady general improvement in Soviet military technology. In addition, there was the ever secretive and always implacable face of the Soviet state, best remembered in the bellicose ranting of Premier Khruschev, who promised, "We will bury you."

Equipped with limited information about Soviet goals and capabilities, American defense planners needed to prepare for the possibility of long-range Soviet bombers (and, later, missiles) arriving across the arctic regions. Later, the challenges grew more grave with the deployment of Soviet missile-firing submarines not far from the U.S. coast. Advanced defense technologies to detect and thwart attacks by aircraft or missiles were desperately needed.

Raytheon's long-running contributions to defense technology in this period were so important to the nation (and to the company) that they bear some special mention. The company participated in building the distant early warning (DEW) line radars across Alaska, Canada, and Greenland. Later, to deal with the dangers posed by submarine-launched missiles, the Pave Paws radars were installed at several locations around the United States, including Cape Cod. Cobra Dane and Cobra Judy—a similar pair of giant, long-range radars using traveling wave tube technology to provide electronically steerable beams—also contributed to security.

These huge, high-power radar systems, which utilized dozens of individual "radiators" in their phased array antennas, could achieve pinpoint accuracy in detecting and tracking missiles by using all-electronic steering of the radar search beam. Because these radars eliminated the relatively slow mechanical process of rotating an antenna, tracking could be accomplished with millisecond response times.

Another Raytheon contribution was the long-lived Hawk program, begun in the 1950s. Advanced versions of Hawk units remain in service to this day in many allied nations.

In the realm of air-to-air missiles, Raytheon either led or participated in such famous programs as the Sparrow, the Sidewinder, and the advanced medium-range air-to-air missile (AMRAAM), as well as outgrowths of these projects for shipboard use, such as the Sea Sparrow, the Standard missile, and the Harpoon missile. Raytheon was also an important subcontractor on the breakthrough Polaris missile program, which gave America a submarine-based, intermediate-range ballistic missile.

Patriot, which began life as SAM-D in the mid-1960s, became a triumph for Raytheon, offering the United States and its allies a flexible, accurate, upgradable, long-range antiaircraft missile that, it turns out, also has significant capabilities against ballistic missiles. This capability was evidenced in the Gulf War, when Patriot missiles were hastily adapted to an antimissile role and achieved hits on Iraqi Scuds in flight—an accomplishment that has been compared to hitting a bullet with a bullet.

Beyond these headline-grabbing products, Raytheon's engineering talent supported much of the fabric of America's defenses with components, specialized radars, and munitions.

Of course, the very success of Raytheon's products in winning the cold war challenged its future when defense procurement plummeted in the 1990s. Today, the company, expanded through acquisitions such as Hughes Aircraft and the defense business of Texas Instruments, ranks as the fifth-largest defense contractor in the United States.

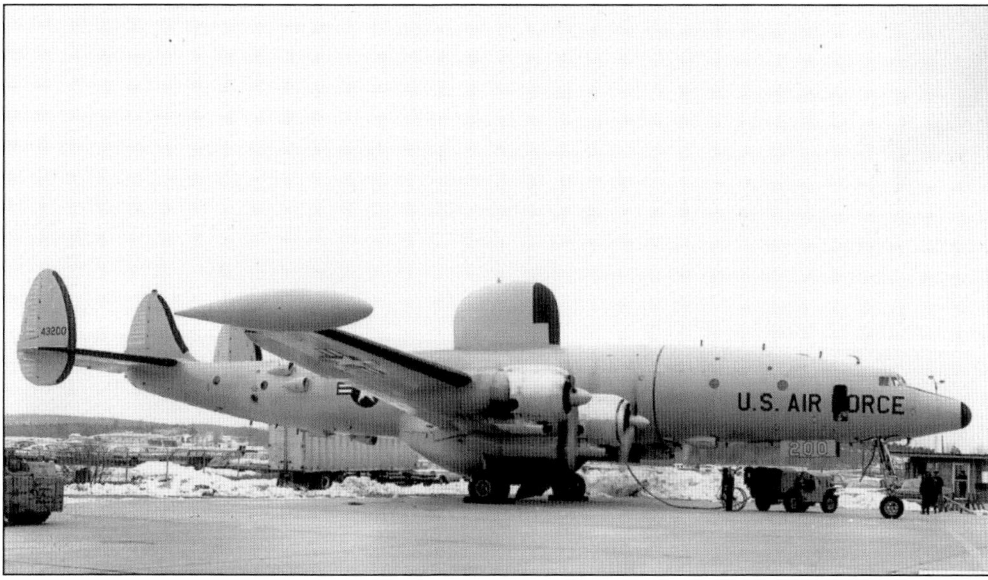

During the cold war, radar patrol planes operated from such places as Otis Air Force Base on Cape Cod. They flew round-the-clock missions off the coast to watch for the approach of enemy bombers. Lockheed Constellation planes were fitted with large radars (featuring many Raytheon components) for long-range search. This costly effort was eventually replaced by ground-based phased array radars such as the Raytheon Pave Paws, which had the ability to scan thousands of square miles of airspace in seconds.

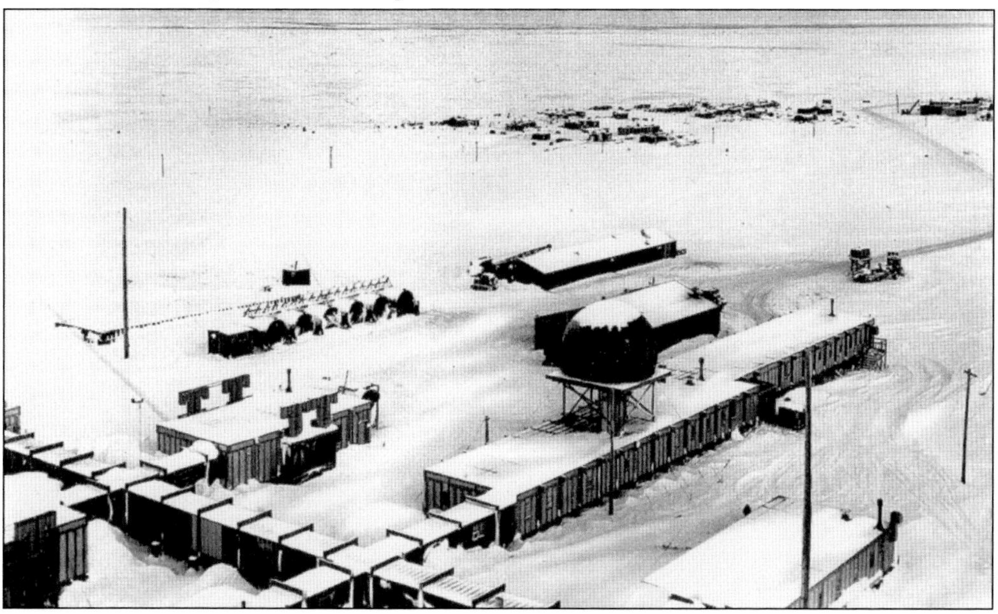

Another major cold war defense project for which Raytheon provided components was the distant early warning (DEW) radar installations that stretched across the edge of the arctic circle from Greenland across Canada and to the Aleutian islands off Alaska. Weather-resistant living quarters were provided for the resident crews, who had to withstand the harsh conditions while maintaining an around-the-clock watch for Soviet aircraft. To test U.S. defenses and monitor electronic signals, Soviet planes were often sent to the edge of North American airspace.

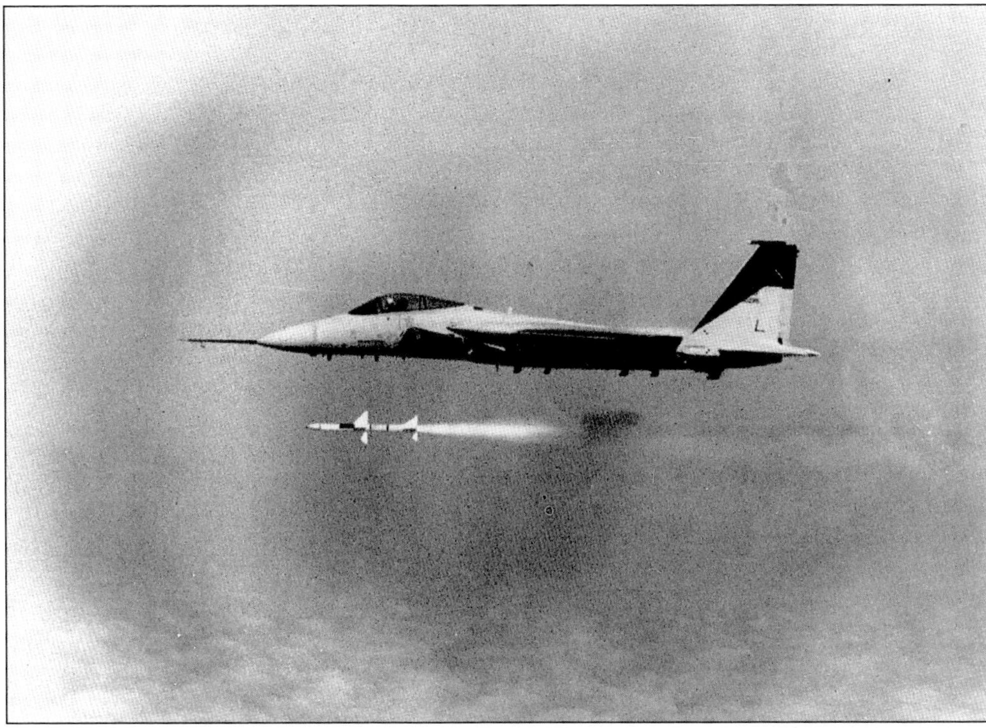

In the mid-1950s, the Sparrow air-to-air missile became one of Raytheon's earliest successes. Its most modern versions remain in service today. A radar-guided missile, it is seen here in a test firing from a U.S. Air Force F-15 Eagle fighter produced by McDonnell Douglas.

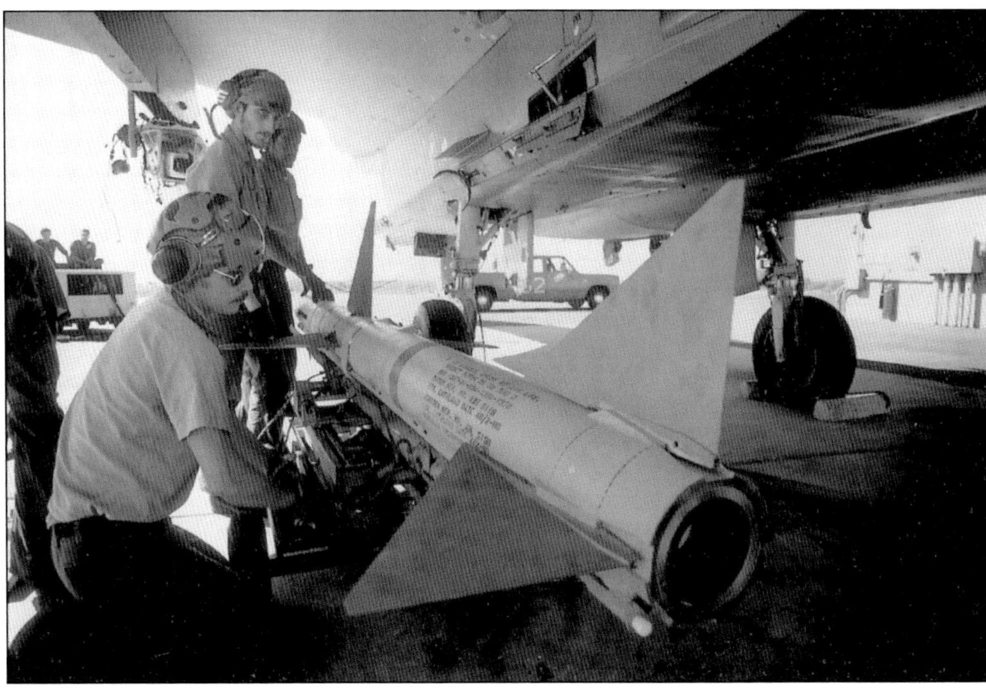

Ground crew members install a Sparrow missile on an air force fighter jet.

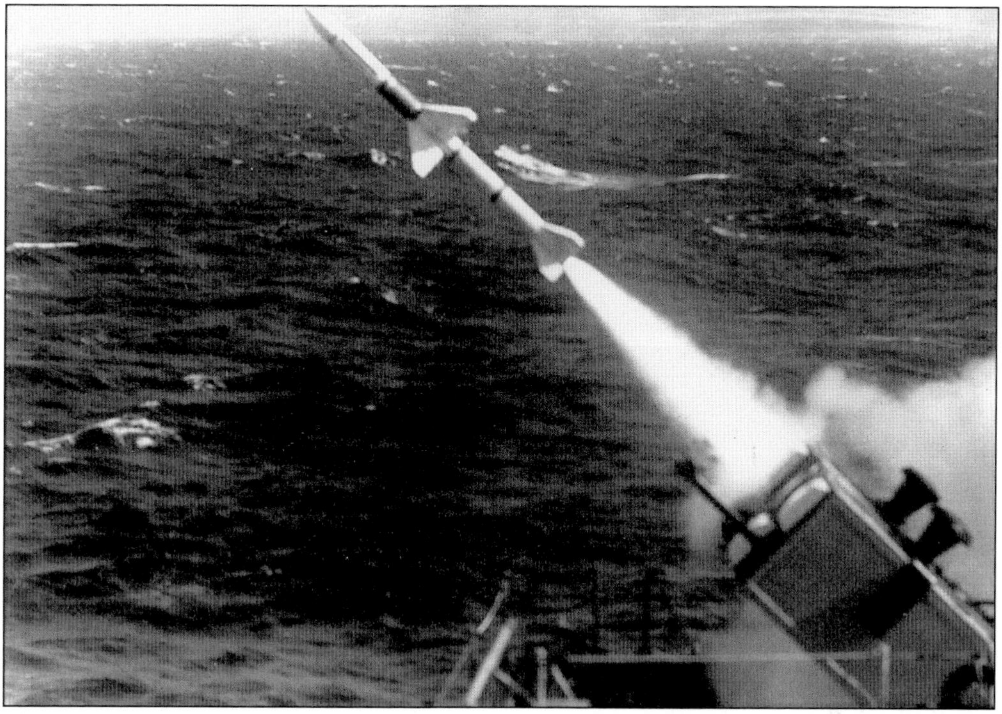

The Sea Sparrow is an adaptation of the Sparrow missile for shipboard air defense. This is a test firing from a multi-pod launcher in such a shipboard installation. These systems first became operational in 1975.

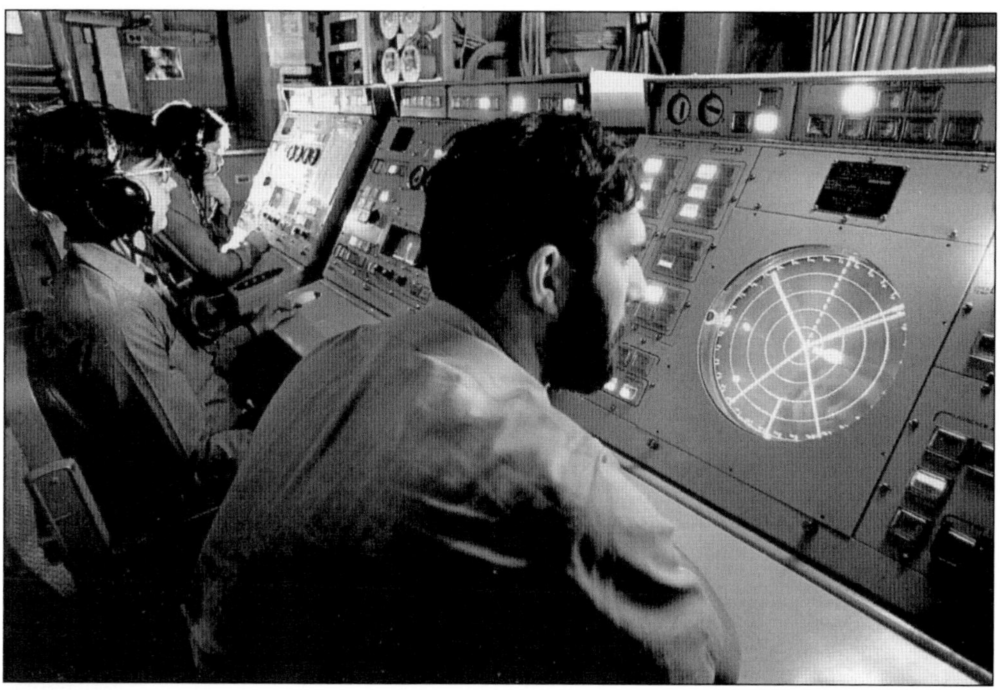

Here we see the missile-guidance and tracking center for the Sea Sparrow aboard a naval vessel.

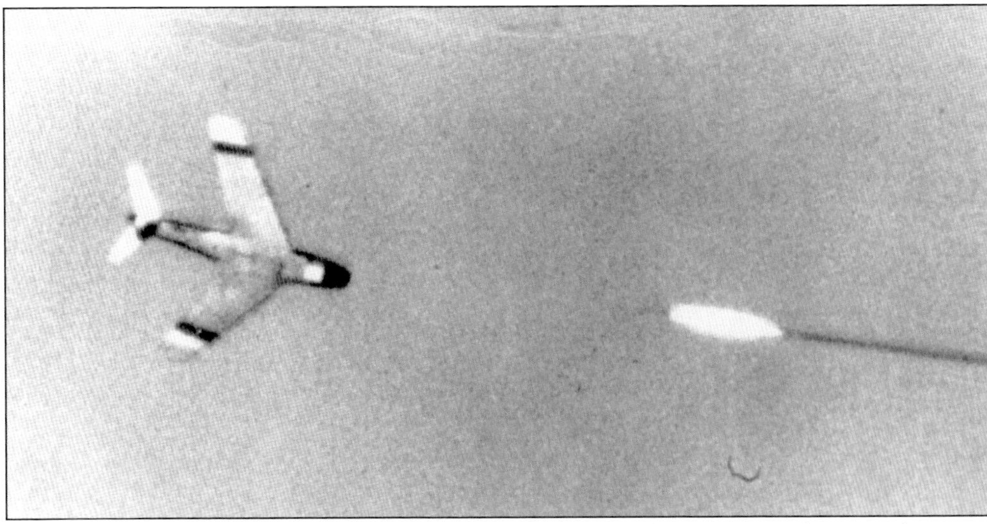

Raytheon's Sidewinder AIM-9 missile has undergone several major upgrades over the years. This heat-seeking infrared missile was first fielded in the 1950s. While successful, early versions could only track a target from behind and often had trouble distinguishing a target in some atmospheric conditions or even in bright sunlight. Raytheon began production of its version in 1964. This photograph shows a Raytheon Sidewinder intercepting and destroying a target drone head-on (a major accomplishment) at the Naval Weapons Center in China Lake, California. This AIM-9L version featured all-aspect approach capability with enhanced maneuverability and accuracy.

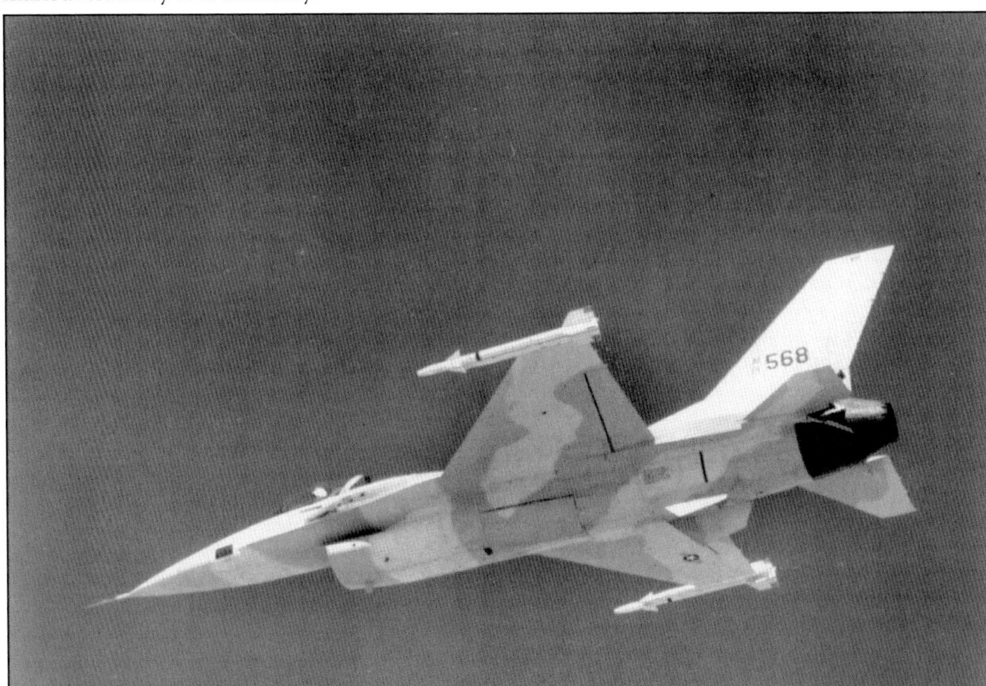

This F-16 fighter plane carries two Sidewinders in a typical wingtip installation. Each weighs 190 pounds and measures about nine feet in length and five inches in diameter.

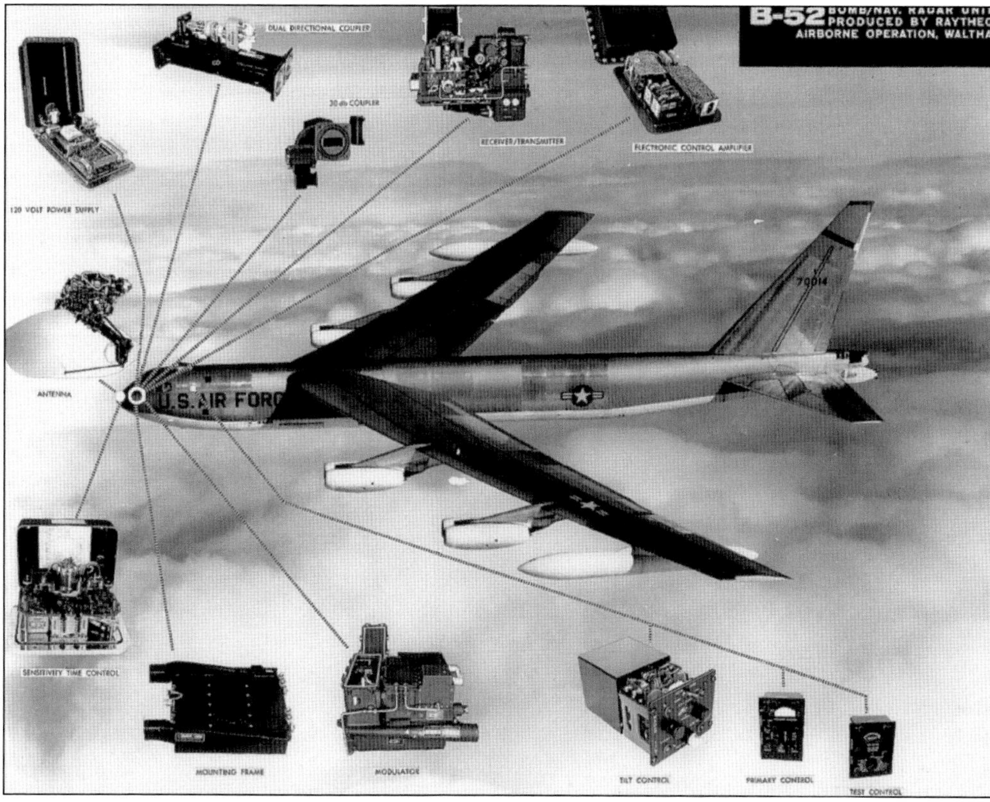

Nuclear-armed B-52 bombers of the U.S. Air Force were one of the country's major deterrents against Soviet aggression. The planes were also widely used for carrying conventional ordnance in Vietnam, both Iraq wars, and Afghanistan. Raytheon electronic components and systems—illustrated around the periphery of this photograph—have been integral to many functions, such as navigation, bombing, and radar.

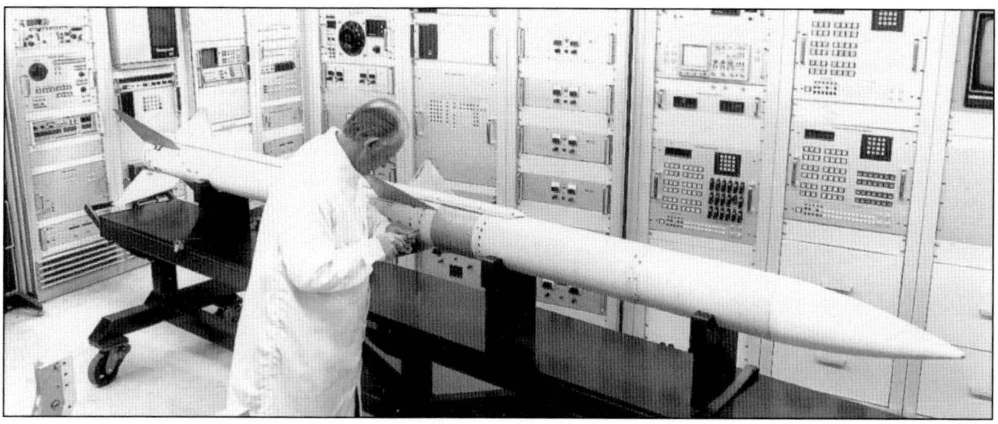

An engineer works on a Raytheon AMRAAM in the Andover plant. The AMRAAM program was begun in the 1970s as a successor to Sparrow. Production by both Hughes Aircraft and Raytheon began in the 1980s. This missile is noted for its high level of operational reliability. It can be launched day or night, in all weather, and its autonomous guidance capability provides the pilot with the ability to maneuver immediately following missile launch, allowing faster engagement of follow-on targets or evasion of the original threat. Over 25 countries have deployed AMRAAM.

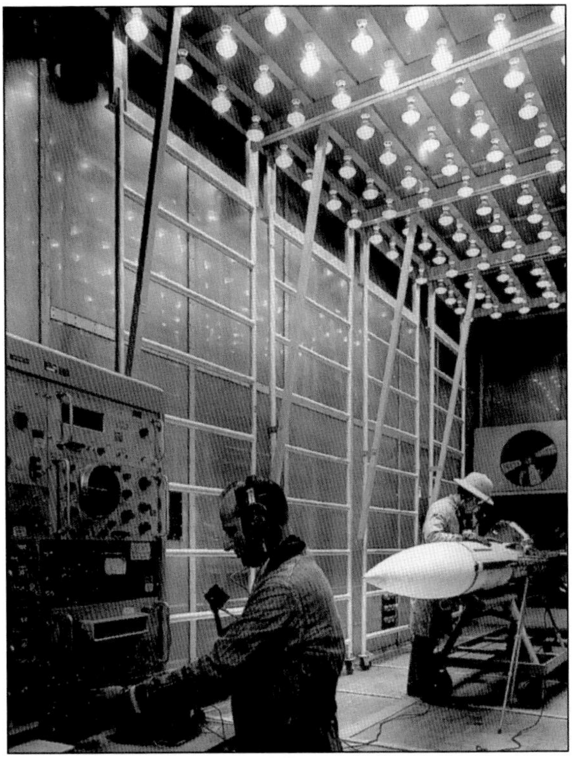

Hawk missiles continued to be an important weapons system throughout the cold war. These Hawk units are being subjected to an electronic check in a special chamber at the Missile System Division in Andover.

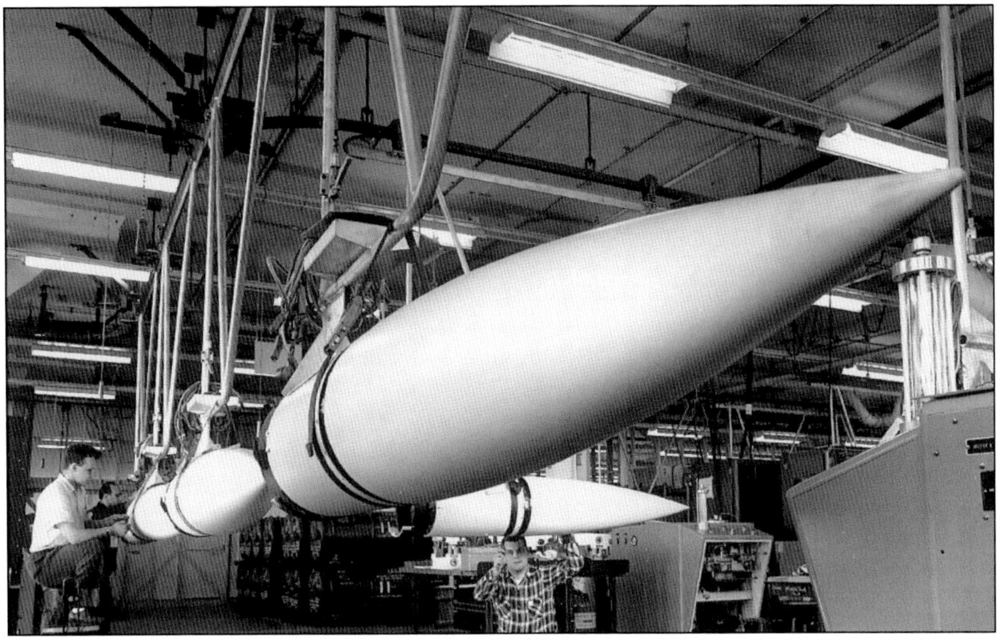

Hawk missile nose cones travel down an assembly line at Raytheon's Andover production plant. Originally named for the bird of prey, Hawk was also associated with an acronym meaning "homing all the way killer." Patriot also had an acronym superimposed on it: "phased array tracking to intercept of target." Pave Paws (see next page) stood for "precision acquisition vehicle entry phased array warning system."

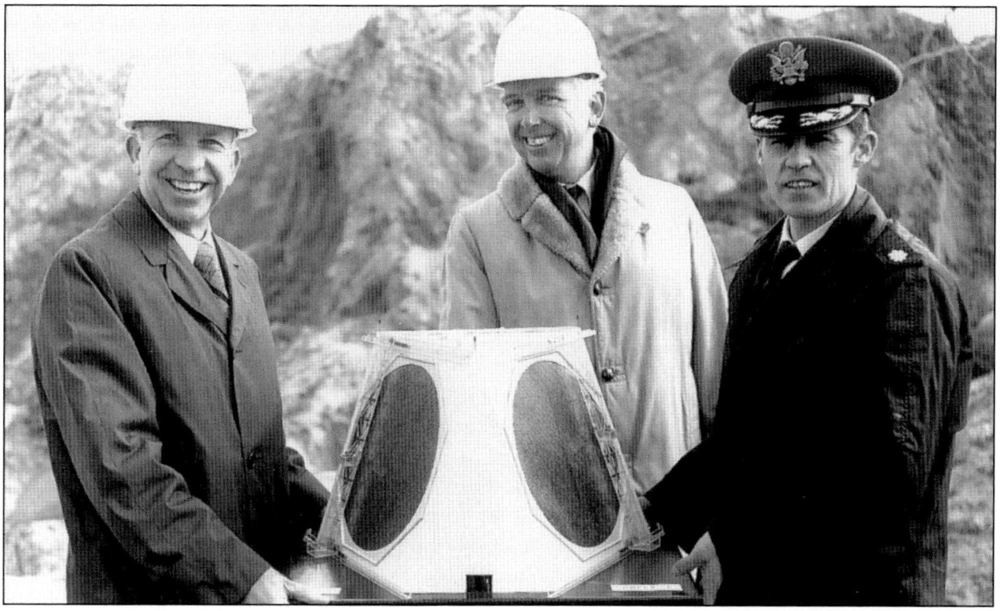

Holding a model of the Raytheon Pave Paws phased array radar system during its construction on Cape Cod are, from left to right, Pave Paws deputy program director Richard Moore, John Caswell of the Raytheon Equipment Division, and Colonel McEachern of the U.S. Air Force. The 10-story radar is capable of long-range target detection and tracking with its electronically steered beams. This capability grew more important when the Soviet Union began to employ submarines armed with nuclear missiles near the coast of the United States. Pave Paws represented the only early-warning capability against this type of threat.

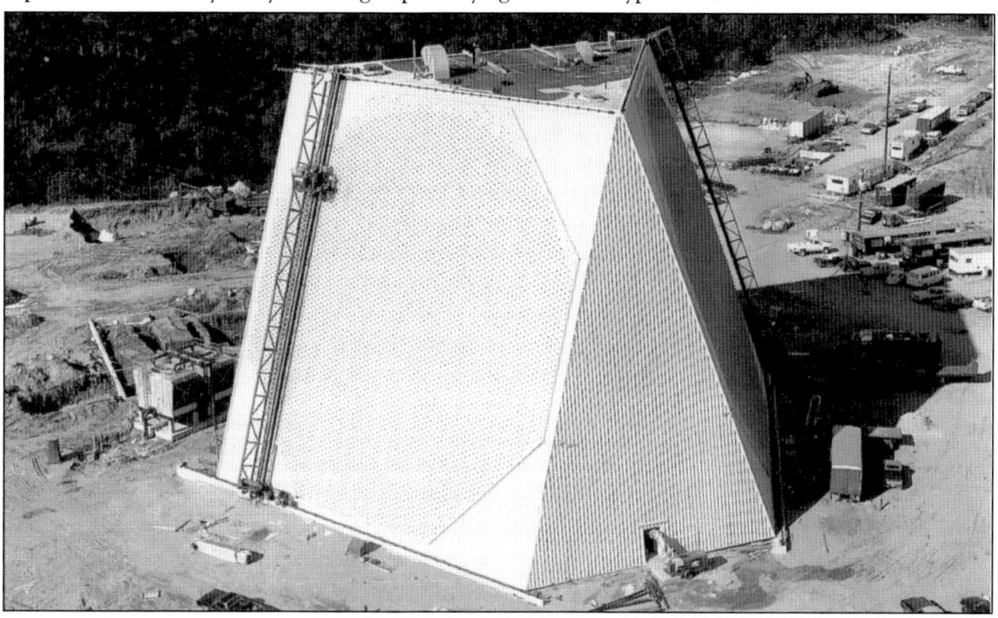

A view of the Pave Paws phased array radar system under construction on Cape Cod shows workers installing components on the multi-element face of the antenna. The system was designed and developed by Raytheon and was constructed at Otis Air Force Base by subcontractor Gilbane Building Company.

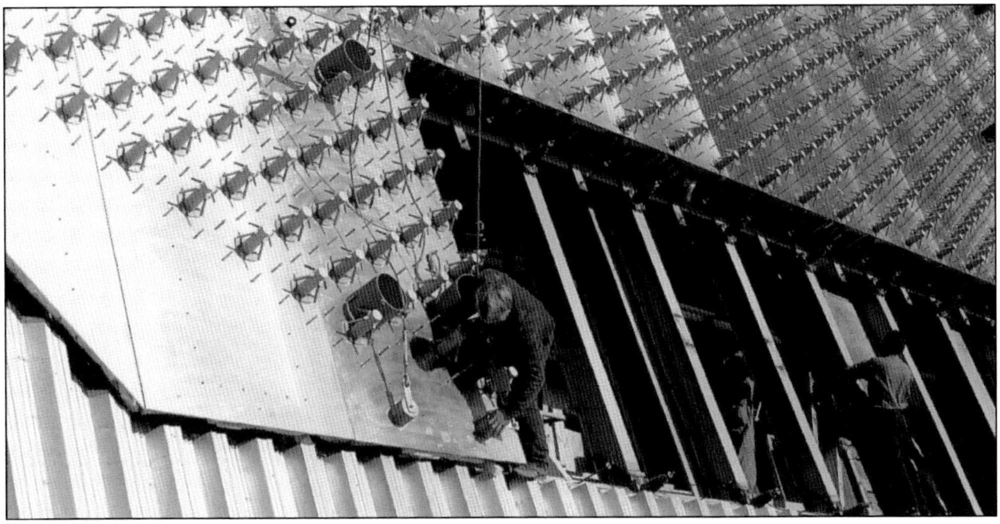

Technicians work on the dozens of phased array elements of the Pave Paws radar at Cape Cod Air Force Station, which was operative on April 4, 1980. Construction of the Pave Paws site at Beale Air Force Base in California was completed in October 1979 and was operative on August 15, 1980. These are the only two operating Pave Paws sites in the United States. There is a decommissioned Pave Paws site at Robins Air Force Base in Georgia; it was closed at the end of the cold war. There was a Pave Paws early-warning radar at Eldorado Air Force Station in Texas, but it was dismantled and moved to Clear Air Force Station in Alaska.

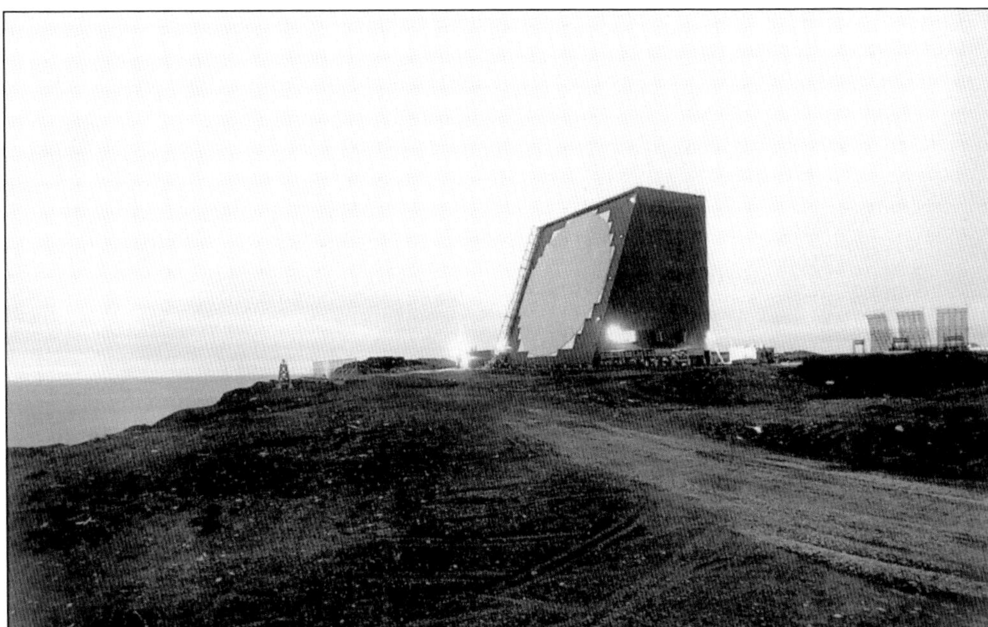

Raytheon's Cobra Dane phased array radar was built at Shemya Air Force Station near the western tip of the Aleutian Islands off the Alaska coast. The giant installation, which includes offices, operating bays, and living quarters, was contracted by the Air Force Electronic Systems Division of Hanscom Air Force Base in Bedford.

The giant Cobra Dane radar in the Aleutians is reportedly capable of detecting a target the size of a basketball at a distance of 2,000 miles. Raytheon executive Walter Stowell is in the photograph.

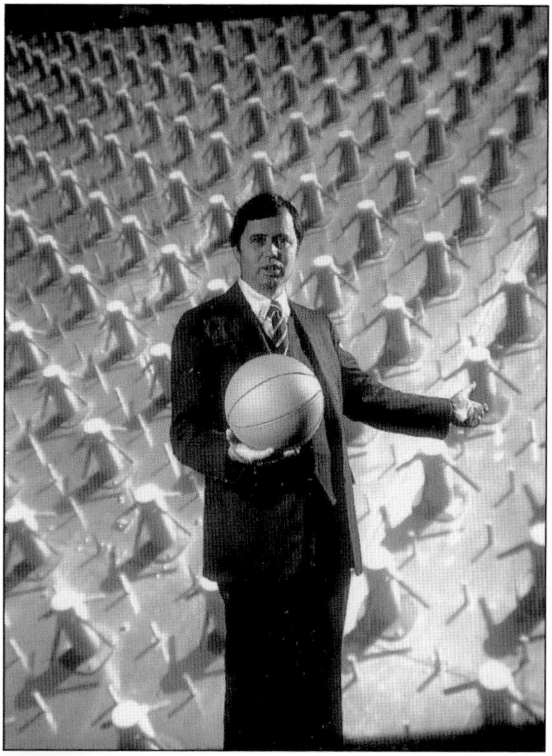

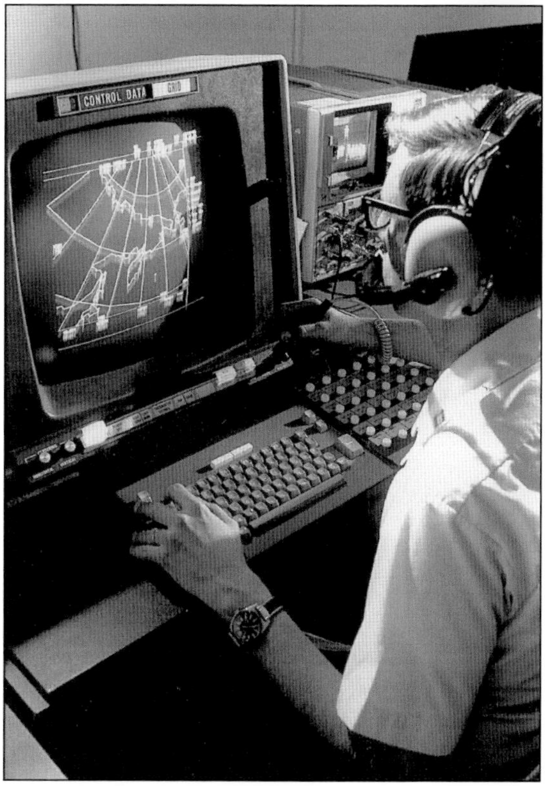

Seen here is part of the control console for the high-powered Cobra Dane radar in Alaska. It regularly tracks Russian missile test launches over the Pacific Ocean.

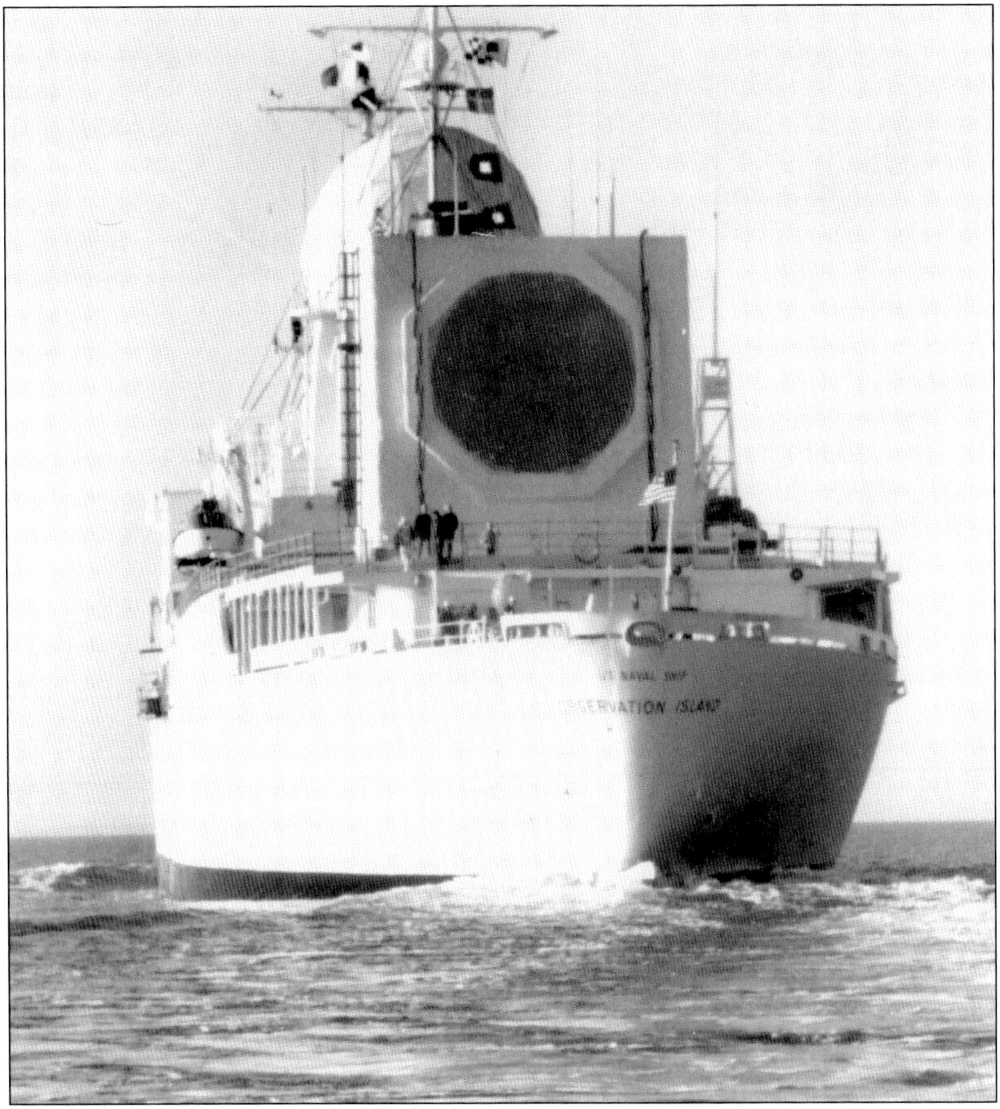

This is a view of the large Cobra Judy phased array radar on the USNS *Observation Island*. The system was designed and developed by Raytheon under contract from the Air Force Systems Command Electronic Systems Division. It is used to collect data on ballistic missile tests.

The Patriot missile system first entered service in the 1980s and has been repeatedly updated with improved hardware and software. It is in service in the United States and several other countries. This 1973 photograph shows a "fly out" test of an early SAM-D missile, later renamed Patriot, from a sealed canister. The test was conducted at the Orlando division of Martin Marietta Aerospace, the principal subcontractor on the program. Raytheon has been the prime contractor for this air-defense system. The Patriot missile has a track-via-missile (TVM) guidance system. Course corrections are transmitted to the guidance system from the ground.

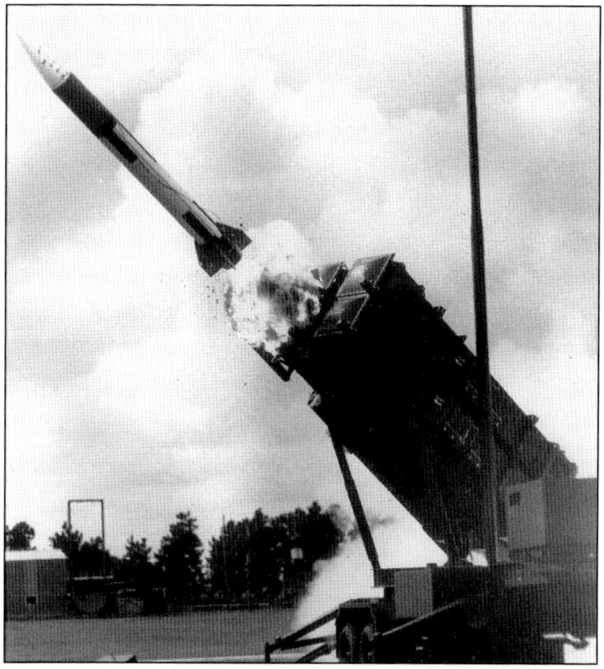

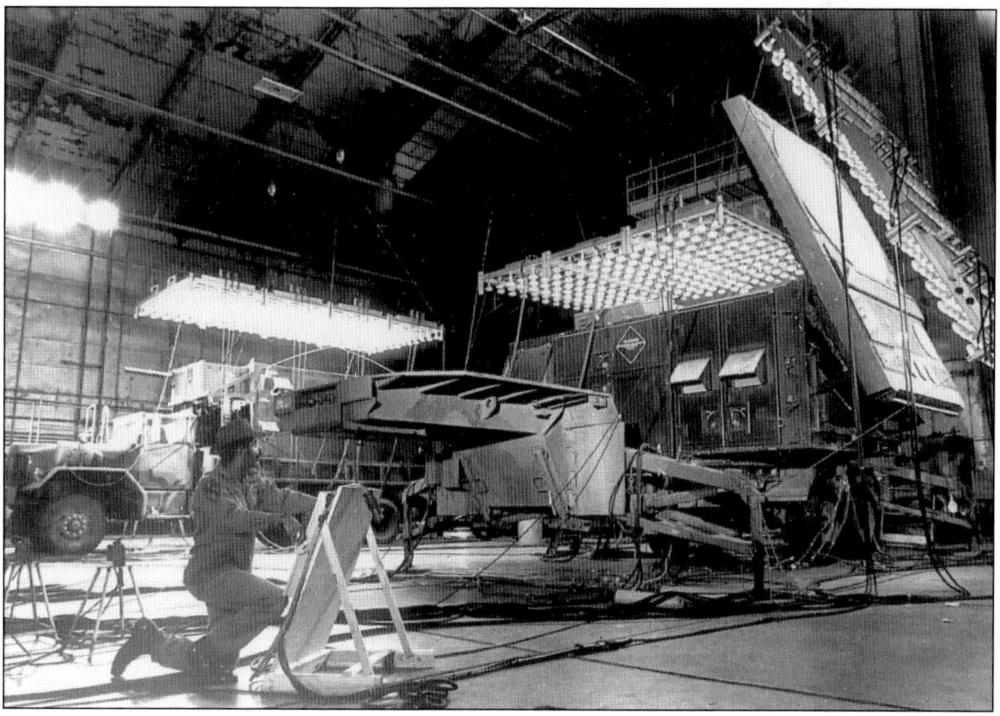

Hundreds of floodlights provided the heat for high-temperature testing of Patriot system elements, including the phased array antenna to the right, in this 1980 test. The climatic chamber was located at Eglin Air Force Base in Florida. The system was subjected to temperature extremes from negative 50 degrees to 120 degrees Fahrenheit.

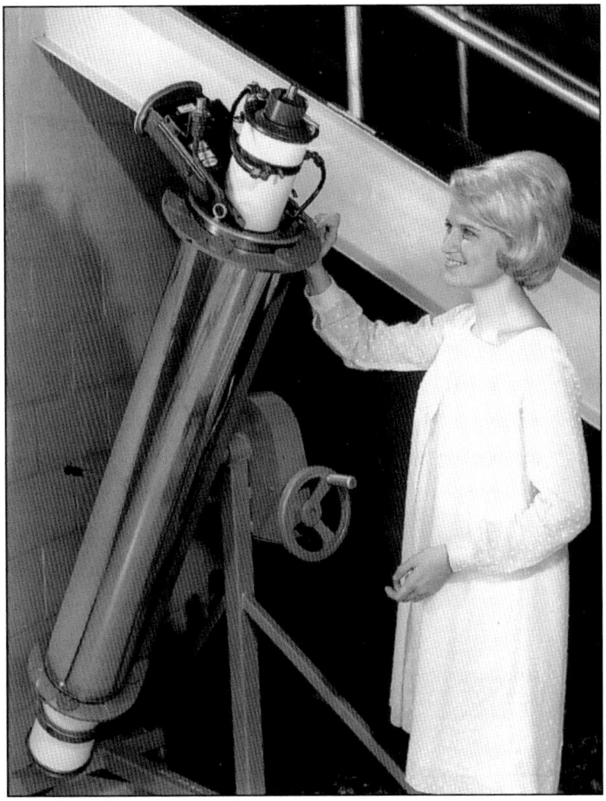

There are 96 of these high-power, Raytheon-developed traveling wave tubes in the phased array Cobra Dane system in the Aleutians. Each is approximately six feet long. They were originally produced in the Waltham facility; production was later transferred to other manufacturers.

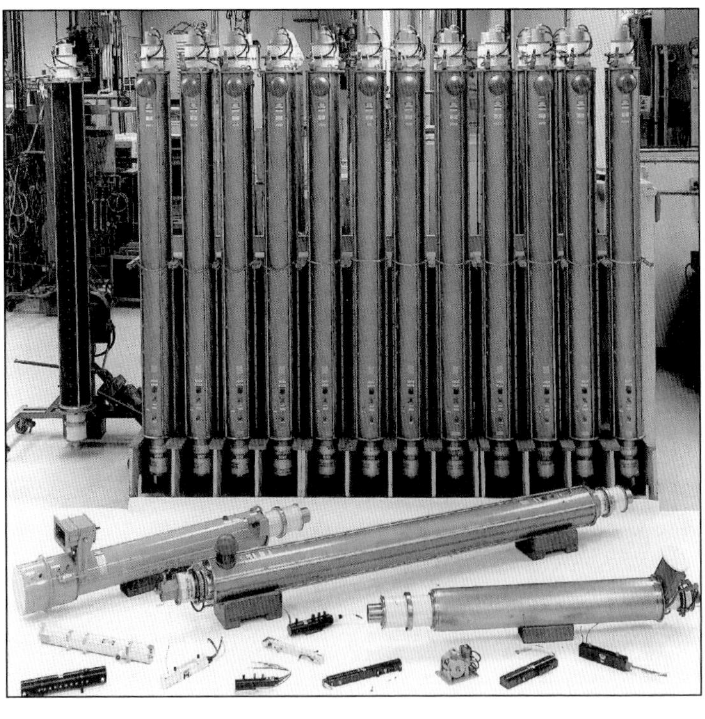

Shown are the 10-foot-long traveling wave tubes for the PPA-200 radar, the six-foot-long tubes for the Cobra Dane, and various smaller tubes used in aircraft radar and in satellite communication applications. All of these tubes were developed and manufactured at the Waltham Microwave and Power Tube facility.

This image provides a size comparison of the 10-foot traveling wave tube and a typical smaller tube developed at the Waltham plant.

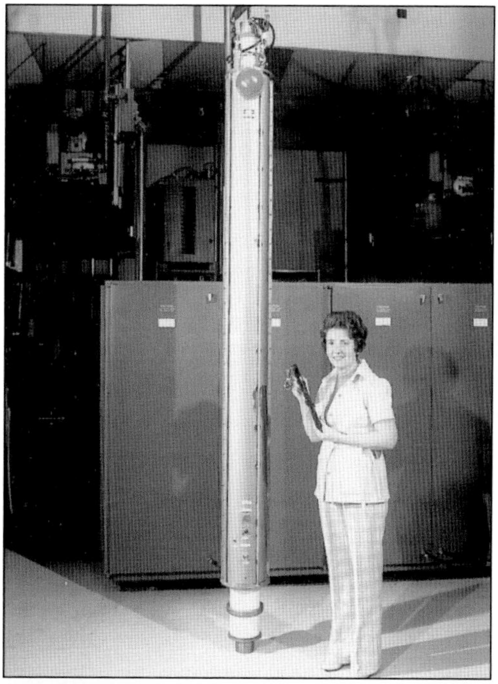

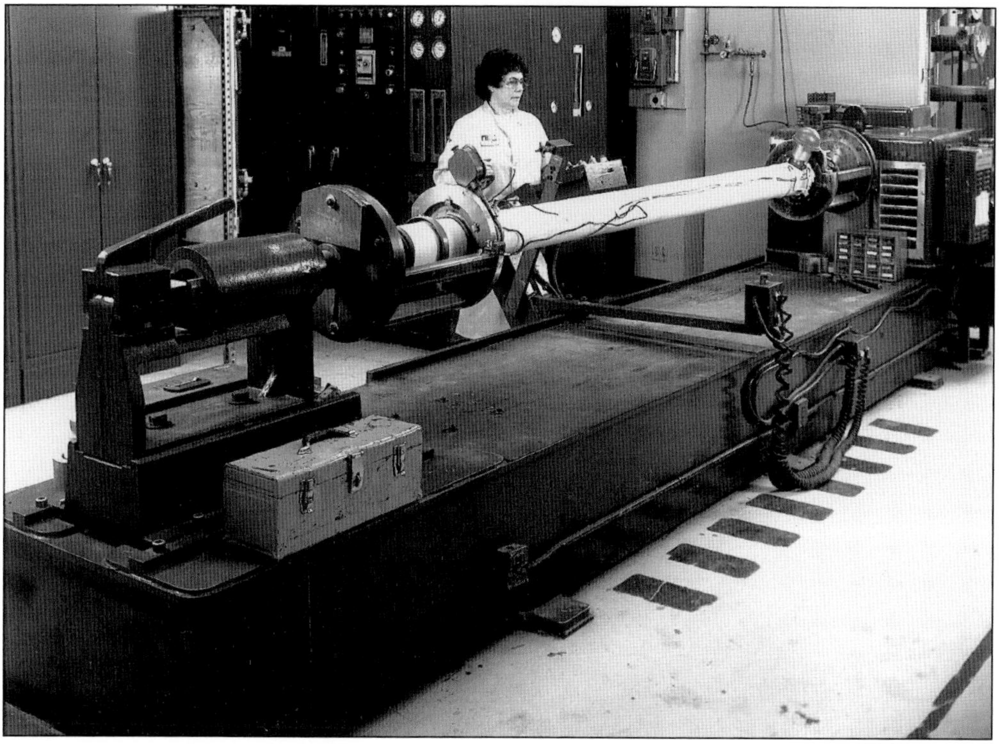

A technician operates a large lathe, which winds the solenoid coil around the outside of one of the 10-foot-long PPA-200 traveling wave tubes. The magnetic field from the coil serves to focus the long electron beam that runs through the center of the tube. Extensive specialized equipment was needed to manufacture these unique high-power devices.

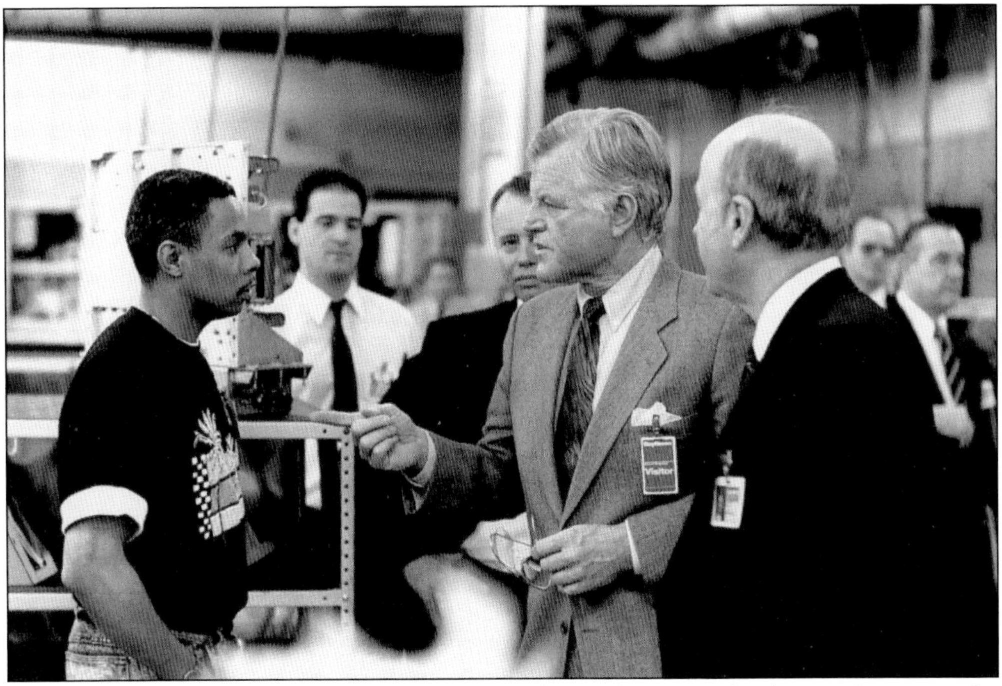

Sen. Edward M. Kennedy is shown here visiting the Andover missile plant and meeting the managers, supervisors, and workers.

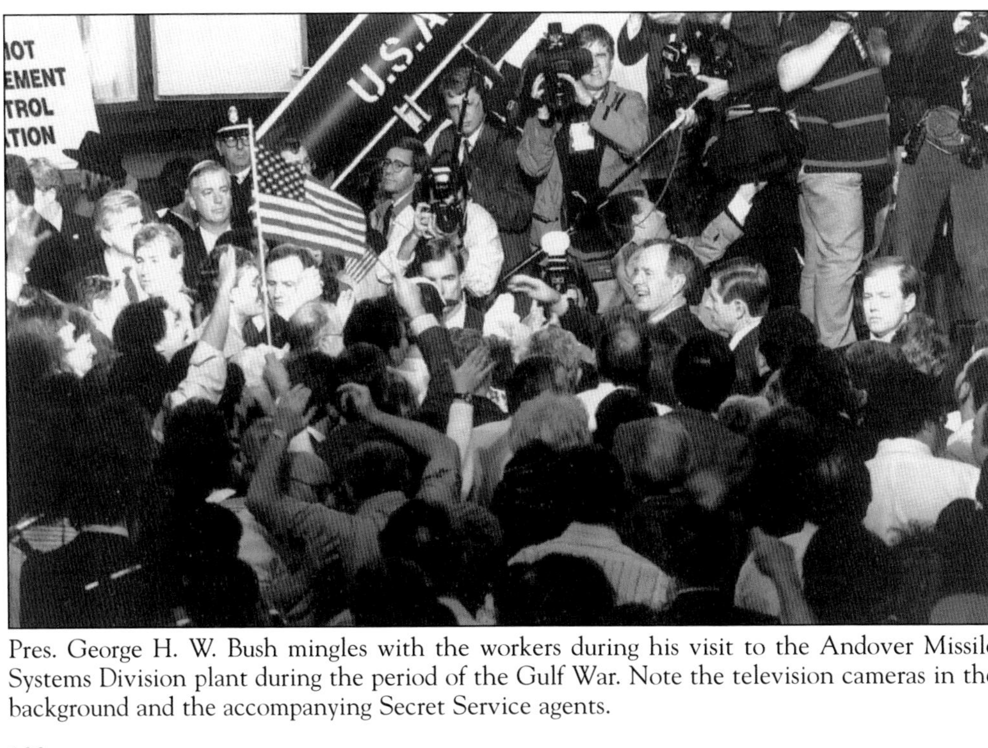

Pres. George H. W. Bush mingles with the workers during his visit to the Andover Missile Systems Division plant during the period of the Gulf War. Note the television cameras in the background and the accompanying Secret Service agents.

The Polaris intermediate-range sea-launched ballistic missile is seen here in a test firing. Polaris, which came into service in the early 1960s, was the first missile with an onboard digital computer. The computer was designed by MIT's Instrumentation Lab (later the independent C. S. Draper Lab) and manufactured by Raytheon.

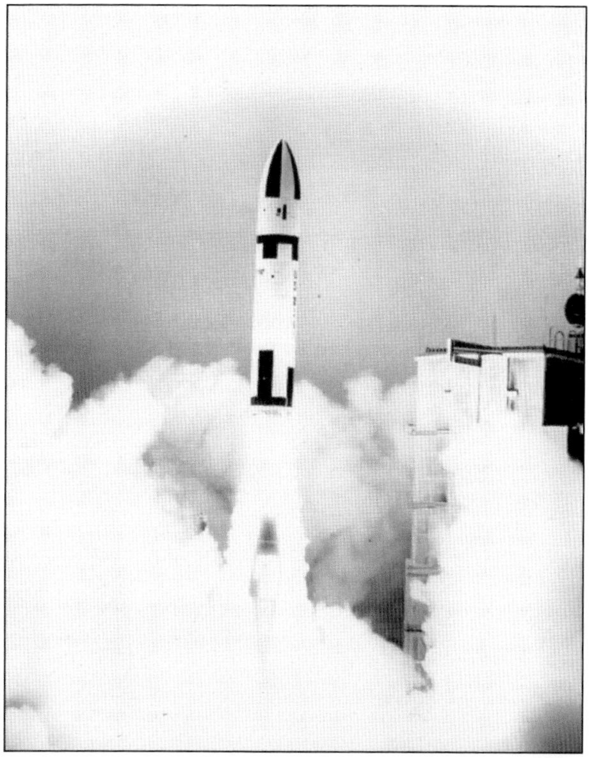

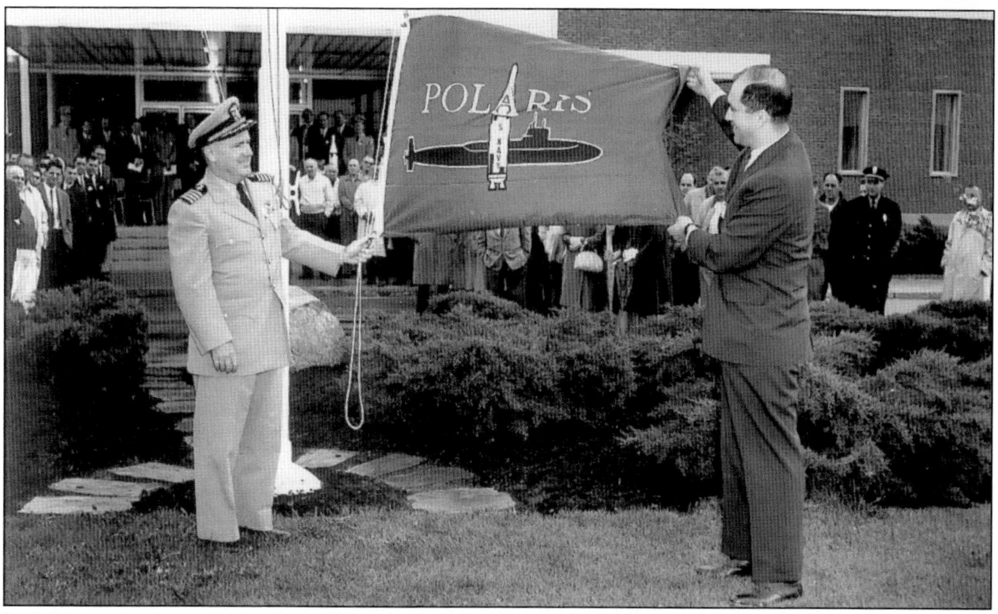

In May 1964, Capt. J. A. O'Neil of the U.S. Navy, director of fire control and guidance for the Special Projects Office, and Raytheon executive vice president Tom Phillips prepare to hoist the Polaris flag at the Space and Information Systems Division in Sudbury. The event was in recognition of Raytheon's work in cooperation with MIT on the electronics systems and computer for the Polaris. The sea-launched missile had a range of 2,500 miles and could strike distant targets with great accuracy.

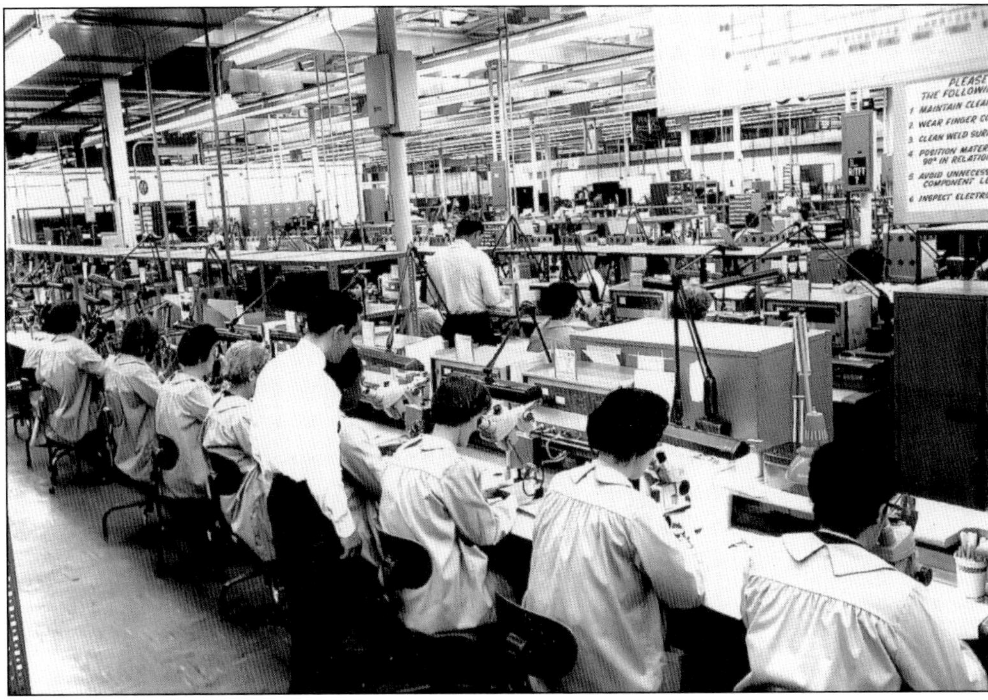

Supervisors and technicians work on the Polaris missile for U.S. Navy submarines at the Raytheon Equipment Division.

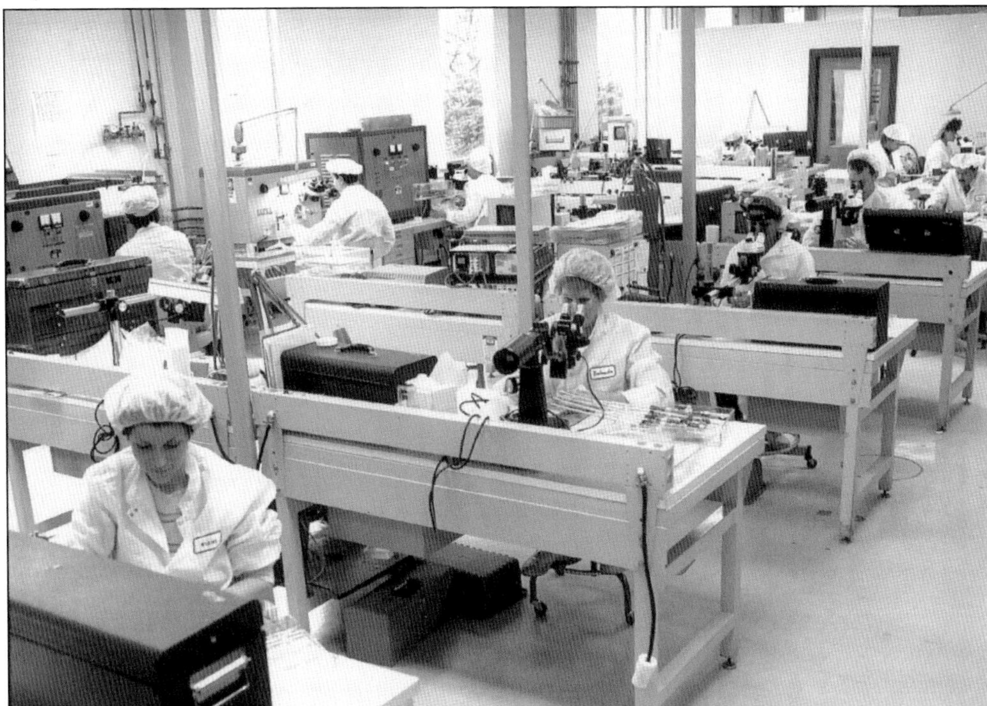

A "clean room" environment was essential for the development and manufacture of traveling wave tubes at the Microwave and Power Tube Division plant in Waltham.

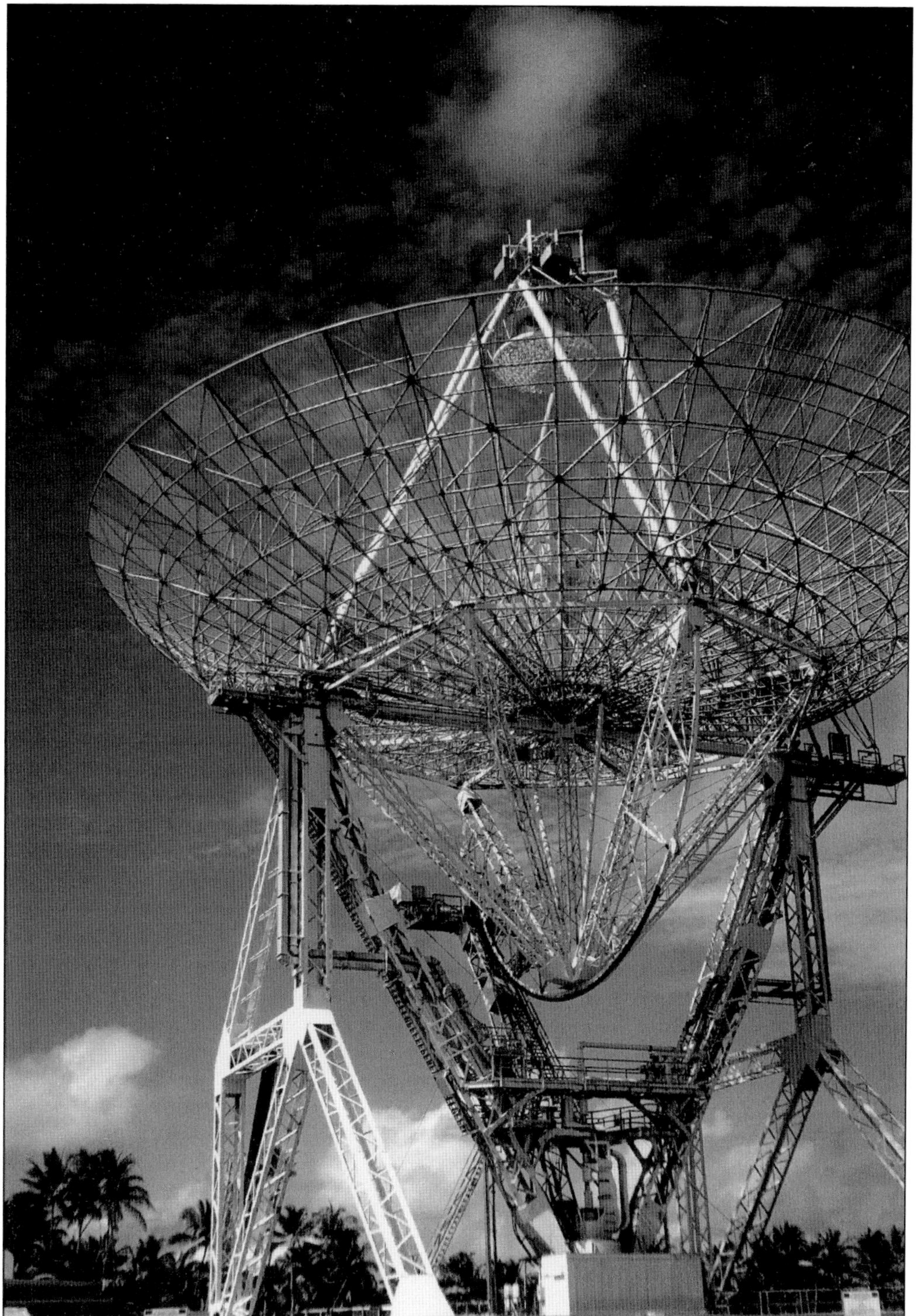

Raytheon operated the giant radar facility on Kwajalien Atoll in the Pacific for the military, providing long-range tracking for missile tests conducted from the California coast. This massive radar antenna can be pointed in any direction and rides on a huge track for 360-degree rotation.

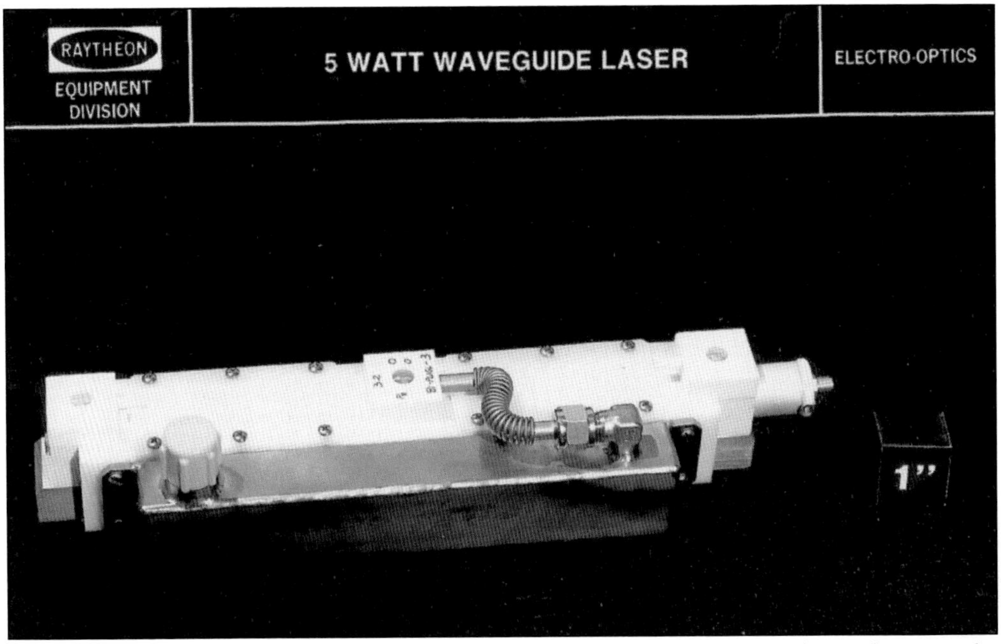

This five-watt ceramic waveguide laser was developed for cruise missile applications by Raytheon's Electroptics Laboratory in Sudbury. It was constructed with ceramic parts and subassemblies from the Waltham Ceramics Facility.

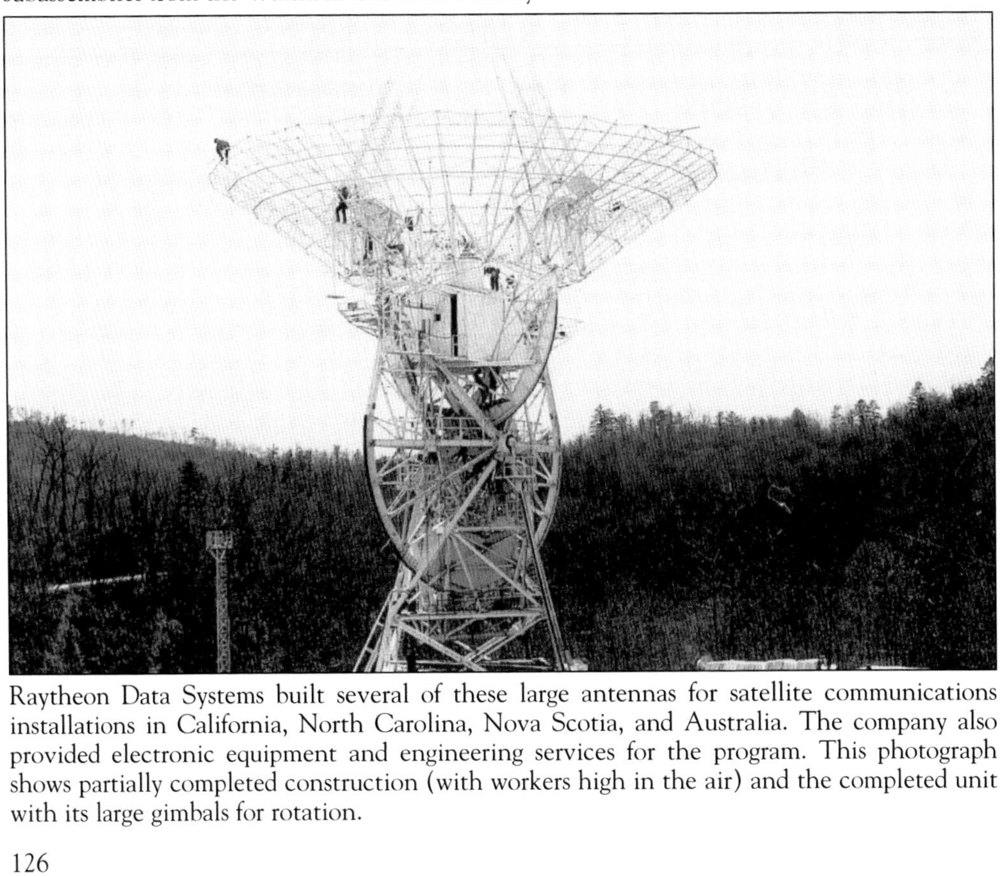
Raytheon Data Systems built several of these large antennas for satellite communications installations in California, North Carolina, Nova Scotia, and Australia. The company also provided electronic equipment and engineering services for the program. This photograph shows partially completed construction (with workers high in the air) and the completed unit with its large gimbals for rotation.

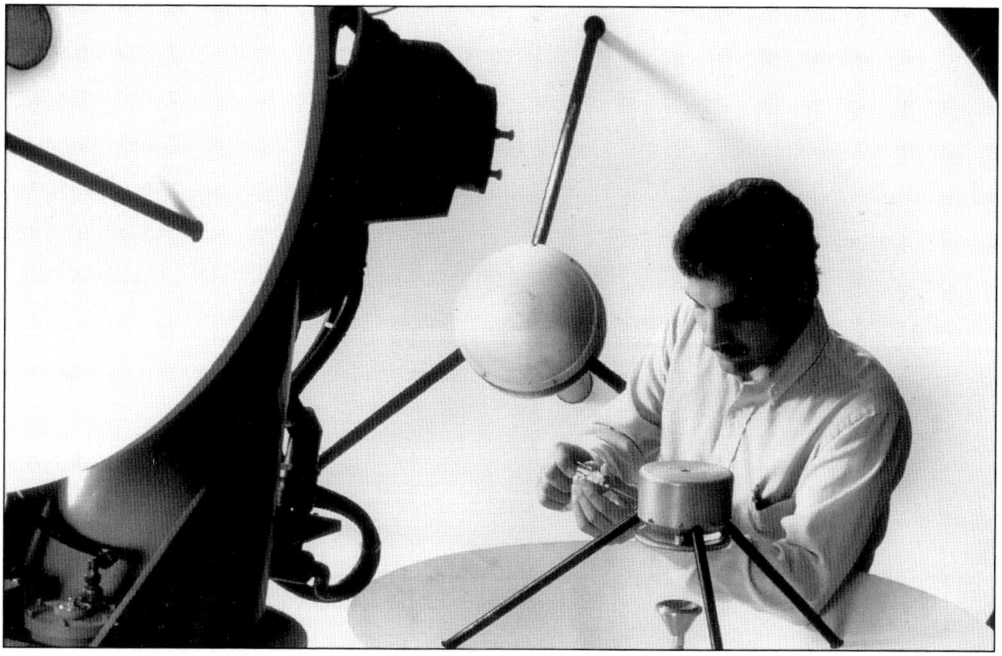

An engineer works on antennas for the U.S. Navy's Satellite Communications Program, known as NESP. The Raytheon Equipment Division participated in this program in the 1980s.

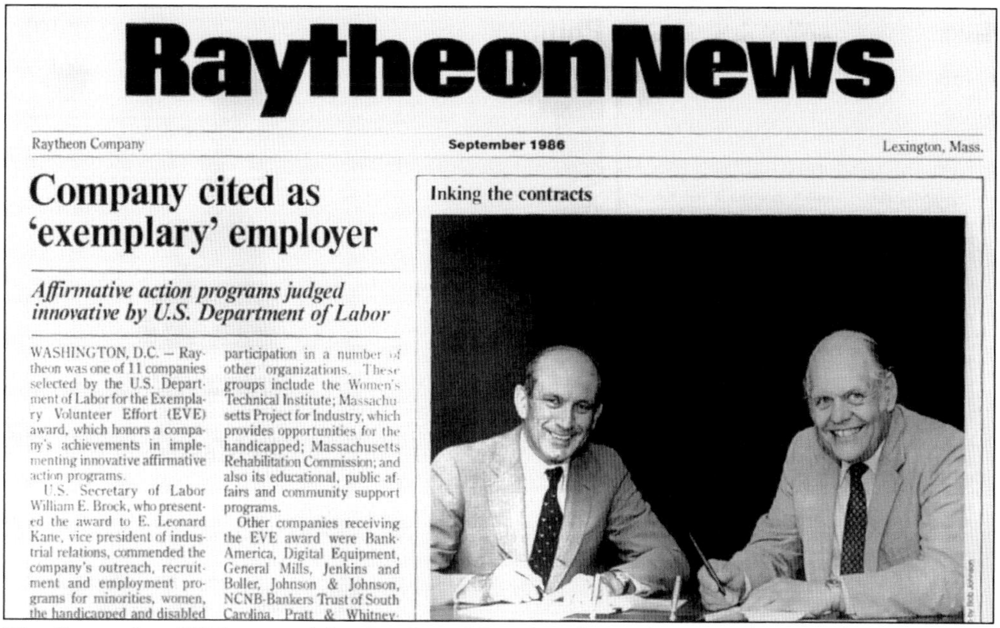

RaytheonNews

Raytheon Company | September 1986 | Lexington, Mass.

Company cited as 'exemplary' employer

Affirmative action programs judged innovative by U.S. Department of Labor

WASHINGTON, D.C. – Raytheon was one of 11 companies selected by the U.S. Department of Labor for the Exemplary Volunteer Effort (EVE) award, which honors a company's achievements in implementing innovative affirmative action programs.

U.S. Secretary of Labor William E. Brock, who presented the award to E. Leonard Kane, vice president of industrial relations, commended the company's outreach, recruitment and employment programs for minorities, women, the handicapped and disabled participation in a number of other organizations. These groups include the Women's Technical Institute; Massachusetts Project for Industry, which provides opportunities for the handicapped; Massachusetts Rehabilitation Commission; and also its educational, public affairs and community support programs.

Other companies receiving the EVE award were BankAmerica, Digital Equipment, General Mills, Jenkins and Boller, Johnson & Johnson, NCNB-Bankers Trust of South Carolina, Pratt & Whitney-

Inking the contracts

The September 1986 issue of the *Raytheon News* headlines the story that Raytheon has been cited by the U.S. Labor Department for its outstanding affirmative action programs to benefit minorities, women, and handicapped and disabled veterans. The Exemplary Voluntary Effort award was given to 11 companies. Also in this issue was the notice that Raytheon and Digital Equipment Corporation were to combine efforts on a program to make a more rugged version of the popular PDP-11 computer for use in demanding military and aerospace environments. The agreement was signed by Raytheon chairman Tom Phillips and Digital president Ken Olsen.

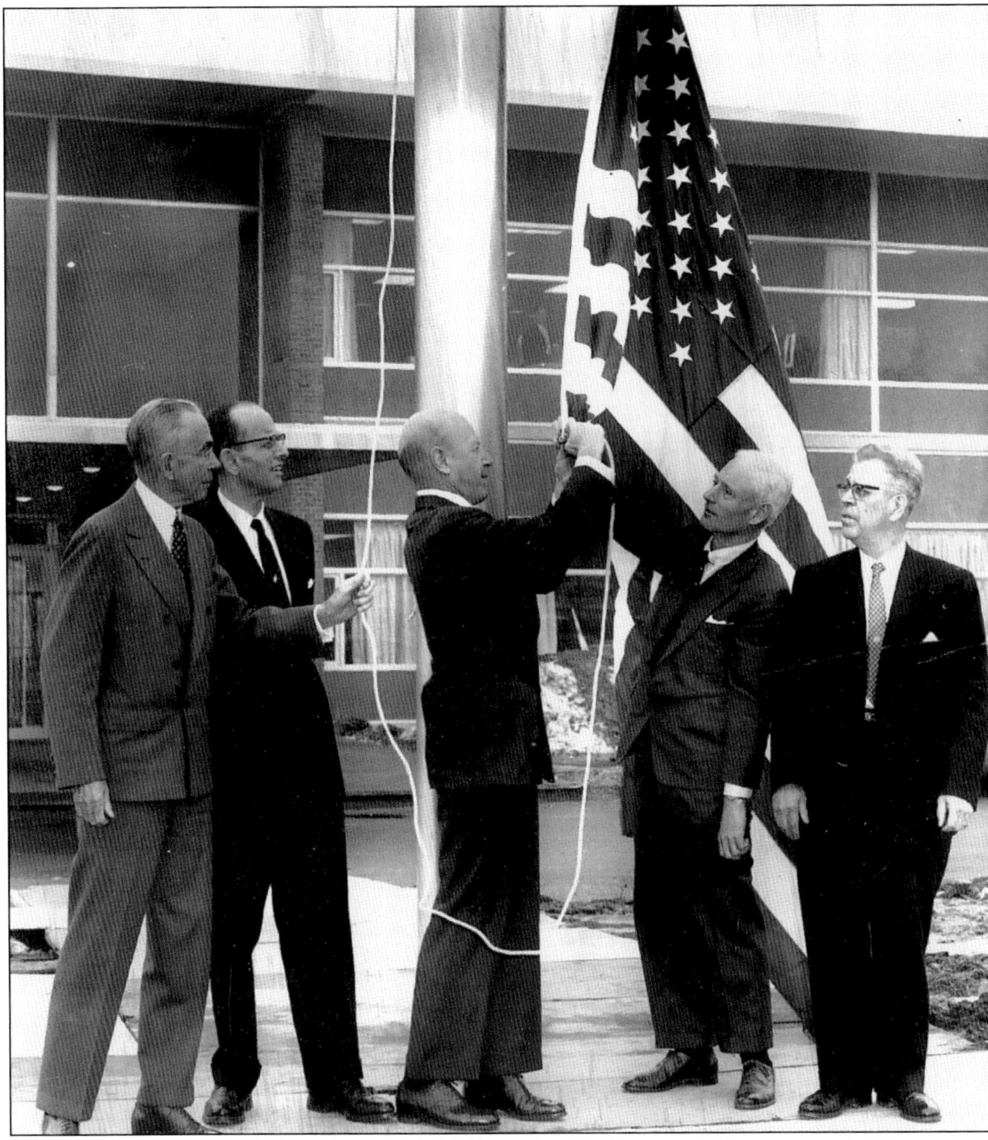

Raising the American flag at the opening of Raytheon's Spencer Laboratory in 1960 are, from left to right, Dean Edmonds (director), Richard Krafve (president), Charles F. Adams (chairman of the board), a Mr. Beckwith, and the lab's namesake, Percy L. Spencer (vice president).

Since its inception, Raytheon has been an entrepreneurial force in the civilian economy and a key contributor to the strength of America's armed forces. In the years subsequent to those covered in this volume, Raytheon has merged with a number of equally historic entities, including E-Systems, Texas Instruments' Defense Systems and Electronics business, and Hughes Aircraft's Defense Electronics business. Indeed, the early stories of these proud organizations each merit a volume of their own. However, the special story of Raytheon, now in its 83rd year, will always be of interest to those concerned with technical achievement, business leadership, and the company's current vision of being the world's most admired defense and aerospace systems supplier.